HEROISM, FLAMING CARNAGE, AND BLOODY TRAGEDY...

In the early months of 1942 two German U-boats arrived secretly off our East Coast. They sank so much shipping vital to the American and British war effort that our naval authorities feared an armada of U-boats had come. And come they did— while American cities on the shore were still leaving their lights on, silhouetting freighters for Nazi torpedoes. The U.S., caught unprepared, was in shock. Churchill sent fishing trawlers to fill our defenses, and they were welcome. The U.S. Navy even appropriated the yachts of the wealthy.

This is the riveting account of how a U.S. defense was heroically mobilized—and how it finally drove the enemy from our shores by the fall of 1943, never to return again.

"A compelling story..."

Kansas City Star

U-BOATS
OFFSHORE

EDWIN P. HOYT

PLAYBOY
PAPERBACKS

*For Rear Adm. Ernest McNeill Eller, U.S.N. (Ret.),
who has guided my career through naval history
for ten years.*

CONTENTS

PREFACE

Most stories of the war against Nazi Germany have been told. After all, more than three decades have passed since the end of the war. But one aspect of that war has never been explored. It is the story of how the U.S. military establishment nearly lost the war for the Allies in the early months of 1942.

In the first six months after the United States was catapulted into war by the attack on Pearl Harbor, the U-boats destroyed nearly six hundred ships, more than three million tons, the equivalent of half the American merchant ships afloat. Most of these ships were sunk in American waters defended by the U.S. Navy and Army Air Forces. Only six U-boats were lost in the western Atlantic in this period, and the first American sinking of a U-boat off the U.S. coast did not come until May 1942.

As Winston Churchill warned from the beginning, American unpreparedness and incompetence in dealing with the U-boats threatened the entire allied war effort more than the Japanese destruction of the American battle fleet at Pearl Harbor.

By March, Churchill was so concerned that he sent a fleet of converted trawlers and another fleet of corvettes to the East Coast of America, men and ships trained in anti-submarine warfare. This was at a time when Britain was besieged everywhere, but with all the defeats and difficulties, the Atlantic war was foremost on Churchill's mind. He knew that if Germany's submarine genius, Admiral Karl Doenitz, could throw enough force against the untrained and unarmed Americans, the tide of battle would be turned for Germany, and Britain's defenses would collapse from hunger.

This book tells why the Americans were unprepared and

what happened, day by day, month by month, during the two vital periods when Doenitz loosed his U-boats against America: from January until July 1942 and again in the summer and fall of 1943.

It is a shocking story. It shows the American high command at its worst. It is a thrilling story, too, of high adventure, danger, and tragedy that occurred in the waters off the American East Coast in those critical months. It is also the story of self-sacrifice, blunder, and heroism.

Hundreds of heroes live in this story, the men who sailed in merchant ships and naval vessels, the men who sent them to sea and sometimes to death, the men who flew planes and blimps, and the men who went to sea in tiny cockleshells to try to rescue survivors of the sinkings.

There are few villains. Even the Germans were brave men doing what they perceived to be their duty. If some German captains abused the laws of war, it will also be seen that they were not alone, as in the tale of *U-85,* whose crew was massacred by an American destroyer.

The story of the war offshore is tragedy and final triumph. Twenty more U-boats, even ten, made available to Admiral Doenitz for his effort against America in the months from January through July 1942, might have turned the tide. The want of those few submarines constituted the legendary "horse-shoe nail." If the British had been forced to their knees, the entire course of World War II could have been changed.

It did not happen that way, but how close it came to happening is the subject of this book.

1
SEA WAR

By the first of December 1941, Americans in the ports along the Eastern seaboard recognized far better than any of their countrymen the horrors of Britain's war at sea; indeed, some had already felt its consequences. The first big British passenger liner torpedoed in 1939, the *Athenia,* carried a number of American passengers. The Cunard liner *Franconia* was tied up at the 48th Street pier in those first days, and observant New Yorkers could see a crew of 70 painters working night and day to change her pristine white hull to battleship gray.

From the beginning of hostilities in September 1939, some Americans had "encountered" the U-boats. In the first week of war, the American freighter *Wacosta* was stopped by a U-boat off the Irish coast and searched for contraband. That same week, a policeman in Queens borough, New York, swore he saw a submarine in Luyster Creek, near the Consolidated Edison plant. One day in 1939, the U.S. destroyer *Leary* went charging out from her moorings in Boston harbor searching for a submarine. There was none there. Another day, President Roosevelt told his press conference that submarines were lurking off New England. They were not.

As the war continued, many mysterious tales were told about the U-boats. One, which originated in Boston, concerned a U-boat captain of great daring.

This captain, went the tale, made it a habit to come in close to the American shore and place his submarine on the bottom near a sunken wreck, where the metal of the known ship would confuse the sound gear of any searching vessel.

Then, at night, this captain would wait for British and Canadian ships heading out of Boston harbor, bound for

Halifax, carrying war supplies for Britain. The U-boat would stalk the cargo vessels into Canadian waters, sink them, and then return to its haven near Boston harbor to lie in wait and strike again.

Several vessels were lost in this way, and the Canadian destroyer men wondered at the apparent omniscience of this U-boat captain. They began searching the area outside Boston harbor for the enemy submarine. Finally, one destroyer captain, who had taken readings at the old wreck when the U-boat was off on a chase, returned and took them again. The sound operator noticed a discrepancy and informed the captain.

The destroyer came to a stop and waited. That night, a British ship was scheduled to sail for Halifax. Sure enough, after the ship passed by, out of the depths rose the submarine and gave chase on the surface. The destroyer captain gave the submarine plenty of room to get out of American waters, then rushed in, surprised the U-boat on the surface, and before she could dive to safe water, depth charged her so severely that she broke up and sank.

To the surface came bits and pieces of flotsam, including a tweed civilian jacket, which was rescued by a boat crew. And when the captain of the destroyer picked up the jacket, he noticed first the label of a Savile Row tailor inside and in the right-hand pocket two stubs from a Boston theater for a performance held the night before.

The story was apocryphal, but it showed how deeply the legend of the U-boats had entered the American consciousness long before the Pearl Harbor attack.

In 1940, New Yorkers had watched the Cunard liner *Mauretania* fitted out with deck guns to become a troop transport. They had read stories of U-boats operating with secret tankers off the coast of Mexico.

After *Wacosta,* a number of other American vessels had suffered the indignity of search by the Germans on the high seas. The freighter *City of Flint* had been captured by the German pocket battleship *Deutschland* and sent to Germany under a prize crew.

There had been tragic loss of American civilian lives at sea, sailing in foreign ships, months before the United States was officially involved. So while the United States had not been at war, some Americans had been immediately involved. And many more knew stories about the sea war.

In the summer of 1941, the American Red Cross and Harvard University Medical School embarked on a project of research in England on communicable diseases. If it seemed an odd time for such activity, perhaps there was more to it than that; Britain's Ministry of Health welcomed the coming of a whole hospital unit to help the beleaguered island no matter the guise under which it appeared. It would be established in five acres of the fields of Salisbury. The Americans would build their own hut-type institution, prefabricated in America and transported across the Atlantic.

So, in that summer, crammed among the cargoes of more than 70 ships, were brass fittings, building materials, kitchen utensils, all complicated equipment to set up a hospital for medical and surgical treatment. Eventually, the installation would consist of 22 green huts among the poppies of Salisbury plain.

On June 3, ten Red Cross nurses sailed aboard the ship *Vigrid*. The ship set out in convoy from Halifax through thick fog. The fog lasted five days, and the convoy had to slow and almost stop while the escort vessels urged stragglers into line. *Vigrid* developed engine trouble, and on the sixth day, she began to fall behind.

Like wolves, German U-boats scouted for stragglers, and on the seventh day, 400 miles from Greenland, *Vigrid* was found, and torpedoed.

The ship's siren screamed. The passengers went to their boat stations. The ten nurses had been instructed well; they appeared wearing warm clothing against the chill of the North Atlantic and over all their life jackets. The nurses and others got into the boats cast away, and all watched glumly in the chill as their ship listed farther and farther.

Margaret Somerville, of Catskill, New York, and Helen Jurewicz, of South Amboy, New Jersey, were in one of *Vigrid*'s boats with the first mate, the chief engineer, and five men of the crew. They did not see the submarine, for it was masked from them by a rain squall. As rain began to come down, they pulled their coats tightly around them. The mate steered the boat through flotsam, which had been their ship's cargo.

An hour after they left the ship, the mate took stock of

the water and food supplies and set up a schedule for the boat. Each person would have 2 ounces of water twice a day, one biscuit a day, and small rations of the meat in the locker, as long as it lasted.

The survivors then sat back to wait.

They amused themselves at first by describing in detail the meals they would eat when they reached home. But the days went by, gray and dreary. After the fourteenth day, when a ship passed, and they waved, shouted, and still failed to attract attention, nobody troubled to talk. At about that time, the food supply gave out.

"We tried unsuccessfully to eat barnacles. . . ."

They sat. They waited. No one moved unless he or she had to. The boat carried a little water-distilling plant, so the men were able to produce a quart of water every four or five hours. They rigged a shelter for the women, who huddled inside.

On the nineteenth day, all the occupants of the boat had almost given up, when suddenly the mate spotted a destroyer on the horizon and shot off a flare. The destroyer turned, and as the castaways saw that they were going to be rescued, their spirits returned in a rush.

They were taken aboard the destroyer and treated to all the amenities a Royal Navy ship could offer in wartime. Soon they were in London, in hospital themselves, to recover from exposure. They did and joined their hospital unit, to be rebuilt from scratch with a whole new set of supplies to be sent later.

Red Cross nurses Marion Blissett, of Detroit, Victoria Pelc, of Auburn, New York, Lillian M. Pesnicak, of Albany, New York, and Rachel St. Pierre, of Newton Center, Massachusetts, were in another boat with ten men.

The boat had scarcely pulled away from the ship when the survivors were shocked to see the long gray snout of a submarine breaking the water. Then the U-boat came to a halt very near them. They saw men on deck.

"Who are you?"

"How many ships were there in your convoy?"

"What were they carrying?"

"What was your destination?"

The boat was silent. The nurses looked at one another and at the men. Not one person spoke a syllable.

The submarine sat there for a moment. Then the sound of engines broke the quiet. The water roiled at the stern of the U-boat, and the submarine moved away on the surface.

These Red Cross nurses reached England safely, too. They were honored for their bravery in coming to help Britain in her hour of need. They met representatives of the British Red Cross and the Ministry of Health. They were taken to London, and Queen Elizabeth received them at Buckingham Palace.

As for the other four nurses in the third lifeboat, they were never found, nor was the boat. They were, like hundreds of other sailors, victims of the cruel war.

In that same convoy, the S.S. *Maasdam* was carrying 16 other Red Cross nurses and the hospital's housemother, Mrs. Ruth Breckenridge, of Winston Salem, North Carolina. The *Maasdam* was torpedoed eight days after *Vigrid*. Several nurses died of exposure.

Since the events occurred in mid-Atlantic, and the rescued were taken to England's shores, the story of the Red Cross nurses was scarcely known in America. That was the way it was with nearly all these war tales. Most Americans, even those whose homes were on the western shore of the Atlantic, and even those who watched the ships that braved the dangers, really had little idea of how badly the sea war was going.

2

UNEASY PEACE

Sunday, December 7, 1941, dawned bright and sunny in Norfolk, Virginia. As the city awakened, and householders went out into the chilly air to pick up their newspapers, they saw headlines that spoke of the danger of war. But the editors' concern was that the United States was drifting into war with Japan. In Norfolk, that possibility seemed remote. The word "war" had no particular shock effect. Norfolk, with its major naval ship building and repair facilities, had already lived for two years in the shadow of the European war.

From the beginning of the European struggle, British ships began calling at Hampton Roads and Norfolk to load supplies for England.

From the time of the president's first declaration of neutrality three days after the European war began, Franklin Roosevelt and other officials said this was Europe's war, not America's.

For more than two years, U-boats had ravaged Britain's lifeline of shipping from North America. Hundreds of ships had been sunk. Still the German navy had been careful to stay well out of U.S. waters. Most of the German submarines did not venture beyond the middle of the Atlantic. Some had come to Canada, to the Caribbean, to strike close to British Bermuda, the Bahamas, and Jamaica, but Adolf Hitler had ordered that the Americans were to be left undisturbed. He did not want the United States to enter the war even though, as each month passed, it became increasingly clear in Germany that U.S. official sympathies were all with England. Hitler was playing for time before he took on the United States, too.

For another reason, some Norfolk citizens paid little attention to the *Virginian-Pilot*'s warning. Many believed the newspaper was a "warhawk" and that the editors were trying to push the United States into the European struggle. Toward the end of the previous July, an explosion had rocked the Little Machipongo inlet lifeboat station near Norfolk, and the nervous sailor on guard there had reported "an explosive shell" had fallen. The newspaper had given the story feature treatment, and a full-scale panic was in the making until investigators learned that someone had left an oxygen tank out in the sun.

When two American minesweepers were painted the dark gray the British used instead of the light gray of the U.S. Navy, the *Virginian-Pilot* said this would help confuse the Nazis. When the New York *Herald Tribune* reported openly the arrival of the British warship *Malaya* in New York harbor, the *Virginian-Pilot* took the *Herald Tribune* to task for violating security. When the British carrier *Illustrious* came limping into Hampton Roads to drydock after a nearly disastrous encounter with German dive bombers, not once did the *Virginian-Pilot* reveal her presence, although the ship was in a U.S. Navy drydock for four months, and British tars with *Illustrious* on their caps swarmed about the city for any German agent to identify.

Reading the *Virginian-Pilot* on December 7, 1941, then, Norfolk citizens believed what their consciences and experiences told them to believe about the danger of war.

In one way, the European war had been a blessing for Norfolk. At least it ended nearly ten long years of hard times that began with the Wall Street crash of 1929. When, early in 1940, President Roosevelt made the decision to rearm the United States, he wanted what he called "a two-ocean navy," and since the Norfolk area was a major naval ship construction center, the shipbuilding brought contracts and new employment. Norfolk prospered.

In the summers of 1940 and 1941, tourists flocked to nearby Virginia Beach and Ocean View. The amusement parks outside the city were more crowded than ever with suddenly affluent workers joining tourists and military men in search of entertainment.

For along with shipbuilding, President Roosevelt's mobilization plans brought thousands of military and naval men to the area. Norfolk became a major base for the Neutrality

Patrol, a U.S. naval command given the task of keeping belligerent activity out of U.S. waters. After Selective Service was begun in October 1940, the army leased the Virginia Military Reservation at the south end of Virginia Beach and renamed it Camp Pendleton. Soon the camp was filled with young Americans training.

The year 1940 closed with retail sales in the community up 28 percent and unemployment ended. Building increased 900 percent. The economic index rose again in 1941.

The military activity did create tensions as the influx continued and increased. When the army proposed building a hospital on the beach near the city, property owners objected: it would lower values. When the navy moved to pre-empt a piece of land far from any habitation, for a practice bombing site to train airmen, outdoorsmen complained that it would ruin the duck hunting.

The Chamber of Commerce was flooded by complaints that the military was overrunning Norfolk and making it unlivable. Military men countered that they were cheated and overcharged by civilians for food, rent, and clothing. Chamber officials met several times with military commanders of the area and civic groups to try to ease the resentments.

By and large, however, Norfolk accommodated itself to the welcome boom and to the concept of American preparation to defend the country against war. The residents were willing to make sacrifices. The European war and the stepped-up U.S. defense effort had already made much change in U.S. life, and in some ways "belt tightening" became necessary.

The summer of 1941 had marked the beginning of real shortages. The Norfolk City Council stopped street improvements; the contractors said they could not get the necessary materials. The hardware stores began to run out of such common items as nails. Gardeners, painters, and fishermen could not find galvanized buckets. Householders searched the stores for electric plugs and switches.

The gasoline supply for civilian use began to shrink. Norfolk's service stations jumped the price of regular gasoline from 17 cents to 21 cents a gallon. Milk went up a penny to 16 cents a quart and then jumped again to 18 cents. Beer went from a dime a glass to 15 cents. Breakfast at the corner drug store rose: two eggs, toast, and coffee cost 20 cents.

To meet other shortages, the federal government asked for direct contributions. A call went out for citizens to search their attics for old aluminum. It was needed to build the 50,000 planes authorized by congress for the army and navy. A Norfolk girl named Kay Larson held an aluminum scavenger hunt. The young people scurried about town to collect saucepans, coffeepots, anything made of aluminum, and Norfolk responded generously. This hunt was written up in the *Virginian-Pilot*. Altogether, in the drive, the Hampton Roads area collected 12,500 pounds of aluminum.

Norfolk was willing and eager to act, to sacrifice.

Everyone in Norfolk that December 1941 knew why there was no asphalt for the streets, why nails were in sort supply, why electrical items could not be found, and why prices on gasoline and food were rising so high.

"It was the war," everybody said. But not many people translated that phrase into trucks and planes and tankers full of fuel, shoes and eggs and field guns, loaded into ships at ports up and down the Eastern seaboard, ships that sailed off into the Atlantic, their captains hoping to make their way to Britain.

The United States might have been able to have "both guns and butter" if the task had been solely to prepare its own defense. But by 1941, the United States was Britain's major source of supply of both military and civilian goods. Only those Norfolk citizens with a keen sense of public affairs even suspected in December 1941 who heavily the United States was committed to the defense of Britain.

The weighting of official American opinion had begun several months before the German armies marched into Poland. In the spring of 1939, U.S. Ambassador Joseph Kennedy in London assessed Europe's immediate future. He predicted war.

"Were Great Britain to be defeated," Kennedy wrote his friend President Roosevelt, "a tremendous, indeed a decisive alteration in the balance of world forces, military, moral and political, would occur to the grave disadvantage of the United States. . . ."

As months passed, the Kennedy position increasingly became the Roosevelt administration's position. Yet when war did come to Europe in September, there was no possibility that the United States would join the struggle. The vast majority of Americans still believed in the viability of American isolation from European struggles.

Franklin Roosevelt was already convinced that the Nazis must be defeated, but he could say that much only in his innermost circle. The country was not ready for war. Congress was not ready.

The neutrality period had been marked by growing government activity toward intervention, although much of this change was concealed from the public. From the beginning of the "Neutrality Patrol" in 1939, the U.S. senior naval officers warned President Roosevelt that it could not succeed. Admiral Stark and several others went to the White House one day in September to point out the difficulties. There were not enough ships to do the job, they said.

At first, the Germans had made neutrality seem easy because they bent over backward to assure a neutral America. Some advisers told Hitler that German-American opinion and native isolationism might keep America from taking sides. But by the spring of 1940, Hitler knew that Roosevelt was sending supplies to England, and when the Americans traded Britain 50 World War I destroyers for bases in British possessions in the Western Hemisphere, the Germans began to regard the United States as the enemy. Yet, in the summer of 1940, the German navy still treated American shipping with kid gloves, although they knew as well as FDR that on any given day a hundred American ships would be at sea or lying in port somewhere, loaded with contraband, destined for England. Long after the Neutrality Act of 1939 theoretically stopped American ships from sailing to Britain, the assistance continued.

The German U-boats began the "War of the Atlantic" against British shipping in the spring of 1940 off the English Channel. Steadily, the U-boats moved westward, but they still avoided the American region where they might meet United States vessels.

In October 1940, eight U-boats, operating in the North Atlantic, sank 63 allied ships, totaling 352,000 tons. That disastrous figure was a military secret, completely unknown to the citizens of Norfolk, where no one realized the desperation to which Britain was reduced. Admiral Doenitz, the chief of the German submarine fleet, wanted 100 submarines. If he had been able to put even 50 onto the Atlantic run that winter, the war would have ended right there. For those eight submarines in one month had sunk as many ships as the United States was building for Britain under the awkward arrangements possible for a "neutral."

The Lend-Lease bill, which went to congress that winter of 1940-41, made the American position absolutely clear to the Germans. Roosevelt proposed openly to build all the ships he could and ship England all the war material possible. In other words, the United States was becoming an avowed production partner in Britain's war. The British would fight and die; the Americans would produce and live.

The German U-boat men became more annoyed, less ready to listen to the official warnings to leave the Americans alone at any cost.

The first act of outright belligerence between American and German warships occurred that April 1941. The American destroyer *Niblack* was patrolling off Iceland which was occupied by British army units. She intercepted an S O S from the Dutch freighter *Saleier* and hurried to her assistance. She found three boats and took on the survivors. As she was doing so, a lookout reported a submarine 1,400 yards away. *Niblack* dropped three depth charges, but the submarine got away. The commander of *Niblack* came back to base at Newport, Rhode Island, to report. He was praised for his attack, not censured.

No information about this incident reached the burghers of Norfolk. A few high-ranking naval officers knew that the U.S. patrol activity had been extended as far as Iceland, but the public had no idea of so much involvement of American ships. The public would have seen the obvious: With American warships dropping depth charges on German U-boats, somebody was going to get killed.

The next incident came on June 9. A U-boat sighted the U.S. freighter *Robin Moor* in mid-Atlantic. She was flying the American flag, but that flag no longer meant neutrality to the U-boat commander. He fired a torpedo and sank her. The crew took to the boats.

Norfolk heard about that sinking; two local men were aboard the ship. Frank Ward, Jr., was assistant engineer, and Virgil Sanderlin was a member of the crew. No one, at the time, knew whether or not they had been saved. (They were.)

When the *Virginian-Pilot* ran the article about the sinking, emphasis was on the warlike act of the Germans. No one asked what the *Robin Moor* was doing in the war zone. Norfolk did not hear about the ships and cargoes that sailed for Britain every day. When Congressman Winder R. Harris of Virginia's Second District took a firm stand in favor of all-out aid to Britain, he did not receive a single letter of complaint or denunciation.

A month after the *Robin Moor* affair, another incident occurred. The battleship *Texas* was patrolling near Greenland a little before dusk when a lookout reported a periscope less than a thousand yards off the port quarter. The alarm rang, the captain altered course and dispatched two destroyers to hunt down the U-boat. But she got away. She was *U-203*, and her captain later reported to Admiral Doenitz that he had tried to get a shot at the battleship, but he could never come to grips with her. By that narrow a margin had a naval engagement been avoided.

Neither Norfolk nor any other American city learned of the *Texas* incident. The U.S. government was keeping a tight veil of secrecy over all its naval operations. So Norfolk did not know that by the middle of summer, 1941, *Texas* and other U.S. warships were operating well inside the area declared as the German blockade of the British Isles.

As summer wore on, the United States assumed responsibility for the defense of Iceland, and with that came deeper involvement: the U.S. Navy undertook to convoy British ships halfway across the Atlantic. It could be only a matter of time until an American warship fought an engagement with a U-boat.

Another confrontation occurred on September 4, 1941, when the destroyer U.S.S. *Greer* was heading toward Iceland on patrol. A British plane signaled that a submerged U-boat lay across the destroyer's path. It was *U-652*.

Greer's crew prepared for action; the ship assumed a zigzag course and slowed to ten knots to allow the sound gear full latitude. She made contact, kept the submarine off her bow for three hours, but did not attack. The captain dropped a pair of depth charges well away from the contact and then left the scene. *Greer*'s commander, Lt. Comdr. L. H. Frost, was issuing a warning; he was not sure what his orders covered. The U-boat was not attacking him; so he decided not to attack it.

The U-boat captain was of a different mind. Since the destroyer had dropped depth charges, he felt free to launch a torpedo attack. He shot one torpedo. *Greer*'s lookouts saw it, and the destroyer then turned and went after the U-boat in earnest. The U-boat fired another torpedo; *Greer* tried to reestablish contact and failed.

Norfolk worked and trained and built ships and sent men to sea, all unaware. Any word that did seep out to the public was so fragmentary that no one could tell that the American course led straight to war.

On September 14, the U.S. destroyer *Truxton* encountered a U-boat on the surface. Each captain knew the other as an enemy. The submarine dived; the destroyer moved to attack. The submarine got away.

In moving onto the Iceland run, American destroyers were openly courting trouble. On October 16, a U-boat wolf pack attacked a British convoy in this area, and five American destroyers came down from Iceland to help. The U.S. destroyer *Kearny* was hit by a torpedo, and 11 Americans were killed and 24 wounded.

This incident was hushed up, too, so Norfolk never knew the truth: "De facto," the American navy was at war with Germany.

On October 31, the *Reuben James*, another U.S. destroyer, was torpedoed 600 miles off Ireland, hardly in American waters. *Reuben James* went down fast, taking all her officers and all but 45 members of her crew.

Once more, the navy tried to suppress most of the facts. That much was impossible, but if many Americans had been killed by the Germans, still the people did not know where or how or why.

On December 7, 1941, in Norfolk then, people were still talking about staying out of the war across the Atlantic.

Norfolk had been working hard all week, and Sunday was the day of rest. Some got into cars and drove into the crisp countryside "to take a ride," a traditional American entertainment of the time. The pious went to church and then to Sunday dinner. Afterward, Norfolk relaxed.

Young people began to drift downtown to the movie houses or to the bars and beerhalls of Granby Street. Sailors came into town on the naval base trolley cars, heading for those same pleasure spots, particularly the Gaiety Theater, which had a girlie show.

At two o'clock, "young marrieds" gathered for "tea dancing" and tuned in to the most popular Sunday radio program of the afternoon, the big band music on WTAR. Old people napped in their chairs.

Suddenly, there came an interruption on the radio.

"Stand by for a special news flash."

And then . . .

"The White House says that the Japanese are attacking Pearl Harbor."

3
WAR!

In Norfolk, with the news that the Japanese had attacked Pearl Harbor, soldiers, sailors, and marines were ordered back to their bases. And as they came in, passes were checked and peacetime laxity became wartime watchfulness; a naval officer's wife, who had, as usual, forgotten her base pass, was turned away from the gate by a sentry who had been letting her through without it for months.

In the town, Police Captain Ted Miller sent officers out immediately to round up the 14 Japanese who lived in the Norfolk area. No one paid any attention to whether they were Japanese or American citizens. Within forty minutes after the first broadcast, they were all in police custody.

Several months earlier, a Coast Guard auxiliary flotilla had been organized in the Norfolk area. Owners of cruising boats had been given reserve commissions, and owners of smaller boats had been enlisted. Now the Coast Guard Reserve flotilla was called to active duty and began a 24-hour harbor patrol. The Regional Defense Council, also organized a few months earlier, began to pull together its lists and take the names of volunteers for civil defense.

In Wilmington, North Carolina, the wife of Governor J. Melville Broughton had just the day before launched the *Zebulon Vance,* the first of 37 Liberty ships, whose building had brought renewed prosperity to that section of the state. The week before, in Raleigh, Governor Broughton had warned his Sunday school class at the Tabernacle Baptist Church that "this country may be at war before we meet here again next Sunday." His prediction had missed the mark by only a few hours. But he was ready: He called together the heads of all the agencies charged with protecting from sabotage such installations as the Wilmington shipyards. Soon, on that afternoon of De-

cember 7 in Raleigh, the counselors began to assemble:
the local FBI agent, the head of the State Highway patrol,
the adjutant general, the head of the office of civilian activities, the Volunteer Civilian Home Guard commander,
and representatives of the local defense councils.

In Wilmington, R. B. Page, chairman of the New Han-
over Defense Council, called a meeting for the next afternoon in his office.

On December 6, Mayor Hargrove Bellamy had suggested
to the Maritime Commission officials at the launching that
Wilmington be given the additional task of loading cargo
for lend-lease. It would add to the city's business prosperity. On December 7, there was no doubt; no one need
worry any longer about what was going to happen to the
shipyards when the 37-ship contract ran out.

Governor Broughton was waiting for a declaration of
war by congress before he called up the Home Guard to
watch over the state's defense activities, especially the railroad and road bridges. Saboteurs, as the governor said,
"could be anywhere."

In Atlantic City, as in Norfolk, the first news of the
Pearl Harbor attack came by radio, over WBAB, the station owned by the *Press-Union*, at 2:32 P.M. For the next
11 hours, the station stayed on the air, alternating local
news broadcasts from its own studios and Associated Press
reports with accounts from the Columbia Broadcasting System's network.

Officialdom had much less to do in Atlantic City than in
Norfolk or Wilmington, for this New Jersey city was pri-
marily a resort. Once Mayor Taggart and Police Chief
Butcher had called up the civil defense council and put
the police department on a 24-hour basis (which meant
16-hour days for the policemen), there was not a great
deal to be done. Some 50 sailors and soldiers on leave came
to police headquarters that afternoon for information,
learned that there was none, and headed off for their posts.

The police assured the community that the city's vital
utilities would be well guarded. Atlantic City Electric Company President Richard Swift assured the citizens that it
was almost impossible for anyone to sabotage the company's new $3 million generator.

Atlantic City, then, remained calm, although someone

heaved a brick through the window of the Oriental curio store run by Mrs. Shige Kato on the boardwalk.

New York City's Times Square was jammed at four o'clock in the afternoon by a noisy, milling crowd that watched the news bulletins racing around the sides of the Times Tower and cheered every gesture of American defiance of the Axis powers. Officially, the activity was the same as the other areas, if larger in scale: Police, port authorities, civil defense, were all alerted.

But what were they to do?

Their actual movement was limited. From Miami to Portland, Maine, defense councils met in solemn session. The business of making schedules, printing cards, planning procedures, began. Air-raid warden schools were established. Auxiliary police began to sign up.

On December 8, the United States declared war against Japan. Since Japan was a member of the Berlin-Rome-Tokyo Axis, or "defense alliance," it seemed certain that Germany and Italy would declare war on the United States within hours.

In Norfolk, on Tuesday, December 9, the army threw up a wall of antiaircraft batteries around the city.

"This city may be attacked by German airplanes any night now . . ." warned the coordinator of disaster planning. "If there are several members of the family, you should have them lie on the floor in different rooms so if one room is hit by a fire bomb, the other members of the family will be able to do rescue work. . . ."

With such alarming words, Norfolk now prepared for war.

On December 12, Germany and Italy declared war. That night, the sirens howled at the Norfolk Navy Base; an unidentified airship had been seen off the coast, and the rumor started that planes had been sighted. The airship turned out to be a navy blimp. No planes appeared.

The first blackout came on Saturday night, December 13. One Freemason Street merchant dutifully shut off his lights, locked the store, and went home, forgetting that the automatic timer would turn on the window display lights at dark. When police summoned him to the shop, shamefaced, he turned off the lights, and Norfolk was very dark, in distinct contrast to careless Portsmouth's bright lights east of the Elizabeth River, beckoning German planes from near and far.

But, of course, there were no German planes within 3,000 miles. There were, however, U-boats preparing to sail for the American shore.

Three days before the German war declaration on the United States, the German naval commander in chief, Adm. Erich Raeder, informed Adm. Karl Doenitz at U-boat command that all restrictions against sinking American ships were removed. So had been the prohibition against operating off the American coast. Doenitz immediately asked Raeder to release a dozen U-boats for operations against America. He was certain the American antisubmarine defenses would be fragmentary. He expected to sink many ships along the Eastern coast of the United States before the American navy could get organized.

Admiral Raeder said that to give Doenitz so many U-boats for that purpose would endanger support of German forces in the Mediterranean theater. He did tell Doenitz he could send six Type VII U-boats to the west. Doenitz would have to make do with them for the moment.

Doenitz went to his map room and looked at his maps and his U-boat roster. He selected the area between the St. Lawrence River and Cape Hatteras as the first zone of attack. He saw that only five of the six Type VII boats were operational at the moment.

These U-boats were 500-ton craft, 220 feet long, with a speed of 7.5 knots submerged but 17.5 knots on the surface. They carried four torpedo tubes, fore and aft, and 14 torpedoes, plus deck guns. Their tanks held enough fuel for a six-week voyage.

Since it might take a U-boat two weeks or more to cross the Atlantic and get on station, Doenitz could only allow a few days for each U-boat to operate before it must head home. Thus, it was imperative that he pick the best men possible.

He chose five of his most experienced captains: Hardegen, Kals, Zapp, Bleichrodt, and Folkers. He interviewed each of them personally and warned them to keep out of sight of enemy forces. They were to attack shipping only when they came on station. If a captain came across a ship of 10,000 tons or more, he might sink it on the way across.

Otherwise, each captain was to await Doenitz's personal orders before beginning operations. He would give them a simultaneous day and time by radio.

In the third week of December, then, the first U-boat set out from submarine pens at Lorient on the French shore. British agents warned London. The word reached the United States just as Prime Minister Winston Churchill and a large party of British officials arrived in Washington to spend Christmas conferring with their American counterparts.

At the Navy Department's two old buildings on Constitution Avenue, the tension began to mount.

Defense against the expected attack was the navy's business. The navy now included the U.S. Coast Guard, which had been placed under naval command by President Roosevelt earlier in the year. And the specific responsibility for command of the territorial waters off the United States coastline was in the hands of a 62-year-old Annapolis graduate and professional officer, Rear Adm. Adolphus Andrews, known to his intimates as "Dolly."

Admiral Andrews' office was on the fifteenth floor of the Federal Building at 90 Church Street in New York City. Below, on the fourteenth floor, was the communications center and plotting room, where the rest of his staff would work in a big bullpen with a few partitioned cubicles along the sides. From these offices, Andrews and the staff were to be responsible for American coastal defenses from the Canadian border to North Carolina. Below that line, Miami and Key West had the authority and the responsibility.

To guard all this undulating coastline of almost 1,500 miles, Admiral Andrews had at the moment at his disposal 20 ships, the largest a 165-foot Coast Guard cutter, and 103 aircraft, most of them obsolete. The vessels could all be anchored in New York City's 79th Street yacht basin on the Hudson River with room to spare. The airplanes would hardly make a stir at LaGuardia Airport.

And as to the efficacy of this defense force:

"There is not a vessel available that an enemy submarine could not outdistance when operating on the surface," the admiral wrote in his war diary. (The top speed of the fastest vessel was 16 knots.) Furthermore, he said, the guns of almost any U-boat the Germans had could out-range the guns of the vessels under Andrews' command.

There were modern warships along the American coast, of course. An entire fleet of battleships, cruisers, destroyers, aircraft carriers, submarines, and other vessels operated out of Hampton Roads. But these were the ships of the Atlantic Fleet. They had to be ready to meet an enemy force. They were not available for defense of the coastal waters of the United States.

Under the overall defense plans of the Joint Chiefs of Staff, the handful of vessels given Admiral Andrews were to be coordinated with the army and navy air services. The army air corps would fly patrols from Westover Field, Massachusetts, Mitchel Field, Long Island, and Langley Field, Virginia. Three army planes from each base would make two patrols daily, as far as 40 miles out at sea. As the admiral knew very well, if there were U-boats off the shore, the chances of their being seen by this wildly scattered defense force were minuscule.

With the enemy on the way, Andrews asked Admiral King for help. King ordered fleet minelayers to mine the approaches to New York Harbor. A week later, Chesapeake Bay approaches were also mined. On December 23, Boston and Portland harbors were ringed by protective screens of mines. That was the most help the fleet could give. Andrews then issued shipping-control regulations. Passenger and freight vessels were routed into the waters most protected and least accessible to the U-boats that were coming.

"Suspected westward movement of enemy submarines now confirmed," said an intelligence report from Washington near the end of December. "Strong indications that sixteen German submarines are proceeding to area off southeast coast of Newfoundland," said a following message.

On December 31, a "submarine periscope" was sighted off the coast of Maine. Planes and patrol boats were sent out. They found nothing.

On January 6, Admiral Andrews received a report from a ship at sea that a whole German fleet was descending on the coast. That would mean battleships, cruisers, and destroyers. The "fleet" turned out to be a handful of fishing boats.

On January 11, U-boat Captain Hardegen's *U-123* was heading west to the assigned position when he happened across the big British passenger steamer *Cyclops*. She qualified under Doenitz's orders. He could not resist the opportunity, although he was 300 miles off Cape Cod, still far from his assigned post. He torpedoed *Cyclops* and sank her.

The ship's captain, Leslie Kerslie, broke radio silence to report that he had been torpedoed. When Admiral Andrews had the word, he ordered the Coast Guard Cutter *Duane* to the coordinates specified by *Cyclops* and sent word to the army air corps' First Bomber Command to try to sink the submarine. The *Duane* found a Canadian corvette picking up survivors. The air corps planes found nothing.

On January 13, Admiral Andrews received several reports of submarines sighted 300 miles east of Nantucket light. They had been seen moving south.

At 11:00 on the morning of January 14, Lt. (jg.) R. H. Braue relieved Lt. Comdr. Bassett as officer in charge at headquarters on Nassau Street. At 11:30, Braue telephoned port authorities that merchant shipping was to be notified of the imminent danger.

Just after midnight, the duty officer at Boston telephoned. A Coast Guard vessel had picked up "submarine noise" south of Nantucket island. Boston and Portland harbors were closed. Newport naval base was notified to send patrol craft out.

At 1:30 on the morning of January 14, a U-boat surfaced and put three torpedoes into a ship 60 miles off Montauk Point, Long Island.

On the evening of January 14, Adeline Edwards, field director of the American Red Cross, at Newport, was notified at Newport Naval Hospital that a vessel had been torpedoed, and there was a possibility the survivors would be brought into Newport.

Edwards began rounding up members of the Newport chapter of volunteer workers, and they assembled at the hospital to wait.

The rumors began.

A ship had been torpedoed . . . Two ships had been torpedoed . . . Every half hour or so, new details were added, most of them imaginary. Shortly after 10:00 P.M. came the official word: *Norness* was the name of the ship. She was a Panamanian tanker. The rescue vessel would bring the survivors to the torpedo station.

Late that night, 38 men were brought safely ashore at the torpedo station.

Two crewmen had been lost in the torpedoing and the confusion of escape from the sinking ship. Two of the 38 had been injured. Since they were civilians, they were not brought to the naval hospital but to Newport civil hospital for treatment. One man was kept there, and another, more seriously injured, was taken to Chapin Hospital in Providence.

The 36 uninjured survivors were kept at the torpedo station overnight. They were treated by naval medical officers for shock and exposure, but they were apparently in good condition.

Captain Fortescue, the naval surgeon, asked Edwards to provide cigarettes, cigars, and civilian clothes since everything the men owned was lost when they leaped from the sinking ship.

Edwards informed the Red Cross volunteers of the need. The chapter president put in orders for warm clothing, and within a few hours, everything was delivered: shoes, socks, underwear, shirts, trousers, lumber jackets, even gloves.

At noon, the survivors faced the tedious processes of officialdom. Immigration officers arrived at the torpedo station and began checking out the status of every man. There were questions to be answered and forms to be filled out. Most of the men had lost all their papers, and the officers had to rely mainly on their statements as to matters of citizenship and identity. Matters were confused because most of the sailors were not Americans but Norwegians, Swedes, and Danes.

The authorities began to make lists. For the next few hours, they tied up the base telephone lines with calls to New York and Boston, as they gave lists of survivors to company officials, the navy, and port authorities.

Then the officials left, and the men waited.

They could not move until the necessary authority arrived from the U.S. Shipping Board in Washington.

There was much to be sorted out. It was all done that day, however, and on the sixteenth, some of the men were moved out. The rest would follow later, to go to Boston and New York, find other berths, and brave the Atlantic once more.

In the next 17 days, 13 vessels would be sunk close to the American coast.

Death had arrived offshore.

4

THE DRUMS BEAT

The operation on which Admiral Doenitz's U-boats were engaged was regarded by the Germans as important enough to merit a code name. It was called Operation Paukenschlag, or Operation Drum Beat. Referring mystically to the Wagnerian dream that characterized the Third Reich, the naval planners saw Paukenschlag as the beginning of the destruction of the West. Now, said the Germans, their hands would no longer be tied by the myth of American neutrality. With all the Atlantic to work, they would have an easier job of sinking ships and destroying the British lifeline.

If Doenitz had been given the submarines he wanted, if the naval master plan had been fulfilled, then this roll on the kettle drums might well have presaged disaster for the West, as the Germans hoped.

In the winter of 1938, when the Third Reich was planning for war, the German navy's Plan Z called for the building of eight superbattleships, a dozen pocket battleships, four aircraft carriers, dozens of heavy cruisers, scores of light cruisers, and hundreds of support ships. There was also a plan for the building of 233 U-boats, a fleet so huge as to stagger the imagination.

But Plan Z went begging. Hitler fancied himself a general, not an admiral. He had little faith in the navy and little understanding of the naval role in a European war. So Doenitz started the war with 56 U-boats, and by the time war with the United States began, he still had only 91 submarines, and they were spread over the Mediterranean, the South Atlantic, North Atlantic, North Sea, and the Arctic Ocean.

In the 17 days after that first attack, however, Doenitz

would show how right he was about the condition of American defenses and what he could have done, given even 20 or 30 U-boats to put on the American station.

On January 17, three of the U-boats worked their way south. That day the Standard Oil tanker *Allan Jackson* was heading north, 60 miles off Cape Hatteras, loaded with 72,000 barrels of Colombian crude oil for delivery in New York.

After midnight, Capt. Felix Kretchmer turned the tanker's bridge over to Second Mate Melvin Rand and went to his cabin to get some sleep. Seaman Randolph Larson was at the wheel. Boatswain Rolf Clausen was down in the messroom playing cards with several others, and Seaman Gustave Nox was just relieving Seaman Hamon Brown as lookout on the forecastle head. At 1:35, two explosions ripped through the ship. The *Allan Jackson* split at the bow, her cargo spewed into the water and caught fire, and the ship began to settle.

Nox and Brown were killed immediately by the explosion.

Rand and Larson were knocked overboard by the force. Boatswain Clausen came on deck, looking for a lifeboat and seamen to man it. Clausen ran to Number 1 lifeboat. It was wrecked. Number 2 boat was jammed in its chocks; Number 4 boat was surrounded by fire that engulfed the ship and spread across the water all around it. Number 3 boat alone remained, and Clausen and seven seamen managed to free it, put it over the side, and jump into it.

Luckily for them, the boat had dropped just aft of an engine-room outlet. A steady stream of water drove the raging flames back from the boat and let the men push away from the fire.

But Clausen found that no one had unlashed the oars, and they could not control the boat. The engine of the *Allan Jackson* was still racing, and the propeller was turning. The boat was being sucked toward the stern. The propeller began to thump against the side of the boat.

Clausen managed to free the oars and push away but then the backwash pushed the boat toward the blazing oil pool astern.

But that backwash also pushed them hard enough to clear the oil. They were safe for the moment. They put the oars into their locks and began to row, away from the split hulk. They rescued one man, Radioman Stephen Verbonich, just before both sections sank.

When the torpedoes struck, Captain Kretchmer was in his cabin. He was thrown to the deck by the force of the explosion, and the cabin filled with flames. He crawled to the bulkhead and managed to escape onto the boat deck through a porthole. He ran along the boat deck and tried to find his crew. He could not see anyone, and then the ship sank under him, the suction carrying him away from the bridge ladder. He went down, struggled, and came to the surface outside the perimeter of fiery water. He found two small boards that would support his weight. He clutched them and drifted away.

Second Mate Rand and Seaman Larson also were washed overboard and found wreckage to support them. The third mate, Boris Voronson, and the junior mate, Francis Bacon, clambered aboard a small raft. They saw Rand and Larson and helped them aboard. Bacon began to get cramps, and lashed himself to the raft. Sometime that night, he died.

The survivors drifted and rowed until dawn, when the U.S. destroyer *Roe* picked them up. Of the 35 members of the crew, only those 13 men survived.

The U-boats followed that same technique night after night. They stayed down all day lest they be spotted by patrol planes and craft. The submarines surfaced after dark to attack. They found it easy, as easy as it had been in the early days off the British Isles, before the English modernized their antisubmarine warfare techniques. As Admiral Doenitz had sensed, the U-boats were dealing with amateurs, civilian captains who had no understanding of naval warfare and naval officers who had never learned how to combat submarines.

Without sufficient warships or planes, Admiral Andrews was virtually defenseless against the onslaught. On January 22, he moved the ship lanes in the Hatteras area 60 miles out to sea to try to confuse the U-boats. The submarines followed immediately, and there was no surcease in sinkings. The change simply meant 60,000 square miles more of open sea for survivors to get lost in.

The U-boats were sinking ships off the American coast at the rate of one a day.

The sinking of the ore ship S.S. *Venore* on January 23 summed up the whole frustrating, deadly struggle.

Venore was an old ship, a tanker built in 1921 and then converted to an ore ship and sold to Bethlehem Steel Company to ply between Cruz Grande, Chile, and Baltimore, carrying iron ore for the steel mills. She was an 8,000-ton vessel, a big prize. Her cargo was obviously essential to the American war effort.

On January 4, 1942, *Venore* had sailed from Cruz Grande with 22,000 tons of iron ore aboard. It was common knowledge in Chile that the submarines were coming, and *Venore*'s captain was worried as he headed north. At the Panama Canal, crewmen got into conversation with soldiers and sailors, and Zeb Scott, the second cook, learned from the scuttlebutt that four tankers had already been sunk off Hatteras. (It was pure rumor, without a shred of fact.)

On January 23, *Venore* was 80 miles off Hatteras. At noon, she came up astern of the British tanker *Empire Sun,* and by twilight, *Empire Sun* was on her starboard quarter. All that evening, the radio officer was busy listening on the naval frequency; earlier in the evening, he had a report that a submarine had been sighted 60 miles east of Wimble Shoals near Hatteras. Dusk closed in and then darkness. By 7:25 that night, the ship was 5 miles south of Diamond Shoals light, traveling in a moderate sea, blown by a Force 4 wind from the southeast. She was making 10 knots. The third mate and the captain shared the bridge. A lookout was stationed forward, and another was aloft. The captain was taking no chances.

Suddenly, off the quarter sounded a tremendous explosion, and *Empire Sun* lit up like a bonfire.

In the glare of the flames, the men of *Venore* saw a submarine on the surface. The U-boat turned toward them, and the men on deck panicked. They streamed toward the boats and tried to lower them. One of the engine-room gang, a Lithuanian whose English was so poor he kept to himself most of the time, climbed up on the poop and jumped overboard. That was the last seen of him.

The captain rang down to the engine room for more speed. The chief engineer came to the bridge to see what was the matter. The captain pointed to the U-boat. The chief engineer raced down off the bridge, onto the ladder that led him back to his engine room.

The bosun and the men were trying frantically to clear the lifeboats, and, like crazy men, they dropped three of them over the side as the ship was moving at more than 10 knots. Two boats smashed immediately, but the third somehow got away with only two men in it.

The submarine had disappeared in the murk, no longer silhouetted against the light from the burning ship. The silence was eerie. The ship moved along, more swiftly as the engines gave every bit of power available. On the bridge, the captain and the third mate strained their eyes but saw nothing.

Then came a lurch, a tremendous explosion in Number 9 ballast tank to port. The chief engineer was on the ladder again, heading upward, and he was blown to his knees. The ship listed sharply to port.

The third mate went to the boat deck to free the remaining lifeboat. The captain headed aft to loosen the life raft on the main deck. That was the last anyone saw of him. The first mate organized the men who slid down the falls into the boat. The radio operator stood at the top on the deck and looked down. The third mate saw him there; then the operator disappeared.

The boat moved away from the side of the sinking ship. Soon they were well away, and the ship disappeared in the darkness.

On the morning of January 24, a plane passed northwest of the lifeboat and circled, then went away. Then the boat passed the two men in the other lifeboat, which was half awash but still floating. There was nothing either boat could do for the other.

The 21 survivors of the *Venore* sailed west that day.

Next morning, Sunday, the survivors were picked up by the tanker *Tennessee*.

Analyzing this and other sinkings at the end of January, Admiral Andrews learned that 3 of the 13 ships sunk had been clearly silhouetted against lights from the shore. Others had been running with lights against all orders. He reported these findings to Admiral King in Washington and recommended that the cities and towns along the shore be ordered to black out their lights at night.

Admiral King reported these findings to the Joint Chiefs of Staff. No one issued an order, for the United States was a democratic republic, not a military dictatorship. But something had to be done. Thus began the laborious task of getting the authority to turn off the shore lights. Simple requests were not effective. Turning off the lights would hurt business.

In Atlantic City, on the Jersey shore, down in Miami, merchants resisted the idea of blackout.

Indeed, as the German captains said, it was a "happy time," like shooting fish in a barrel.

Admiral Andrews called Washington every day asking for help. Give him ships, he asked. But in Washington, Admiral King said there were no more ships to give Andrews. There were few enough ships for any purpose. The destruction of the battleship fleet at Pearl Harbor had necessitated a change in plans. Cruisers, carriers, destroyers, had to go west to replace the sunken fleet. Smaller ships had to go east to shore up the convoy-protection forces. And the battle fleet must be retained for the possibility of a major naval engagement.

Nimitz in the Pacific had a much higher priority than Andrews on the U.S. East Coast. The answers that came back to New York were clear and unequivocal. There would be no more ships. There would be no more bombers.

What was available to Andrews indicated the desperate situation of the American defenses. King said two blimps at the naval air station at Lakehurst, New Jersey, could be assigned to coastal defense. At the air station in Salem, Massachusetts, were a number of unarmed flying boats. He could have them, too. He could also have a few land planes stationed at Portland, Maine. These were, again, aircraft capable of flying patrols not farther than 40 miles out to sea.

That was absolutely all.

5

ONSLAUGHT

The Americans only suspected, but the action in January was just the beginning of what Admiral Doenitz had in mind. Doenitz kept pressing the high command for allocation of more U-boats to the Western Atlantic, and his pleas were heard. In Berlin, the machinery was put in motion.

Along the East Coast of the United States, among those few men who knew what to expect in weeks to come, there was a feeling of absolute helplessness. Death lurked just offshore, at the 100-fathom curve at which the continental shelf drops off into deep water. This was the favorite hunting ground of the U-boats. Along this line, they could strike, submerge, go deep, and then surface to strike again.

There seemed to be almost nothing the U.S. Navy could do to stop them.

In London, Winston Churchill had sensed what was going to happen and sent several messages to Franklin D. Roosevelt with suggestions about dealing with the U-boat menace. Churchill's ultimate answer: Use the convoy.

Roosevelt read the messages. He turned the convoy suggestion over to Admiral King for action. King took it up with his staff, which had nowhere near the confidence in the convoy that the British had (or the experience, either.) Indeed, the whole exchange was marred by a residue of sentiment in the U.S. Navy about the Royal Navy that went back to the War of 1812, a sort of inchoate resentment against anything British—"limey."

So the convoy plan was put well down on the list of defensive measures instead of at the top. Only by stripping the Atlantic fleet of fighting ships could it have been done, and that to the naval mind was unthinkable.

President Roosevelt did not give this matter much personal consideration, for he had many other matters on his mind in these first days of the war. If he had done as Churchill after personal experience in two wars—seen the U-boat threat as a menace more dangerous than any Pearl Harbor attack—he might have changed the course of the sea war. A prompt response, use of planes and ships from the fleet to protect coastal shipping, would have discouraged Doenitz immediately. But there was no hope of it for several reasons. First, the Americans knew virtually nothing about fighting submarines. Second, the Americans could not agree among themselves on a single strategy for defense of the continent. Army, navy, and air forces all wanted to lead the van. There was almost constant quarreling among the members of Roosevelt's staff. And even FDR had as many bad ideas as good ones. One of the more harebrained was his suggestion that Air Corps General Arnold send 50 pilots down to South America for "a few weeks" to teach the Latin Americans how to use depth bombs.

The trouble was that there were as few pilots as there were planes to man in these desperate days, and almost none of them knew anything about depth bombs.

The public, of course, was unaware of the state of defense. Partly, this was because Admiral Andrews had invoked censorship on naval activity along the East Coast. This meant newspapers and radio stations did not discuss the weather or the sailings of ships or interview naval officers and men, although they did interview the survivors of torpedoed ships once they came ashore, and these stories filled the East Coast press.

Even so, it had become apparent that the United States was not in any immediate danger of air attack or invasion. So what had begun as alert verging on hysteria relaxed. The press seemed to be more concerned with economic measures, such as the president's statement that half the national income would go to produce war goods and new federal regulations on the sale of tires and automobiles.

The newspapers said nothing about the bright lights that burned all night in the coastal cities, beacons for the U-boats and shadow boxes along which their prey traveled.

Under censorship, broadcasters and newspaper editors grew restive. Not all shared the view of Norfolk's *Virginian-Pilot* that military matters should be kept secret, so many ignored the rules where they could. Even the *Virginian-Pilot* changed its views when U-boats appeared off the coast. As long as the war had been Britain's, it could be regarded loftily. When it came to the American shore, it suddenly changed guise and became a matter of "public interest."

On Saturday, January 31, an "unidentified rescue vessel" landed 30 survivors of the torpedoed 6,000-ton tanker *Rochester* at the naval operating base at Norfolk. The sinking of the *Rochester* marked the seventeenth strike of a U-boat against shipping off the U.S. coast. It was the first time that a U-boat had made a surface attack in broad daylight and the first attack on shipping off the Virginia coast.

All these details appeared in the *Virginian-Pilot* story, and naval intelligence protested. The newspaper had as good as told the Germans how successful their attack was, how badly defended the coast was, and had given an outline for future action.

In spite of censorship pressures, the press was rising to the story of the U-boat war. That same day, the Associated Press sent out a national dispatch reporting on the sighting of a U-boat off Cape Hatteras by the crew of the freighter *Bellingham*. The naming of the ship was information for an enemy.

One reason for the press attitude was that so little real information, or even explanation of the need to limit information, was seeping out of Washington. The administration had decided to play the war cards "close to the chest." This meant editors were not taken into the confidence of the federal authorities, as they ought to have been (and would be a year and a half later). They were not told how precarious the national situation was at the moment, with the Philippines under siege and all but lost, Japan moving everywhere in the Pacific, and the Germans on the march in the East and in the Mediterranean.

Oddly enough, even journalists within the administration added to the confusion and misinformation. Secretary of the Navy Frank Knox, publisher of the *Chicago Daily News*, issued a series of extremely misleading and untrue statements about the naval war. In December, even before the U-boats had arrived, he boasted that the Americans had "found the answer to the U-boat menace." In the fourth week of January, when the U-boats were beginning their effective war along the coast with no opposition, a navy spokesman claimed that 14 U-boats had been sunk, with the clear implication that the U.S. Navy had sunk them.

Not one submarine had even been damaged by American defense forces at that time.

Any successes, and they were few, were those of Canadian and American forces operating out of Newfoundland and Iceland, not those of the U.S. coastal defenses.

The merchant ship *W. L. Steed* was sunk off the New Jersey coast by a U-boat that came to the surface, stood only 200 yards away from the ship, and poured 17 shells into her from its deck gun. It was as if the Germans were taking target practice in their own protected waters.

The ships traveling alone were no better than swimming ducks. On February 4, the 3,600-ton Panamanian freighter *San Gil* was torpedoed in the same general area. The Coast Guard cutter *Nike* hurried to the scene, and found 38 survivors in boats 15 miles south of Fenwick Island light.

Two hours later, one of the handful of search planes reported a "very suspicious" freighter 30 miles east of Cape Lookout. The pilot was sure he had spotted no fewer than ten 7-inch deck guns. Was she a surface raider?

The searchers did not even know what they were looking for.

Toward evening of that day, the tanker *Indian Arrow* was moving along the Jersey shore, alone. It had been a quiet day aboard ship, and radio operator Edward J. Shear was lying on his bunk in the radio shack when suddenly, just after 6:30, he was slammed out of it onto the deck by a tremendous concussion.

Shear jumped up, ran to his key, and began to tap out the message with the ship's identification letters: S O S KDHP S O S KDHP S O S KDHP. Help, I have been torpedoed. Help, I have been torpedoed. Help, I have been torpedoed.

That message was picked up by Chatham radio station on Cape Cod.

"What is your position?"

Radio operator Shear did not know. He ran out of the shack and found Capt. Carl S. Johnson. The captain began to give him the position, but his voice was drowned out by the explosion of a series of six German deck-gun shells.

The shells started fires; the ship began to burn. She was already listing heavily.

The power failed, and the radio went dead before Shear could reply to Chatham. He tried the auxiliary radio, but it was out, too.

Feeling that the ship was going, Shear ran on deck and jumped over the rail. *Indian Arrow* went down as he swam away from her side. As the ship sank, flotsam arose from the wreck, including a hatch cover. The operator found this and clung to it.

With torpedoing and shelling, the crewmen forward had rushed to the boats and got two boats away before the *Indian Arrow* went down. The crewmen aft were not so lucky; the torpedo had struck just aft of the engine room, and only two men escaped from that compartment, and one more from the sleeping spaces above.

As the boats went over the side, *Indian Arrow* was already sending pools of blazing oil around the ship. One boat stayed in the shadow of the hull just a little too long. *Indian Arrow* groaned and rolled over on the boat, crushing it. No men came up from the wreckage.

The other boat managed to get clear. In the darkness and the blazing oil, the men rowed to get past the flames. As they came out of the ring of blazing light, 300 feet from the sinking ship, they saw the submarine on the surface. It ignored them.

The men of the boat found the radio operator clinging to his hatch cover and took him aboard. Then they headed for the shore. They had no trouble finding the way, for they could see the lights of Atlantic City brightly shining off to the west. Their ship had been framed for the U-boat against the glow.

A few minutes after the messages and the sudden end to them indicated possible trouble aboard *Indian Arrow,* a seaman at Fifth Naval District headquarters looked her up in the registry. She was a Socony Vacuum tanker. At 7:20, Fifth Naval District sent a message to the company. What was the last reported position of their tanker?

The message, of course, arrived at night, and Socony

Vacuum was still on a peacetime schedule. So no one read the message till next morning, and it was one o'clock in the afternoon before the navy had a reply.

"Near Winter Quarter shoals lightship."

A patrol vessel was sent to that point, hoping to find survivors. The duty officer at Fifth Naval District also telephoned the duty officer at Langley Field, the army air base. He asked the army to send a plane to search for survivors.

The army's answer was an unequivocal "no." Langley Field had its orders: No planes were to be dispatched on unauthorized missions. Authority could only be secured from the commanding general, First Air Force in New York.

Disgusted, the Fifth Naval District turned to the naval air station at Norfolk. Four planes were sent out, and one of them spotted the bow of *Indian Arrow,* still floating, 30 miles from the position noted by Socony Vacuum.

At Fifth Naval District, the admiral heard of the army's refusal to help and sent the army liaison officer up to Langley to see what was the matter. He got no more cooperation had than the navy. He was told to go see First Air Force.

It took a call from Admiral Andrews to First Air Force's Maj. Gen. Follett Bradley to begin the unraveling of the confusion, as the survivors of *Indian Arrow* drifted and rowed toward the beckoning shore. They fell afoul of the current and were carried south and east, and then they rowed west again. Finally, after a day and a half in the boat, they were picked up, not by the navy searchers but by a pair of Jersey cod fishermen, Capt. Frank Marshall and John Shaw, in the 24-foot skiff *Gitana.*

As they were coming ashore, in the same waters where *Indian Arrow* had been hit, a U-boat sank her sister ship *China Arrow.*

Four ships, then, had been sunk virtually at the doorstep of Atlantic City in less than a week. The word had reached the newspapers, and they were quarreling with Admiral Andrews and with the Navy Department in Washington about official censorship. So when the survivors of *China Arrow* were landed at Lewes, Delaware, the Fourth Naval District actually invited reporters to the scene to get the story. The sinking of this ship, and of *W. L. Steed, San Gil,* and *Indian Arrow,* became national news stories, sent by the press associations across the nation. For the first time, the public was told all the details: how *Indian Arrow* was torpedoed at night; how *China Arrow* was sunk in broad daylight; how *W. L. Steed* had been shelled from only 200 yards away; and how *San Gil* had been torpedoed at night against the lights.

So Atlantic City and the other cities along the East Coast of the United States were learning about the U-boat war. But on the boardwalk, every night the lights still blazed.

Blackout?

It would ruin business, said the merchants.

6

WHEN DEFENSE
WAS NO DEFENSE

Admiral Andrews and his staff could add as well as could
Admiral Doenitz. They knew the basic capabilities of the
Type VII U-boats, and from Naval Intelligence they knew
that the boats they faced must be Type VII because they
(and the even bigger U-boats just in construction) were
the only craft of the U-boat fleet capable of journeying
across the Atlantic and returning without refueling.

Andrews believed, in early February, that they were
facing the second wave of U-boats. Actually, the last of
the first five had not been dispatched until January 25. All
this damage off the Jersey coast and Cape Hatteras was
being caused by two boats, not a whole flotilla, as the
defenders imagined.

The press even now seemed somehow to miss the point
that the Eastern U.S. coast was the focal point of an
attack. Norfolk's *Virginian-Pilot* seemed more worried
about the peril from Japanese submarines to the West
Coast. Two U-boats that had participated in the Pearl
Harbor attack had then journeyed east and shelled installations off the California coast and sunk several ships
off California and Oregon.

The *Virginian-Pilot,* in discussing the Atlantic attacks,
spoke of the "German submarines which have been attacking American commerce in the Atlantic coastal lanes" as
if the emphasis were the same.

Of course, there was no way for the editors of the
Virginian-Pilot to know what was in Doenitz's mind, and
Washington did not help them much. But across the
Atlantic, Winston Churchill did know. He was growing
ever more alarmed as the sinking reports from the West

reached his desk day after day. They told their own story: The American defenses were totally inadequate.

To show the seriousness with which he regarded the situation, the prime minister, hard pressed as he was at home, ordered 24 precious trawlers to America. They were small ships, simple trawlers, not converted trawlers. They had not been changed one iota since they had been brought in from coastal waters and stopped the fishing. The British sacrificed them in these desperate hours to meet needs Churchill said were more immediate even than their own.

When Admiral Andrews learned that the trawlers would come, his delight was an indication of the desperation to which the Eastern Sea Frontier (the new name of Admiral Andrews' command) had been reduced. Not only were the trawlers tool-less, "not even a spanner," as one officer said cheerily, but they were not equipped for service in southern waters, such as those off much of the American coast. They had no ventilation, and their amenities were Spartan. These ships had been built for short voyages around the North Sea and the cold waters off Scotland. They were also coal burners, whose cranky furnaces were used to the hard anthracite Cardiff coal. Andrews knew of all these serious problems and rejoiced. They were ships, and he was going to have them.

Andrews also asked Admiral King for the assignment of at least two destroyers to help deal with the critical situation he faced off New Jersey and the Chesapeake. The events of the first week of February indicated a number of U-boats were out there. The attack, said Andrews, was in "full fury."

Since most of the destroyers of the Atlantic Fleet were located around the Virginia Capes, it was possible to have them if King would only agree.

Admiral King seemed to respond favorably. On February 5, Andrews was told he had the use of no fewer than seven destroyers: *H. P. Jones, Roe, Ludlow, Wainwright, Mayrent, Trippe,* and *Rowan.*

The Eastern Sea Frontier lost no time in making assignments and sending the destroyers to sea on patrol. The trouble was that the first of the U-boats to arrive on the coast had run out of ammunition and supplies and had gone home, and the last of the five, dispatched on January

25, had not yet completed the two-week voyage across the Atlantic. So the seven destroyers had no contacts. Suddenly, the sinkings stopped. Admiral Andrews' plaints rang hollowly in the halls of the Main Navy Building in Washington.

But by any standards, deprived of the seven destroyers, Andrews' defenses were pitiable. Two months into the war, the only armed patrol planes on the coast were located at the Norfolk naval air station, and the Atlantic fleet complained that their use for antisubmarine patrol would interfere with the fleet training program.

When Andrews asked for planes, Admiral King suggested that 42 PBY flying boats would be available in March or April, but that was a long time off for men who could almost see the submarines out there, roaming at will. In this lull, King decreed that no matter what happened offshore, the squadrons would be brought up to fleet strength before the shore patrols would have any planes. No one seemed bothered by the anomaly of squadrons training while the enemy went unmolested.

One excited young officer of Eastern Sea Frontier came to Admiral Andrews to announce that he had discovered 40 PBYs at Elizabeth City, North Carolina. They were being armed and made ready for duty. Why couldn't the Eastern Sea Frontier have these?

Because they were bound for Britain, said Main Navy.

Couldn't someone at least ask?

But Winston Churchill said the British need was greater and more immediate. The only way the U-boats could be kept down at all was to patrol off the French coast. And patrol bombers alone could reach out to midocean and offer some protection to the convoys on their dangerous journey from the point where the Western defenses ended and the Eastern convoy defenses began. Beyond bomber range, in that great middle section, the convoys had only their handful of escorts to save them from destruction if they could.

In the end, all the young officer's "discovery" accomplished was the speeding of delivery of the PBYs to England.

Andrews had an ally in Adm. Russell R. Waesche, commander of the Coast Guard. Waesche complained to

Admiral King that since the Coast Guard had been taken over by the navy, it had not only lost its entity, but Coast Guardsmen were not being properly used in their specialties. His protest, particularly about the deprivation of patrol planes, was so vigorous that he managed to secure a commitment for 40 patrol planes, but it was only a commitment. The planes would not come until March.

All along the coast, Andrews and Waesche searched for vessels that might help in this emergency. For even though the submarines had left, Andrews knew that more would soon be on the way. (They were already almost finished with the voyage.)

Admiral King authorized the use of 70- and 80-foot Coast Guard cutters as patrol craft, which pleased Waesche and Andrews as well. The ships were to be fitted with 1-pound guns, .50-caliber machine guns, and depth-charge racks. If sound gear could be found for them, they were to have it.

The search turned to the yachts of the wealthy. That month, 23 of them were turned over to the U.S. Maritime Commission to be made into warships.

Alva, the $3-million yacht of William Kissam Vanderbilt, joined the fleet and became a patrol vessel. The naval officer chosen as her captain had a few surprises in store for him.

On the first night aboard, he climbed into the bed in the big stateroom and went to sleep. Next morning, rolling over drowsily, his sleep-fogged eyes focused on a panel of buttons on the bulkhead a few inches from his nose.

The captain pressed a button. He heard a noise, and then a bar, complete with bottles, came sliding out of the paneling alongside the bed.

He pressed a second button and found his whole bed moving. The bulkhead slid away, and the bed traveled through the space and came to a stop directly beside the bed of his executive officer in the adjoining cabin!

It did not take long for the navy to rectify these military defects.

Only slightly less dazzling than the rakish *Alva* were William B. Leeds' $2-million *Mona* and Miss William Boyce Thompson's *Alder,* which had carried a peacetime crew of ten.

Boston financier Robert Herrick gave his yacht for the duration. So did New York's Arthur Lehman of the banking firm, Henry Ford, the auto builder, Huntington Hartford, the A & P heir, Joseph Davies, the business magnate, and Mrs. Jesse Hall Du Pont, of the chemical and munitions company.

The craft ranged from 36 to 316 feet in length. Thirteen of the largest ones went to the navy, seven to the Coast Guard, the rest to auxiliary service. It was not too much to say that these private yachts were the sinew of U.S. coastal defenses in that winter of 1942.

The civilian effort was far more important than most Americans ever knew. All up and down the East Coast, the inadequacy of military coastal defenses had led to the buildup of coastal patrols manned by civilian air pilots flying their own planes, at their own expense most of the time. They were unpaid volunteers.

In Charleston, the patrol squadron was Civil Air Patrol No. 8, or Lucky Eight, as its members called it. Lucky Eight operated out of James Island Airport, under Capt. S. B. Mahaffey.

The patrol group was responsible for a long segment of the coast, flying eight missions a day, four north and four south, looking for U-boats. Between missions, pilots and air crewmen relaxed at Andre's restaurant on Folly Road, their unofficial headquarters and clubhouse.

One February day, the war came home to Lucky Eight. Clarence Rawls and Drew King climbed into their patrol plane after routine briefing. They were to fly along the Grand Strand this morning. They took off, circled the field, and then headed out to sea.

Somewhere out there, something happened, and the plane never came back. Searchers went out to find them, but there was nothing down below but the cold and empty sea.

In Charleston that night, there was mourning for casualties of the war. The U-boat menace had become real.

7

THE ADMIRALS TAKE STOCK

When Kapitaenleutnant Hardegen of *U-123* returned to German submarine headquarters in February to report to Admiral Doenitz, he told how it had been in American waters and urged that the admiral send every possible boat across the Atlantic.

Doenitz already knew part of the story, but it was even more persuasive in person. Hardegen's *U-123* had sunk the *Norness* in January. She had then moved down the Long Island coast, going very close to shore as she discovered there were no defenses. Twenty miles off Southampton, *U-123* had sunk the British tanker *Coimbra*.

Hardegen had then turned south during the last few days of January and headed for Cape Hatteras. It was *U-123* also that had sunk the Esso tanker *Allan Jackson*. Then she sank the *Norvana,* a small freighter, and the *City of Atlanta.*

In detail, Hardegen told how he had been blessed with a surfeit of targets off Wimble Shoals. One night, he saw three ships moving around the light buoy at the northwest end of the shoals and five more, all lighted up like Christmas trees, coming at him in another line.

At that point, *U-123* had only two torpedoes left. Hardegen had brought the boat to the surface then and opened up with his deck gun on the tanker *Malay*. He torpedoed the Latvian freighter *Ciltvaria* and also sent his last torpedo into *Malay* as she ran for the safety of Norfolk, blazing and badly damaged. He thought she had sunk; in fact, she made it to safety. After that last encounter, Hardegen had turned toward Europe, to claim the sinking of 100,000 tons of shipping on this war patrol.

In fact, Hardegen had sunk eight ships with a combined displacement of 53,360 tons and had damaged several others. The other four U-boats in this first wave had sunk another 140,000 tons. Put in terms of war goods the Americans were trying to send across the Atlantic, the German effort by five U-boats in about a month had cost the allies the following:

    400 tanks
    60 8-inch howitzers
    880 25-pound guns
    400 two-pound guns
    240 armored cars
    500 Bren carriers
    52,100 tons of ammunition
    6,000 rifles
    4,280 tons of tank supplies
    20,000 tons of stores
    10,000 tanks of gasoline

Based on an analysis made by the logistics experts, in order to destroy this much equipment by aerial bombardment, the Germans would have to fly 30,000 bombing missions.

No wonder P.M. Winston Churchill was so worried. The British were using 750,000 tons more of supplies each month than were coming through by convoy. The situation grew worse by the day.

Churchill sent a special message to presidential adviser Harry Hopkins to call Roosevelt's personal attention to the immediacy of the problem. Roosevelt did not reply. What could he say? Admiral King and Admiral Andrews did not have the answers. The defenses simply were not effective, as those five U-boats had discovered. They had left the American shore, chaos behind them.

One sign of it was a mutiny by men of the merchant marine. Early in February, half a dozen ships, loaded for England and British colonies in the south, were tied up in New York harbor. Their civilian crews flatly refused to take the ships to sea, to face U-boats without any protection. They had no confidence in American defenses.

The quarrel had been building for some time. The men of the National Maritime Union felt badly abused, and the union called for, and got, a congressional investigation of naval practices. As far as treatment was concerned, Trinidad, in the Caribbean, was singled out as an extreme example. American seamen landed from torpedoed ships were not allowed to enter the U.S. naval base canteen at Trinidad. When they complained, they were ignored by the American consul even though they had only the clothes on their backs. They found it hard to come by razors, soap, and toothbrushes.

The seamen were also victims of the old British class system: Their officers were quartered in hotels and invited to all the clubs. The stranded seamen were taken to temporary camps so carelessly made that the tents did not have floorboards, and the toilet facilities consisted of outhouses.

Also, when the merchant ships reached West Indian ports undamaged, civilian seamen were kept aboard the ships, while naval enlisted men were allowed to go ashore.

But now came the greater issue: safety. Until it could somehow be solved, the seamen said, they would not sail the ships.

Many captains agreed with the men, but owners and enough captains sided with the authorities to push the men back into service with real and implied promises.

The hiatus, in the middle of February, between the successive waves of U-boats resolved the problem, it seemed. But nothing had changed; the coastal defenses were still totally unorganized.

What had seemed to be improvement was quickly ended. The second and third weeks of February had brought surcease of U-boat losses along the coast. So Admiral King whisked away the seven destroyers he had "given" Admiral Andrews.

King, unfortunately, completely misread the intentions of the Germans. Doenitz's enthusiasm for the western Atlantic was so strong that he ordered all new U-boats to proceed to western France as soon as they were ready for service. It was his intention to load them and send them to the American theater.

In February, six more U-boats were ready for dispatch to America, as the first wave returned. This time Doenitz sent them to begin at the south, in the Caribbean. He wisely estimated that whatever defenses the United States was pulling together would be concentrated in the area the first five U-boats had just left.

And so, as Admiral King took back the seven destroyers to dispatch them to the mid-Atlantic, the U-boats were moving toward the Caribbean. There were no U-boats at all operating in mid-Atlantic at this time. Seven boats were deployed for protection of German-held Norway, where Hitler expected an invasion (which did not come). Three were off Gibraltar, preying on British ships heading into the Mediterranean. That was all. Doenitz was disrupting Anglo-American defenses with just 16 U-boats in service. But Admiral Andrews had almost nothing at all.

Admiral King was playing a double game: Andrews was almost immediately "assigned" three more destroyers. But by now he knew that meant he would have them for a few days, and then they would be jerked away.

Once more, in February, the British pressed the Americans to institute the convoy system. They argued that it was the one effective protection against U-boat losses. Pushed, in turn, by President Roosevelt, Admiral King moved: He called on Admiral Andrews to present him with a plan for convoy operation.

Admiral Andrews was stunned. The operation of convoys presupposed the existence of protective forces, and he had no protective forces. But an order from the commander in chief was an order. Andrews called his naval district commands and his staff and asked for advice.

Two weeks later, Admiral Andrews responded to Admiral King's demand.

Every day there passed through the Eastern Sea Frontier between the Carolinas and the Canadian border some 120–130 ships that needed protection against the enemy. There were two ways, said Andrews, to protect those ships.

One way was convoy. He had available for convoy in mid-February 9 suitable escorts that could make 14 knots or better. He had also 19 other vessels that could make between 12 and 14 knots.

Altogether, then, he could assemble 28 vessels for convoy duty. That meant stripping every harbor of every defense vessel. Still, he would not be able to give any air cover. He had no long-range bombers and could only call in emergency for the use of the fleet planes at Norfolk.

He recognized that convoys would persuade the reluctant seamen to man their ships, but without air cover, the convoys would be blind.

The second means of protection, the admiral said, was to concentrate his forces in the danger areas and be ready to rush out to fight if the threat appeared.

Given what he had for fighting, he advised against the convoy. What he was really saying was that it was impossible to divide 28 vessels into even two convoys, one northbound and one southbound, every day.

There was one bright light in all this darkness. Patriotism was bursting out across America. Before December 7, the country had been sharply divided on the war. It had not been easy to persuade civilians that there was any need to change the way they did things.

The uproar raised by the merchant seamen brought congressional focus on the shore defense effort. In his history of U.S. naval operations, Samuel Eliot Morison blames the newspapers for forcing the navy into using destroyers for shore defense when they should have been involved in fleet operations. ("Hunting hornets all over the farm," said Morison, quoting a remark by President Woodrow Wilson from World War I.)

But the uproar indicated a vital change in America. Congressmen were demanding investigations of defense efforts. Newspapers exhorted the public to go easy on tires, watch the gas in their cars, and give up cigarettes for the duration, as well as meat, aluminum, grease, and a hundred other things.

The War Production Board was restricting use of tin, copper, and lead. Spices were in short supply. So was tea. Tires were rationed already, so now was retreading. Gasoline rationing was expected momentarily, and there was talk of rationing of farm fertilizer and farm machinery. Tin containers were prohibited for use in tobacco, beer, and dog food.

In Norfolk, the duck hunters had raised an outcry when the navy threatened their treasured hunting grounds. That was back in 1941. This was 1942, and when, on February

6, the navy condemned 508 acres of land for the naval air station, including the Norfolk Golf and Country Club's clubhouse, nobody even whimpered.

It wasn't the admirals' war any longer. It was America's war.

8

OIL ON THE BEACHES

With the dangers outside and the refusal of some ships' crews to go to sea, Admiral Andrews was forced to a new plan that would promise ships a degree of safety. He announced that henceforth ships would move "inside," making as much use as possible of inland waterways. Where that was not possible, the Eastern Sea Frontier would concentrate defense craft and keep all vessels close to the coast so the handful of aircraft could keep an eye on them. Up north, where the Canadians had escort vessels, he would run convoys from Cape Cod to Halifax.

But for the sort of convoy duty that entailed, the British way, he would need 64 more vessels, and he did not have them. So there would be no convoys anywhere else.

The Germans continued to be astonished at the ease with which they could attack in American waters. The second wave sent out by Doenitz arrived in the Caribbean. On February 16, a submarine surfaced and shelled an oil refinery at Aruba in the Dutch West Indies. That same day, six small tankers were sunk off Maracaibo. Two days after that, a U-boat appeared in the Gulf of Paria and torpedoed two ships anchored off Port of Spain.

All this occurred under the noses of American naval defenders who had established bases and created a Caribbean Defense Command in the south.

Having achieved maximum surprise and forced the cessation of shipping from several ports, the U-boats turned north again. This time they headed for Florida.

On February 19, the *S.S. Pan Massachusetts* was sunk off Cape Canaveral, a tanker again. Doenitz had been very specific about tankers. She was the first ship lost in the newly organized Gulf Sea Frontier.

Within a matter of hours, *Pan Massachusetts* was followed by the tankers *Cities Service Empire* and *Republic*. But these were torpedoed much farther south, in the Jupiter-Palm Beach area. It was apparent that more than one submarine was at work. Actually, there were two: *U-128* off Central Florida and *U-504* in the south.

Florida began to get a taste of what was to come that spring as oil from the sunken tankers drifted onto the white sand beaches.

Naval patrol craft, Coast Guard cutters, and planes combed both areas, but they found nothing. It was much too easy for a U-boat to surface, attack, and dive again. There was no way a handful of defenders could cover all that ocean. They learned about submarines for the most part when they attacked.

Occasionally, however, a search plane had luck. *U-504* was hanging about the Jupiter area, and that night she surfaced to charge batteries. Just after midnight, a navy dive bomber was dispatched from Miami's air station on patrol. Lieutenant Ostromm, the pilot, found the moon bright and the sea calm. At 1:15, he was over Jupiter Light when he sighted something: the periscope, conning tower, whole hull of a surfaced submarine. Ostromm dived and attacked and swore his bomb hit the crash-diving submarine as it went down.

That same night, up north off Central Florida, the tanker *W. D. Anderson* was chased by a submarine but managed to escape.

For two days, the naval men congratulated each other on Ostromm's "kill." Then, on the night of February 21, war came ashore at Jupiter Inlet.

The shore there has a peculiar structure which brings ships closer to land than any other place on the coast of Florida. The Gulf Stream slides in near Jupiter Inlet, carrying with tremendous force the ships that are in its grip. In the days of sail, many a bark and brig was washed up on that shore, and many a life was lost in the storms of winter.

In October 1939, Jupiter Inlet residents had a taste of war when the flotsam from a scuttled German tanker washed up. But after that "World War II was only a black headline in our morning paper and a voice over the radio," one resident said.

Jupiter Inlet's tranquility was shattered on February 21 by an explosion that shook the night and rattled every window in the community. Dishes fell off the shelf and broke. One householder went running from room to room to see if some member of the family had fallen out of bed. Lights went on. Telephones began to ring.

What had happened?

In an hour, the people of Jupiter Inlet began to learn when two lifeboats came ashore, and from them climbed men dripping oil.

They were crewmen of the tanker *Republic*, which *U-504* had found and torpedoed in sight of land.

That night, Capt. Alfred Anderson shepherded his men into the houses of the Scrantons and the Bartletts, where they were made welcome and given baths, dry clothing, food, and drink. They stayed only a few hours; Captain Anderson made a telephone call, and navy trucks arrived to take the survivors to a hotel in Palm Beach.

Next morning, the whole community went out to see the ship, grounded just offshore in 6 fathoms of water. The stern rested on the bottom, and the bow rose high.

Leonard Smith and Kenneth Myers, two of the more intrepid youths of the village, decided to take a boat out and have a closer look. They brought the boat up alongside the hulk, avoiding the oil patches that were steadily moving inshore to coat the beach. "Smitty" climbed aboard. He saw nothing at first but bits of clothing and wreckage trapped in the hatches. Then he heard a yapping, and out of some hidden crevice came a little wire-haired terrier. The dog ran to him, barking and wagging its tail.

"Smitty" rescued the terrier and lowered him into the boat. Then he beckoned Myers on deck. They managed to launch one lifeboat and tied it to the stern of their work boat. They found several hundred feet of good hemp cable, too.

"Smitty" took the tiller on the way in, and Myers held the little dog. They brought the two boats in, moving far around to the south to navigate the inlet.

The young men were elated at so successful a salvage.

But as they came in to dock, towing the lifeboat, they were faced by stern Coast Guardsmen. The prize was impounded, the cable confiscated, and the dog picked up by a Coast Guardsman. The two youths were ordered to appear next day before the naval commander of the district. The charge was looting.

But friends intervened. They pleaded the youth of the pair and that young Smith was scheduled to appear in Miami Beach next day for induction into the army.

The last argument won the day. The charges were dropped, and the Coast Guardsmen went away.

The Coast Guard had other more serious worries just then. A few hours after the two youths had visited the wreck of *Republic,* men working at the inlet and drivers on the ocean road watched as the tanker *W. D. Anderson* blew sky-high. She had escaped *U-128,* only to come into *U-504*'s operating zone.

Most of the 34 men of *W. D. Anderson*'s crew were in the mess room when the submarine attacked. Two of them finished dinner and took their coffee up onto the fantail. Then they saw the torpedo coming. Frank Terry dove straight out from his deck chair into the sea and swam under water as long as his lungs held out. He surfaced, saw burning gasoline all around him, ducked, and swam again until his lungs seemed about to burst. He came up and found himself clear of the flames.

His friend hesitated for a fraction of a second and was never seen again. Nor were any of the other 32, all blown up in the fiery blast that rose 100 feet in the air, as what was left of the *W. D. Anderson* sank in 40 fathoms of water.

A Coast Guard vessel came out, and as the flames on the water died down, it combed the area. The Coast Guardsmen found nothing and were just finishing the last sweep before abandoning the search when a lookout spotted a single swimmer, laboring. They pulled Frank Terry into a boat, covered with gasoline and stiff with cold. He alone of the crew of the *W. D. Anderson* survived.

The coastal defenders obviously still had no defense. But the people of Florida and the other coastal states could only guess at the truth, for the navy told them anything but the truth. On February 25, Secretary Knox announced that three U-boats had been sunk and four "probably damaged" since January 1. The actual score: zero. The hunters had enthusiasm but little else.

On February 28, a lookout at American Shoals light off the Florida coast heard gunfire and saw a merchant ship turn and begin to list. He reported a submarine attack (*U-504* again), and a PBY was sent out from the naval air station at Key West to investigate and hunt down the U-boat.

An hour and a half later, the pilot of the PBY reported a periscope 15 miles from the light. He dropped floats and circled to attack. Five minutes later, he saw his quarry and moved in. He dropped two depth charges.

Following the aircraft's contact reports, naval authorities dispatched several surface vessels. The Coast Guard cutter *Triton* came up along with the destroyer *Hamilton* and the patrol boat *PC-449*. Fifteen minutes later, *Hamilton*'s sound man declared he had contact with a submarine, and the destroyer attacked with depth charges. A patch of oil 25 yards square came to the surface. Then sound contact was lost.

Three more seagoing craft arrived on the scene, and they formed a 6-mile scouting line. At three o'clock, *Triton* made a sound contact and dropped seven depth charges. Ten minutes later, she made another contact and dropped six more depth charges. Her captain's action report gave the details:

"Where the starboard Y-gun charge exploded an unusual agitation was observed, with quantities of air and foam coming up. In a few seconds a large black object, projecting 2 feet out of water and tapering 20 feet back to the water, arose in the center of the area, and then slipped back under the water."

The sailors aboard ship swore that they had seen the submarine, and that black form was the under side of the hull as she sank. Nobody saw a conning tower. There was no more oil.

The captains of *Triton* and *Hamilton* conferred. They agreed that they had sunk a submarine.

They also agreed that there should be another around the area, so they continued the search. At five o'clock that afternoon, sure enough, *Triton* made another contact. She went in with her last few depth charges, and *Hamilton* crossed over her stern and dropped three more.

This time nothing was heard.

These searchers were a determined lot. They reformed the scouting line and reversed course. They had traveled 21 miles from the point of the first contact, and then they spotted an oil slick 500 yards long and 100 yards wide. Just there, *Hamilton* made another sound contact; obviously the submarine was moving along slowly under the surface.

Hamilton moved in to attack. She dropped three depth charges. Then the Y gun jammed. She sheared off, and *PC 449* came in to drop more depth charges.

All was quiet then. No oil was seen. There was no debris.

The captains of *Hamilton* and *Triton* conferred once more. This second submarine must be damaged or sunk. But it was getting late, and *Hamilton*'s ability to fight was impaired, and *Triton* was out of depth charges. It was time to go home.

They headed for port then, preparing their action reports: one U-boat sunk, one U-boat badly damaged.

When they returned to port, their reports were correlated with those of the naval air station's PBY. In the debriefing that had followed the mission, the pilot and copilot of the patrol bomber had sworn they saw that submarine before they dropped their depth charges. But the port blister gunner had also looked down, and what he saw was a whale.

In the end, the claims of *Hamilton* and *Triton* were quietly forgotten. At Gulf Sea Frontier, they knew the whales had taken a dreadful beating that day.

9
THE FATE OF *JACOB JONES*

If the defenders at sea seemed fettered by inexperience, so, too, were those ashore. Norfolk took civil defense seriously, and in February began the training of air-raid wardens. Some 1,800 wardens received five hours of instruction in their duties that month. Auxiliary police were training to take the places of the men called away to war and to augment the force, just in case of need. Auxiliary firemen were being trained by the fire department.

The head of the emergency public-works department was planning for future demolition of buildings wrecked by bombs. The decontamination division was ready for gas attacks. In February, 58 instructors were trained to teach others the methods of combating gas warfare if it hit the coast.

The medical service established casualty stations and assigned doctors, nurses, and aides to every one of them.

The city itself was more or less relaxed about the war in spite of all this activity. There had not been a total black-out since the practice attempts of December. Nothing had happened, and no enemy planes had swooped in; in mid-February, it seemed unlikely that they would ever come.

In this period of respite from U-boat attack, Admiral King urged speed in laying more minefields along the coast to discourage the submarines. King had already ordered contact mines laid between Cape Cod and Cape Ann. Again, however, it was the same old problem: Where would he find the minelayers? The minelayers *Monadnock* and *Miantonomah* were supposed to be made available for the task, but they could not do it until January, said the fleet, and then in January's last days, the fleet said they could not do it until February 20. On February 20, the weather was so bad offshore that the minelaying was postponed until March 1.

In New York, it was the same situation, complicated by another factor. Admiral Andrews observed that it would be too dangerous for ships to run through minefields unless he had at least 20 patrol vessels to bring them in and out. He did not have them. Before the end of February, he had managed to persuade Washington not to put the mining plan into effect.

At the beginning of the third week of February, it seemed that perhaps all these precautions would be unnecessary, anyhow. The U-boats had gone. Shipping moved along the road undisturbed. Soon the nervous merchant seamen regained heart. Perhaps it was all over. But then came the reports from Florida.

On the night of February 26, the tanker *S. P. Resor* was traveling south of Manasquan, off the New Jersey coast, when she was torpedoed by a U-boat.

On shore, Police Sergeant William Briden of Belmar saw a sheet of flame rise 200 feet in the air. She was so close to shore that rescue boats set out from the bank to try to reach her. They found three men, and that was all.

As morning came, smoke could be seen drifting northward in the wind, past the place where the big liner *Morro Castle* had burned in 1934.

Then two days later came an even more audacious attack. The U.S. destroyer *Jacob Jones* sailed from Brooklyn Navy Yard on the day after the sinking of *S. P. Resor*, on patrol for Admiral Andrews. *Jacob Jones* was at the disposal of the Eastern Sea Frontier command until she was detailed elsewhere. On this day, she was ordered to share a search area with U.S.S. *Dickerson* down along the Delaware capes. Her area extended from Barnegat to the lighted buoy that marked the 5-fathom bank. She was to cruise along the 100-fathom curve about 40 miles offshore during the daylight hours and then at night to move in toward shore.

Jacob Jones passed the burning bulk of *S. P. Resor*, off Sea Girt. She stopped and spent two hours searching for survivors but found none.

At 7:58 that night, *Jacob Jones* was in position to begin patrol, and she began traversing the area, moving at 15 knots. The night was calm, although a little hazy, and the full moon shone down on a quiet sea.

At four o'clock in the morning, the watch changed. The ship was at Condition 2, alert, but not alarmed. The crow's nest was manned by a lookout, and men were forward on either side of the galley deck house, looking ahead for signs of trouble. She was not zigzagging but was moving straight along.

An hour went by on the new watch. Then a torpedo slammed into *Jacob Jones* forward, and almost immediately another struck aft.

The impact was devastating. Fireman 3c. George Edward Pantall was watching the gauges in Number 2 fireroom when suddenly his feet went out from under him, and he was on the floor plates. The pressure in the boilers dropped 50 pounds as fast as the needle would travel. Pantall picked up a life preserver and headed up the ladder.

On deck, Able Seaman Adolph Ring Storm was standing his watch on the starboard side of the top of the galley deck house. He, too, was knocked down by the impact. He got up, climbed down the ladder to the main deck and began to help others try to free the lifeboats. It was apparent that the *Jacob Jones* had received a mortal injury.

The torpedo forward must have hit the magazine, for it could not have done so much damage unaided. When the debris and smoke cleared from the explosion, there was no bridge and no charthouse. "Officers' country" had disappeared, and so had the petty officers' quarters.

The second torpedo did almost as much damage. It hit 40 feet forward of the fantail; the whole after part of the ship was carried away.

So it was obvious that the *Jacob Jones* was in her death throes. One look at the deck, where it was rolled up like a bamboo rug from the space above Number 1 fireroom to the galley deckhouse, was enough to shock a man who had lived atop this steel housing for months.

All the officers but one had been killed in the explosions. That single officer was so dazed that he could not function. Seaman "Dusty" Rhodes took charge and put the 25 men who were on their feet to work trying to free the lifeboats. Most of them were jammed in their skids, and it was almost impossible to get any purchase on the deck to tug at them because the blast aft had broken the fuel tanks. What deck remained was covered with a layer of slippery oil.

Soon, Rhodes saw that their efforts were of no use. They could not free the lifeboats. And the ship was faltering.

He shouted, and the men turned to the life rafts. They got four of them over the side, and the men began to jump aboard, three or four of them on a raft. For some reason, 14 men crowded aboard one raft.

George Pantall found himself the last man aboard, and he jumped into the water and swam for a raft. He and his companions paddled away from the ship as quickly as they could.

What they were afraid of happened soon enough. *Jacob Jones* began to go down, and as she went, the depth charges aft went with her. When they hit their set depths, they began to explode. Where *Jacob Jones* had been, up came a huge blast, a column of water, a sheet of flame, and a roar that shook them all. That raft with 14 men on board was right in the line of explosion. All were killed.

At six o'clock in the morning, it was all over, and the sea was quiet, gulls showing occasionally overhead, the surviving men slumped on their rafts, still stunned by the events of the previous hour.

Two hours went by. Then one of the handful of observation planes assigned to shore defense happened by, and Army 1st Lt. L. R. Blackburn, Jr., looked out and saw men in rafts below him. The plane circled and began to call up the navy on the assigned frequency. Soon there was an answer: U.S.S. *Eagle 56* was not far away, and she responded.

The army flier was intelligent. He gave the course and location as best he could and then went on about his business, which was to try to find the submarine if he could in this vast stretch of sea.

Forty minutes later, *Eagle 56* came upon an empty lifeboat, and 20 minutes later, the crew saw the first raft. The searchers picked up three men.

There were four bodies still on the raft, said the survivors.

The captain considered. It was important to find the other survivors. Bodies could wait. He ordered the raft taken in tow, and they went on.

But the raft was not designed for fast tow.

In a few minutes, it began to break up, and the four bodies were swiftly sent to the deep.

The *Eagle* boat went on, casting off the wreckage of the raft and continuing the search. By ten o'clock that morning, the boat had picked up 12 survivors and saw no more in the sea. Calling in to station, the captain ordered to Cape May with the survivors. A water tender, Carl Smith, died on the way in, and cut the number of survivors to 11.

Two days more were involved in the search, but no other survivors were found. *Jacob Jones* had gone down and had taken nearly all her crew with her. She was the first naval ship to fall victim to Doenitz's assault on the American coast. Admiral Andrews knew then that at least one submarine was working the Jersey coast. But how many others were there?

Next day, the tanker *Oregon* came up along the Jersey shore just as dawn began to break. She was zigzagging along in a fair sea with three lookouts on watch.

Suddenly, they saw a submarine surface. Men poured out of the conning tower and manned the deck gun. The U-boat fired a shell into *Oregon*'s starboard side, amidships.

All eyes turned to the U-boat.

In came another shell, this one from the port side. Another U-boat!

The shells knocked out the radio shack, so not a word of the attack could be transmitted. The submarines remained on the surface, concentrated amidships, and continued to shell the ship for an hour and 15 minutes. A boiler exploded, much damage was done, but the ship did not catch fire.

When the shelling began, the crew tried to abandon ship, but the submarine on the port side turned its machine guns on the men who were fumbling with the boat. The crew ran around the other side, and 26 of them got away. Four others dove overboard and made it to a raft. One of them said that one of the U-boats tried to run him down as he swam away from the ship. It came so close that he could see the hull of the U-boat clearly enough to report later that it was welded, not riveted.

So the U-boats were back offshore, in force.

10
THE WINDS OF MARCH

After Admiral Doenitz persuaded the German high command that the U-boat results were such that more U-boats should be assigned to the American station, Admiral Andrews had the unpleasant intelligence in a few days. Knowing then that the U-boats had come again in greater force, he asked Admiral King for more destroyers. But Admiral King said there were no destroyers to give him except on the same loan basis as that under which he had gotten *Jacob Jones*. King said he had no choice in this matter. The convoys were calling more loudly for ships than the coastal defense forces. He did not seem to understand how much damage the U-boats could do off the American shore.

Survivors now began to complain that their ships had been easily seen by U-boats because they were silhouetted in the sea lanes against the bright lights of the cities and towns along the shore line. So many told this story that Lt. Gen. Hugh A. Drum, commander of the army's eastern defense command, decided that the lights must be turned out.

Orders were issued. Issuance, however, did not mean compliance. At Atlantic City, in Miami, and in scores of cities and places in between, the lights still shone brightly along the American coast at night, beacons for the U-boats out hunting their prey. Businessmen said there was no danger of bombing, so why should they turn out the lights?

The newspapers were full of the news of sinkings. On March 1, more than 100 survivors were landed at a Canadian port, and they indicated that eight ships of their single convoy had been torpedoed on the voyage across the Atlantic. That sort of news made the British squirm. They knew how useful and encouraging were such reports, to the Germans.

The report was correct. Traveling across the Atlantic, *U-155* had found convoy ONS-67 600 miles northeast of Newfoundland. Within 300 miles were five more U-boats, some of them on their way to the U.S. coast. The U-boats had a field day, and six of the sunk ships were tankers. After dealing with the convoy, the U-boats proceeded to their assigned stations.

In Atlantic City, on Monday, March 2, the boardwalk was full of people enjoying a clear bit of early spring weather. Suddenly, the strollers heard explosions out at sea. They saw nothing, but now they knew the war was out there, offshore. On March 3, the newspapers reported the shelling of an ore ship off the Virginia coast, another torpedoing, more refugee sailors coming into port.

This time, there was a slightly different note. No fewer than three submarines had come up on the ore ship *Marore,* just off the American coast, and sent her to the bottom.

The Windward Passage between Haiti and Cuba was a favorite hiding spot for submarines as it had been for buccaneers in the days of Morgan and Blackbeard.

The S.S. *Barbara,* an American passenger freighter of the Bull line was moving through the passage on the night of March 7 when she was torpedoed. Most of the crew escaped in life rafts, but Q.M. John Tourin and Boatswain Charles Rooney were cut off in the after section of the ship. They were about to swim for the rafts when they saw a gangway secured to Number 5 hatch. They cut it loose, threw it overboard, and paddled away on their float as the submarine began to shell the ship. A Puerto Rican passenger joined them. Soon, however, the gangway waterlogged, and they had to hang on to it to keep afloat.

They were joined by sharks, which circled them constantly but kept at a distance when they paddled and splashed their feet.

They had been covered by bunker oil as they swam from the ship, and in the hot Caribbean sun, it caked on them. Their thirst began to grow.

On the afternoon of the first day, planes passed overhead, but there were so few and flying so high, the survivors knew the planes were not looking for them.

On the afternoon of the second day, the Puerto Rican passenger let go his hold, and soon the sharks deserted the others.

The two men held out until the fourth day, when a scouting seaplane spotted them in the water and called a destroyer that picked them up.

They were lucky men. The sinkings were coming so rapidly that the slender forces of the United States in the area could scarcely cover the region.

Most seriously alarmed again was Winston Churchill, who saw in what was happening the death knell of his England.

"I am most deeply concerned," he wrote Franklin Roosevelt on March 12, "at the immense sinkings of tankers west of the 40th meridian and in the Caribbean Sea."

In two months, the sinkings had aggregated 600,000 tons. The rate of sinkings of tankers was so great that if it continued, the British would soon be out of oil.

As if to emphasize Churchill's words, on March 14 came one of the most spectacular sights ever witnessed by the strollers of Atlantic City's boardwalk: two tankers making their way up the coast hugging the shore and a submarine throwing shells at them.

The ships rounded Brigantine Island and were lost to view in the bend, but just then, up shot a sheet of flame, and from the sea came a roar, as one tanker met her doom.

The U-boats were so confident that they did not even bother to submerge after an attack. That same day, March 14, off the biggest American naval base of all, Norfolk, after torpedoing a small steamer, one U-boat stayed up four hours, shining a yellow light in the conning tower.

The headlines were bold and disturbing. Across the water, the British were aghast that so much information was being given to the enemy, confirmation of the success of the U-boat war.

The question of convoys was raised again by British and American naval officers. Admiral Andrews again counted the patrol vessels and said that it would require far more ships than he had to undertake the task.

Yet everyone knew the convoy system could not but help the situation.

On March 15, Admiral Andrews sent what amounted to a plea to all commands with which he was associated: Let them beg, buy, or steal vessels capable of carrying guns and depth charges. He was even willing to accept the Menhaden fishing boats, although they were capable of making no more than 5 knots and were no match for even a disabled U-boat.

From this plea, Andrews received the welcome, if inadequate, news that his associates had been able to find five more yachts, varying between 75 and 175 feet, that could be outfitted for patrol.

But the best news came from England. The British trawlers would arrive at Halifax during the second half of the month. They could be outfitted, and it was estimated that by April 1, 14 of them would be ready for service. It was the first break in the deadly pattern that had existed since December 7. There was more good news: Churchill, who had begged for escorts a year earlier, was stripping away five of his invaluable corvettes to send to the Americans. There could be no more certain sign of his deep concern over what was happening in the West.

Those reinforcements, or reverse lend-lease, meant that as of the beginning of the following month, the Eastern Sea Frontier would have 94 ships in service to patrol from Canada to the Gulf frontier in Florida.

The constant pressure on President Roosevelt from London produced its effects, too. Harry Hopkins had only the most general appreciation of the war at sea, but he did transmit the messages that "former naval person" was rocketing across to FDR. In his own way, Roosevelt communicated the sense of urgency to King and the others. On March 16, Admiral King ordered a meeting to produce a plan for convoys along the East Coast from Canada to the Caribbean. From New York, Capt. T. R. Kurtz, chief of staff to Admiral Andrews, and Capt. F. G. Reinicke, the New York port director, went down to Washington to participate.

Once again, the men who sent the ships to sea argued the case.

Every day, they said, 35 ships moved from the Caribbean northward, and a similar number went south. That meant a convoy northbound should leave every three days from Key West, said the convoy planners.

It would not be a convoy as the British knew it, obviously. There were not enough escorts. Instead, the ships would try to take advantage of the protection of coastal waters and daylight.

The northbound convoys would assemble and leave Key West at two o'clock in the morning. At daybreak, they would be at Rebecca shoals. There they would form into columns and pass through the dangerous Florida Straits. The next morning, they would be at the north end of the straits and would sail northward. In four days, they would reach the Virginia Capes. There the Chesapeake Bay traffic would be detached, and the ships from Baltimore and Norfolk would come out. That evening, the convoy would be off the Delaware Capes, where the Philadelphia-bound ships would drop off. Five days out, at six in the morning, they would make Ambrose Light off New York, and the New York-bound vessels would go their own way. The rest would head northward by way of Long Island Sound and the Cape Cod canal, and at Boston, the remaining northbound ships would join the BX convoys headed for Halifax.

The southern convoys would operate in the same fashion except that they would move west, or inshore of the northbound convoys.

The plan would be fine, said the men who would have to carry it out, if Admiral King had six groups of escorts to give the convoy forces. They needed 31 destroyers and 47 corvettes or patrol boats to cover the seaboard in this fashion.

The two captains went back to New York and reported to Admiral Andrews the plan devised in Washington. Andrews ran a check on his strength at the moment. He had three destroyers assigned to him on temporary duty, no corvettes, and eight available patrol craft.

On March 18, President Roosevelt wrote Churchill. "My navy has been definitely slack in preparing for this submarine war off our coast . . . You learned the lesson two years ago . . . We still have to learn it. By May 1 I expect to get a pretty good coastal patrol working. . . ."

But even President Roosevelt did not seem to grasp the immediacy of the threat.

Churchill was aghast.

May 1? The war at sea might be lost by then. What did Roosevelt and the Americans believe the Germans were doing at that moment? What was the U.S. Navy doing?

Criticized, the U.S. Navy blustered back.

"Those of us who are directly concerned with combating the Atlantic submarine menace are not at all sure that the British are applying sufficient effort to bombing German submarine bases . . . It seems that the R.A.F. is not fully cooperative. . . ." said King.

And Roosevelt sent Churchill a petulant message to that effect. Perhaps the petulance indicated more surely than any argument how little the Americans could do to slow the U-boats in their rampage. Churchill seemed suddenly to understand that impotence and sent a placating message to Roosevelt. He would send an air armada against Lübeck, and he would try to concentrate on U-boat nests.

As FDR wrote then, there simply was no way the Americans could cope with the U-boats until they learned how.

11

"SHUT OFF THAT
GODDAM LIGHT . . ."

The failure of the American defenders was as much organizational as lack of planes and ships. The U.S. Navy did not know how to make best use of the material at hand, a fact over which American naval officers and civilian captains were often at odds. Partly, the failure in these early months could be attributed to the U.S. system. In Britain, merchant officers were automatically members of the naval reserve and had at least a rudimentary understanding of naval practice. Not so in the United States.

On the night of March 18, S.S. *Liberator* was traveling along off the New Jersey coast, bound from Galveston to New York. Her captain was nervous. The radio bands were alive with submarine reports. His state of mind that evening was not improved when, in quick succession, two nearby ships were torpedoed and set afire within his plain view.

Just after two o'clock in the morning, the captain was on the bridge when a lookout called attention to a low and unfamiliar silhouette two miles off the starboard beam.

Liberator was armed with a 4-inch deck gun to protect herself from submarines and surface raiders. Without hesitation, the captain ordered the gun into action, and the gun crew opened fire.

The U.S. destroyer *Dickerson* was patrolling off Cape Lookout as part of her temporary duty for Admiral Andrews' antisubmarine efforts, not far away from *Liberator*.

When a lookout reported the presence of the blacked-out freighter, 3,500 yards away, Lt. Comdr. J. K. Reybold, captain of the *Dickerson*, took note, came up for a check, and at 1,500 yards turned away, satisfied, presenting the destroyer's beam to the merchant ship.

Suddenly, there came a tremendous crash on the bridge. A 4-inch shell plowed through the starboard spray shield. The shell exploded in the chart house, killing a seaman, the sound operator, and the radar operator. The radio transmitter was knocked out, as were several other vital components of the ship's electrical system. The flag locker was smashed, and the flag bags broke open, spilling their pennants over the deck in a torrent of color. Two officers on the bridge were knocked unconscious, and, worst of all, the captain was sorely wounded.

The executive officer was asleep in his bunk when the shell burst. In a moment, he was on his feet and on the bridge. He ordered the destroyer turned and headed for Norfolk so the wounded might be given attention. They traveled for 15 minutes on the new course before the "exec" sensed that something was amiss, checked the compass, and discovered that the repeater had been knocked out, and they were 80 degrees off course. He corrected the error and sped for the base at 27 knots.

The captain died before they reached Norfolk.

The area off Cape Lookout, then, was deprived of its single antisubmarine patrol vessel.

Admiral Andrews was aghast. The accident and its aftermath emphasized all that he had been saying. He issued new pleas to Admiral King for more destroyers. The answer, as in the past, was a short and unequivocal "No."

The shortage of patrol planes and patrol craft brought growing resentment from merchant captains. Many of the "old sea dogs" had little use for the U.S. Navy and preferred to follow their intuition in dealing with the U-boats. One day a patrol plane came back from its brief flight, and the pilot reported that he had seen 30 ships, 15 of them out of their proper lanes. In other words, the merchant captains were traveling as they pleased, with little regard to the shipping instructions.

Because of that independence, submarines were not the only menace to navigation.

Nor could the captains always be blamed. S.S. *Raritan* was a case in point. She set out from Colombia in late February with a cargo of coffee for New York City. At the Panama Canal, the naval authorities gave her captain two coordinates as a check on his proper course. When he reached one point, off Jacksonville, he was to head for the second point up north off Diamond Light, zigzagging and taking the usual precautions all the way.

But when *Raritan* was in the middle of the Caribbean Sea, the defense plan was changed. The captain was notified that he was to move in close to shore, in light of the system that was supposed to protect ships by bringing them in so close the U-boats would not get them.

The middle of March was accompanied by foul weather off the Eastern American coast, so threatening to *Raritan* that the captain spent ten solid days on the bridge. He did not, in fact, have his shoes off all that time.

On the tenth day, the captain was exhausted, eyes red-rimmed, surviving on a constant infusion of hot coffee. He was doing as ordered, keeping inshore in these unfamiliar waters. That day, having nearly reached her destination, in heavy weather, *Raritan* grounded on a shoal 18 miles off Cape Fear. The navy sent patrol boats, and they took the men off, every one of them. The rescuers were just in time, for the seas were already breaking over her, and next day she broke up and sank.

No submarine could have done a better job of dealing with *Raritan* than the naval command had done.

Such confusion seemed to be the rule in this fourth month of war, as on the night when S.S. *Olney* was steaming off Fernandina, Florida, and was approached by a navy patrol boat.

The captain of *Olney* saw the boat coming and watched. When the patrol boat was a mile off, her captain turned a bright searchlight on the beam of *Olney*.

"What ship is that?" brayed the naval officer through his electric megaphone.

"Shut off that goddam light," screamed the captain of *Olney*. If he had had a gun in his hand, he would have shot it out. And when he got back to shore, the captain told the story of the jackass naval officer who turned a searchlight on his ship right in the middle of the U-boat zone.

It was just one of dozens of such stories, all of them reflecting badly on the U.S. Navy, whether illuminating naval incompetence or damning naval arrogance, as did the tale of the captain of S.S. *Malchage*.

That ship was ready to sail from Norfolk on March 18, and her captain went ashore to the port director's office to pick up his sailing orders.

Part of Admiral Andrews' protection of ports was the antisubmarine net that protected the Norfolk region's waters from the sort of invasion U-boat Comdr. Guenther Prien had made into the British fleet base at Scapa Flow in 1939 to sink the battleship *Royal Oak* as she lay at anchor. The captain of *Malchage* was given recognition signals so the net would be opened for him to pass through. Since it was not certain that he would make it to the outer defenses on the eighteenth, he was also given the recognition signals for the next day.

Malchage sailed late, and anchored that night near the antisubmarine net, still in the safety of patrolled waters. Next morning, getting under way, she was challenged by a naval patrol boat, and the captain used the signal for the nineteenth.

The officer in charge happened to be a spit-and-polish young regular of the "old school," even if just recently out of Annapolis. He stopped the merchant ship, boarded, and raised absolute hell with the captain. *Malchage* had sailed on March 18. What right did the captain have to be in possession of signals for the nineteenth?

The implication that he might be a spy infuriated the captain of *Malchage,* and harsh words were passed, the reverberations of which reached Admiral Andrews in New York.

Both captains had a point, Admiral Andrews decided. The behavior of some merchant officers left much to be desired, as did the attitude of some naval officers. But naval intelligence was just then seriously worried about the condition of port security up and down the coast.

Too many merchant captains and too many seamen were talking too much, and intelligence attributed at least some of the ever-increasing U-boat successes to breaches of security. The merchant captains, or too many of them, just did not seem to give a damn.

One reason for this attitude, where it existed, might have

been the overkill of government and press on the subject of espionage a few months earlier.

After 1939, German espionage had made a vigorous effort to establish agents in the United States. When war broke out between Germany and England, Carl Herman Schroetter of Miami was traveling in Germany. There he was recruited by the German *Abwehr* and ordered to return to Miami to become a "stationary agent."

It was not hard to persuade him, although he was Swiss born, not German. He had two sisters living in Germany, and the *Abwehr* made it clear that their continued good health would depend on his willingness to undertake this task for the Fatherland.

So Schroetter returned to Miami and waited for contact, as ordered. He had a perfect cover for what was wanted: He operated a charter boat out of Miami, *Echo of the Past*. He was established, he had a Social Security card, a driver's license, all the identification anyone in America needed. Now, he was told, he was to keep his eye on ship movements, and he did so, in his charter boat.

In March 1940, the Germans sent Kurt Frederick Ludwig to be resident agent in New York. His specific assignment was to secure detailed information about American preparedness. Ludwig's arrival made no stir at all, for he was an American citizen, although he had grown up in Germany and was a thoroughly converted Nazi.

Ludwig set up residence in Queens and recruited several agents among the members of the German-American community. Soon he was in touch with Schroetter in Miami, demanding that Schroetter send him regular reports of ship and military movement in the South.

By this time, Schroetter had burrowed into Miami in a manner that displayed his "patriotism." He had volunteered for election duty and was made a register clerk in voting precinct Number 34, Dade County. None of his fellow workers even suspected that the quiet, studious worker went home at night and made up coded messages, transcribed them in secret ink, and sent them off on their way to Germany.

All during 1940 and in the spring and summer of 1941, agent Schroetter sent those reports to Queens. One day, a British warship off Miami laid down a smokescreen to discourage an inquisitive charter boat that was nosing about while the ship was engaged in torpedo practice. Schroetter was on the job.

He found it hard from the boat to get much information about the growing Miami Naval Air Station, so he got a night job as cook at the Greyhound Club, a place near the station frequented by officers and men. The reports continued.

Master spy Ludwig, in New York, was so confident of his own cover that he took a trip to Florida in the spring of 1941 to meet Schroetter. He was accompanied by his "sister," pretty Lucy Boehmler, whom he encouraged to be friendly with American servicemen they met in bars.

Ludwig and Boehmler stopped here and there on the way South, while Ludwig photographed her against such scenic beauties as the Norfolk naval ship repair yard and finally arrived in Miami, where they conferred with Schroetter. They went down to Key West, where Ludwig photographed his sister against the backdrop of the naval base and the air station, and they came back to Coral Gables, where the Ludwigs settled down in a rental for a few days and spent their evenings at the Greyhound Club.

Back in New York, Ludwig felt perfectly safe until the summer, when President Roosevelt began issuing open warnings about the peril to America in the successes of Nazi Germany. Then the FBI began picking up German agents.

Still sure of his cover, Ludwig was nonetheless nervous. He risked a call to Schroetter, asking him to pick up a small boat in which Ludwig could escape to Cuba. Schroetter said it was impossible. Everything on the waterfront was under close watch; he would not destroy his own cover.

Ludwig panicked then and fled to Seattle, hoping to get passage to Japan. But the FBI arrested Lucy Boehmler and others of the New York ring, and soon they had Ludwig. Almost as soon, they got Schroetter in Miami, and with that arrest, the heyday of German spies in the United States was declared ended by the FBI, a claim roundly endorsed by the American press.

But in 1942, with U-boats off the American shore, there were enemy agents in America, and naval intelligence knew it. The agents behaved in various ways, from inciting riot to actual espionage. One captain told how, when he reached port with a crew of 30 men, he lost 13 of them the first day, men who had been persuaded by "friends" to jump ship because of the inordinate dangers offshore and the "rotten deal" they were getting.

The bars of Brooklyn, New York's waterfront, and New Jersey's port cities were honeycombed with sympathizers and workers of the enemy. One of the most notorious places was the Highway Tavern in Jersey, which naval intelligence kept under constant surveillance. Another was the Old Hamburg in Manhattan, and still another danger was Schmidt's bar in Bayonne.

Seamen assembled at Schmidt's, drank and got drunk, and swapped stories of their adventures at sea. In the telling, out came the information about ships and cargoes and convoy practices; it was no good telling how your ammunition ship had damned near blown up unless you made clear that it *was* an ammunition ship.

One of the bartenders at Schmidt's was a German agent, and he was quick to stand drinks on the house during these exciting tales. He was above suspicion; he was "one of the boys," who had served aboard the S.S. *America* for several years and had shipped out on many another vessel.

Also, the son of the proprietor, young Schmidt, had for several years been in the commissary department of Standard Oil of New Jersey, and so he knew the tanker men very well. These two agents functioned for several months before Naval Intelligence got on to them and finally took them away.

The bars were not the only danger spots. The agents worked in a dozen different ways. A favorite ploy was for an agent to collect the names of seamen and the names and addresses of their wives. Then, when a sailor went to sea, his wife would receive a telephone call:

"Is Charlie there? Has he gotten back yet?"

And the sailor's wife would be sure this was a friend of Charlie's who knew all about his business; she would talk, and it was not long before the caller knew all she did about her husband's movements.

The navy warned captains. Posters were put up in the hiring halls, along the docks, in the bars, and in the ships. "Loose talk sinks ships."

But many captains did not believe. Some of them appeared tight-lipped at port directors' offices, took their sailing instructions without comment, sailed, and then ignored all they had been told.

"Too much goddam red tape," said Capt. E. R. Kemp, the master of one merchant vessel. And he became a terror of the naval authorities of the Eastern seaboard because of his never-ending criticism of navy methods and his open discussion of his destinations. He broke all the rules, and he got away with it.

And that was that until one night in March when Captain Kemp was conning his ship off the Jersey coast, in his own fashion, doing precisely as he pleased, no zigzagging, no special watch, and a torpedo slammed into the ship's side.

The navy knew about it when the radio operator sent out the message that the ship was sinking. By that time, it was a little late to convince Captain Kemp that sometimes the navy knew what it was talking about.

12

"THE ANSWER IS NO."

In March, the U.S. government cracked down on the reporting of losses. The British had been pointing out for months that newspaper headlines and articles naming ships and places could not help but play into the hands of the German enemy, and President Roosevelt had responded. In February, the newspapers were full of reports of sinkings. In March, the reports ceased abruptly under a change in censorship policy.

Yet, in March, the people who lived along the Eastern shore became more aware of the seriousness of the war out beyond the breakers. The intensity of U-boat activity was such that oil and debris began to drift in to beaches from Montauk to the Florida Keys. The Germans' second wave of U-boats was decimating shipping offshore. In this wave, Hardegen's *U-123* would sink 11 ships, and Lieutenant Commander Mohr's *U-124* would sink nine. The impact was frightening: on the night of March 18, the night that *Dickerson* had been so sorely hurt and forced out of action, the U-boats did a particularly nasty evening's work. They hit three tankers off Cape Lookout and two freighters off Hatteras.

Ironically, one of the freighters was *Liberator,* the ship that had shot up the only destroyer in the area and sent her back to Norfolk with a dying captain. But what the U-boats were after was tankers. And that night they came upon five of them in an unescorted convoy. They were: *Papoose, W. E. Hutton, E. M. Clark, Acme,* and *Esso Baltimore.*

The U-boats attacked *Acme* first. When they put a torpedo into her, the freighter *Kassandra Louloudi,* which was nearby, went to the tanker's assistance. The same U-boat torpedoed *Kassandra Louloudi* and sank her, while *Acme* floated, was ignored in the rush of action that came next, and was eventually saved:

Papoose was hit, and her crew took to the boats. The Germans provided light for them to see by, making a flaming torch of *W. E. Hutton.*

That night, the U-boats missed *Esso Nashville,* but three days later, they found her off Frying Pan Shoals. And *Esso Nashville*'s story of that night of March 21 was one of the most amazing and certainly one of the most heartening to come out of the first months of the war off the American shore.

The tanker was built in 1940 by Bethlehem Steel Company at Sparrow Point, Maryland. She was a 13,000-ton ship, on this voyage carrying 78,000 barrels of fuel oil for New Haven, Connecticut. Her captain, Edward Peters, was an experienced skipper, and he was also a respecter of the naval authorities and their regulations. The tanker had sailed from Port Arthur, Texas, on March 16 and had followed her routing instructions faithfully until the night of March 20, even through the dreadful attacks of March 18 when she had been so lucky as to escape the U-boats in the murk.

She was blacked out on this night of March 20, when she reached a Frying Pan lighted buoy at 10:56.

It was a dark, drizzly night. The stars were blanked out by a thick layer of cloud. The wind was blowing briskly from the southwest. *Esso Nashville* was heading northeast at 12 knots.

At midnight, Second Mate Johannes Boje took the bridge watch with Seaman Theodore Niedzwiecki at the wheel and Seaman Harvard Brown on lookout atop the wheelhouse. Captain Peters was a thorough man, so a second lookout, John Littlefield, stood on the forecastle head, looking out across the ship's bow into the darkness.

The captain was below in his cabin, trying to go to sleep.

Twenty minutes later, Captain Peters felt a thud against the ship's side, as if they had brushed by some obstacle. He jumped from his bunk and headed for the bridge.

As he reached the bridge, he was nearly thrown off his feet by a tremendous crash on the starboard side aft, and he stopped wondering what it was he had come to investigate. He knew.

The crash of the torpedo forced the ship to heel sharply to port. A huge gout of oil spouted up as high as the foremast and flooded *Esso Nashville* with oil. Although the air was full of smoke, and the captain saw sparks where the torpedo had hit, the oil did not burn.

The captain rang the engine room. There was no answer; communications had broken down in the explosion. But, as a painstaking seaman, he had already discusssed emergency procedures with Chief Engineer Aloysius Kist, and down below, when the explosion came, the chief immediately stopped the engines.

Men came running from all over the ship. But they ran with purpose, for Captain Peters had conducted his lifeboat drills regularly and strictly. Now each man knew what he had to do, and there was no panic even though every light in the ship had gone out, and the men were groping their way by flashlight.

Esso Nashville had been equipped on that voyage with 38 rubber lifesaving suits, and the captain had made sure each man knew how to use them. Most got into their rubber suits. Some did not.

The men headed for the boats. All were put into the water without mishap. Third Assistant Engineer Henry Garig had gone down to the engine room on hearing the report of the dud torpedo, and he led his men to his station, the Number 4 lifeboat. The boat was lowered, with 21 men in it. It began banging against the side of the ship, and Garig called six others in life suits to follow him into the water. They clung to the gunwales of the boat, while the others pushed off and rowed away from the tanker.

Oiler Leonard Mills had not had time to get into his life suit, and he was wearing only shorts and a life jacket. One of the men who could not swim panicked and yelled for a life preserver. Mills took off his life jacket and gave it to him, although he was 56 years old, without a lifesaving suit, and the other man was younger and wore a rubber suit.

Garig told Mills to take back the jacket.

"That's all right," said the oiler. "I can swim, and he can't."

He was one of the first to jump into the water, even without a rubber suit.

By the time lifeboat Number 4 had cleared the ship, it was raining hard, and the wind was blowing. The water was the cold Atlantic of early spring, enough to kill a man by exposure in a few hours.

They rowed toward shore, then gave up and rested on their oars to await daybreak. When the dawn came, they saw their ship, half a mile away. She had obviously broken her back. The midships lay low in the water. Bow and stern stuck up so high that the two masts almost joined.

As the sky lightened, Garig saw that the ship's flag had been raised at the stern, upside down in the international signal of distress.

Shortly after daylight, the Coast Guard cutter *Tallapoosa* came along and picked up the survivors of lifeboat Number 4. Garig told the captain someone was aboard the ship, and the Coast Guard cutter *Agassiz* headed toward the tanker.

Someone was, indeed, still aboard. It was Captain Peters.

After he had issued the order to abandon ship, the captain observed the four lifeboats lowered in an orderly fashion. His boat was Number 2, and the crew waited for him, while he went to his cabin to get his secret papers. He found the cabin full of smoke and gas and was forced to retreat and abandon his orders.

As he stepped down the pilot's ladder, Captain Peters slipped on the oily metal and fell into the water between the ship's side and the boat. The ship had swung around so that Number 2 boat was to windward of the hull, and the captain feared the boat would be crushed against the ship. He waved the boat away and told the men to pick him up later.

Chief Mate Hansen, who was also in the boat, tried to grasp the captain, but he and two others slipped and lost their grips, and the boat began to yaw dangerously toward the wrecked vessel. They struggled and cleared it and then went back to look for the captain. They called to him. There was no answer, so they rowed to the stern and kept on rowing until they were 3 or 4 miles from the ship.

The captain had broken his leg in the fall, and it gave him much pain and also hampered his swimming. The oil on top of the water did not help any, either. He tried to swim for three-quarters of an hour but made so little headway that he looked up, saw the ship close by, and decided to take his chances back aboard her.

As he swam painfully, he could see that she was lying, decks awash amidships, and he boarded her easily forward of the mainmast. He dragged himself back to the engineers' quarters aft and lay down on the second assistant engineer's bunk to rest. When he felt stronger, he found a bandage, tied it tightly around his swollen leg, and went on deck. He lashed a white bed sheet to the rail on the windward side of the ship and ran up the ensign, upside down, on the flagpole on the poop. He tried to get into one of the life-saving suits to warm his body, but he could not make it and gave up.

Then along came the *Agassiz*. The captain jumped off the stern of *Nashville* and swam toward the cutter. The Coast Guardsmen lowered a boat, and he was saved.

For some reason, too many men (21) had headed for boat Number 4, and none for boat Number 1. Third Mate John Kerves went to his station and soon saw that he and radio operator Thomas Rhiel were the only men left aboard. Together, they launched the boat; rather, it launched itself, slipping on the oil deck and falling the few feet into the sea. Rhiel burned his hands on the lines trying to hold it back.

Kerves sculled the boat away from the ship's side, and they tried to rig the sail but could not manage it in the dark. The mast and lines were slippery with oil. They sat in the boat until dawn, then managed to get the sail up. They sailed a quarter of a mile off the ship's stern and saw no one or any lifeboats. They did see flares about 5 miles ahead of the ship. Then they turned toward shore and began to move. That morning, they were picked up by the destroyer *McKean*.

Lifeboat Number 2 was manned by Chief Mate Hansen, 2nd Mate Boje, and six men. It was also picked up by *McKean*, which continued patrol and then landed the survivors at Norfolk on March 22.

Boat Number 3 also got away, with Chief Engineer Kist in charge, with eight other men. They moved away from the ship to be sure they were not carried down by suction if she sank. They rowed until dawn and then sent up flares. In the glow of the flares, Kist saw the conning tower of a submarine, a mile away, and they hurried away from it.

Later that day, they were picked up by the *Agassiz* and reunited with the captain.

Esso Nashville broke up that day even as tugs were coming to take her to shore. When U.S.S. *Umpqua* arrived on the scene, the stern section only seemed salvageable, and it was towed to Morehead City, North Carolina. Within the week, the survivors of *Esso Nashville* were landed ashore and began to reassemble. The remarkable aspect of the whole story is that in that terrible night, not a single man's life had been lost.

Esso Nashville's story of heroism, good sense, and good luck was too seldom the case in the Eastern Sea Frontier. The war was four months old, and still Admiral Andrews and his staff were trying to protect American waters without enough planes or ships.

The admiral was a handsome, stylish, and self-assured man. He had weathered the storm of publicity that threatened him after the great French liner *Normandie* burned at her mooring the month before, while under navy command. Several times each month, he wrote, telephoned, or traveled to Washington to see Admiral King to argue the case for more planes and more ships assigned to the Eastern Sea Frontier.

At the end of this month, even Admiral King was convinced: The losses were growing constantly and were hard to contemplate. More than a ship a day was going down, and even without Churchill's constant nagging, King knew something had to be done to change that situation.

On March 28, through President Roosevelt's personal intercession, 70 OS2U-3 aircraft, which had been produced for the British and assigned to them already, were taken back and given to the Eastern Sea Frontier. King also relented regarding the fleet and released a fleet air squadron to Andrews for offshore patrol.

This force, fewer than 100 planes, would make all the difference in the world. Andrews suddenly had something with which to fight back. Or he soon would have, for the new planes had not yet arrived.

They could not arrive soon enough. As the month came

to an end, the U-boat rampage continued. The tanker *Dixie Arrow* was sunk on the day that the impending arrival of the planes were announced, and the freighter *Equipoise* and the passenger ship *City of New York,* which had sailed all the way from Capetown safely until she reached Hatteras Inlet, was torpedoed.

The destroyer *Jesse Roper* picked up one of *City of New York*'s boats and found in it an extra passenger; a pregnant woman who had been taken into the boat and had given birth, even as a quarter of the passengers and crew of the ship perished in the sea. In honor of the rescuers, the baby was christened Jesse Roper Noharovic.

While waiting for the planes, Andrews and his men turned to the smallest vessels. In the emergency, even if they could not stop sinkings, they could rescue more survivors. The numbers of bodies washing up on the beaches were mute evidence of that.

Andrews then organized the volunteer Inshore Patrol, whose task was rescue, checking of aliens along the shore, examination of suspicious craft, and report of contacts with anything at all suspicious. The authorities wanted to know about excessive purchases of gas and oil by any boat owner; it was perfectly feasible for enemy agents to make assignations with U-boats, meet them offshore, and feed them information about ship movements.

The Inshore Patrol would also watch out for floating objects, report debris and menaces to navigation, and keep a sharp lookout for enemy mines.

Alfred Stanford, the commodore of the Cruising Club of America, had proposed earlier the use of sailing vessels for such purposes. Stanford said that U-boats would not suspect sailing boats and ships; they could disguise themselves as fishermen if need be. They were silent runners; they could watch and listen for submarines very effectively.

So desperate were the defenders of Admiral Andrews' command that they considered this idea. He could assemble 80 such vessels, said Commodore Stanford, for observation and patrol at 10-mile intervals from Cape Cod to Halifax and from Ambrose light to Hatteras. They could cover almost all the area offshore.

The commodore had 36 such vessels, all lined up with

their civilian crews, ready to go by the end of March. Only the red tape held them up, he said. Admiral Andrews was interested: He had to have some kind of weapon with which to fight, and if this was strictly nonregulation, so were the U-boats offshore. He appointed Comdr. Vincent Astor of the U.S. Naval Reserve to examine and supervise such a plan. With a little luck, they might be in operation by the first of June.

At the end of March, Admiral Andrews might wonder if the defenders of the shore would ever see the first of June.

The total losses in the month of March equaled those of January and February combined. Directly off the U.S. coast, the U-boats had sunk 27 ships, and in the waters of America (out to 300 miles), they had sunk 53 ships. Including Canadian waters and the Caribbean, the total ran to 79 ships, so disastrous a month that American insurance companies stopped writing insurance policies on cargo vessels.

Sitting in his New York office, Admiral Andrews added up the totals: At that rate, the U-boats would sink two million tons of ships in a year!

If Andrews was concerned, his worry was at least matched by that of Winston Churchill across the Atlantic.

Churchill could not understand why the Americans had failed so miserably to absorb the lessons in offshore warfare learned at such cost by the British over nearly three years. President Roosevelt had stated the case in a sidelong comment in a letter. Where the American navy had failed, the president admitted ruefully, was in a doctrinaire approach to naval warfare. Admirals Stark and King and all the rest had refused to think of vessels of less than 2,000 tons as important. The British corvettes and frigates had made no impact at all. Thus, when war began, the United States was woefully deficient in patrol and escort vessels. The American admirals had never seriously considered that the continental United States might be placed under siege.

For three years, the British and Canadians had been building corvettes and frigates, but even this had not impressed the Americans. These small, fast vessels were specifically designed to protect shipping and fight submarines.

The United States was just now building a force of small ships. It would be months before a significant number could be available to Admiral Andrews and the fleet.

On March 30, Admiral Andrews asked for more destroyers.

Four submarines had been sighted at widely varied places in the Eastern Sea Frontier in the last few hours. Another two boats were believed to be lurking just then off Hatteras at the 100-fathom curve the U-boat skippers liked so well.

The admiral's statistics were impressive. Forty-nine percent of the ships sunk in the entire world that month were sunk in the Eastern Sea Frontier area. More than 500 ships had made the run across the Atlantic to England safely, for the activity in mid-Atlantic had slowed down as Admiral Doenitz diverted his submarines to the Western Hemisphere.

There were 73 destroyers in the Atlantic fleet, he pointed out to Admiral King (who knew the numbers very well).

In the Caribbean, where 27 percent of the world's shipping that month had been sunk, the navy had 28 percent of its destroyers on duty. In the north, where only 6 percent of sinkings had occurred, the navy had placed 41 percent of its destroyers. And on the Eastern shore of the United States, with nearly half the submarine activity occurring anywhere, the high command had allocated only 5 percent of the destroyers of the fleet.

The shore defenders had done everything they could. They rerouted ships (to the disgust of merchant captains, who hated changes in routine). They had tried the theory of sailing only in daylight hours, making the ships hole up at night along the shore.

But the problem was escorts and patrol craft. On an average over the month, Admiral Andrews' command had the use of two destroyers each day. U.S.S. *Dahlgren*, for example, had been ordered to service with the Eastern Sea Frontier for a week but had actually served three days. They had *Dickerson* and *Roper* for eight days. They had *Dupont* and *Cole* for 48 hours.

The American defenders had still not sunk a single U-boat. They had not even seen one, yet all during March, at least six and sometimes eight, U-boats were operating off the American coast.

The destroyers, said Admiral Andrews, were the key to his defenses. Could he please have some more of them?

The answer came swiftly enough from Admiral King. It was NO.

13
THE Q-SHIP CAPER

Desperate times make men undertake desperate missions, and there was no more cogent illustration of the state of the times in January, at the end of the first week after the U-boats appeared off the East Coast, than when Admiral King called on Admiral Andrews to fit out Q-ships to fight the submarines.

Andrews responded that since the U-boats were concentrating on tankers, a converted tanker would be best. Barring that, the Q-ship ought to be "of such a relatively insignificant appearance that upon sighting it a submarine would not submerge."

So, in February, a Q-ship operation was launched.

There was nothing new about Q-ships. They were used in World War I with some success to entrap German U-boats. Q-ships were heavily armed warships camouflaged to look like the most innocent of merchantmen. Almost always, they were converted merchant ships, but by the time the naval dockyards finished with them, there was little resemblance between the new and the old save for the silhouette. Armor, big guns, depth charges, even tubes and torpedoes were fitted to these ships and hidden so the undersea enemy would not suspect.

But the Q-ships of World War I operated against smaller, much less powerful submarines than the Type VII U-boats that Admiral Doenitz was sending across the Atlantic. Even so, the situation of the defense was so precarious that no possible weapon could be overlooked, so Project LQ was born.

Project LQ was so secret that the communications were to be made by word of mouth. Nothing indicative was to be put in writing.

Three vessels were selected for the program. One, the

Wave, was a Boston trawler, 133 feet long. She was to be called U.S.S. *Eagle.* The other two were small interisland cargo ships, the S.S. *Carolyn* and the S.S. *Evelyn.* They had belonged to the A. H. Bull Steamship Company of New York City. They were bought by the U.S. Maritime Commission by two gentlemen named Huntington Morse and S. H. Helmbold and then secretly taken to the navy yard at Portsmouth, New Hampshire, for conversion.

There, the two 3,000-ton cargo ships were given four 4-inch guns, four .50 caliber machine guns, six single depth-charge throwers, and an assortment of .30 caliber machine guns, sawed-off shotguns, automatic pistols, and hand grenades. *Eagle,* being smaller than their 318 feet, had only one 4-inch gun, and while the two cargo ships would have crews of six officers and 135 men each, *Eagle* would carry only five officers and 42 enlisted men.

The names of the cargo ships were changed as further protection. *Carolyn* became U.S.S. *Atik. Evelyn* became U.S.S. *Asterion.* But the commissionings were not made a matter of record in the navy yard, and all written information about these ships was kept in a top-secret file in the custody of the vice chief of Naval Operations.

In order to mask the arming of these ships, Admiral Stark, who was chief of Naval Operations, opened a joint account in the Riggs National Bank in Washington and deposited there $500,000, which could be drawn out by either F. J. Horne or W. S. Farber. Also, Stark told the bankers he might from time to time want to transfer some funds to other people. Almost immediately, he did so: He wrote a check for $50,000 to the Eagle Fishing Company, L. F. Rogers, master. Then he wrote a $100,000 check to Asterion Shipping Company, K. M. Beyer, treasurer, and another to Atik Shipping, E. T. Joyce, treasurer. These were all naval officers encharged with the fitting out of the secret ships.

Early in March, all was ready. Admiral Andrews then called in the commanders of the three ships, Lt. Comdr. L. F. Rogers, a reserve officer of the *Eagle* and two regulars, Lt. Comdr. G. W. Legwen of *Asterion,* and Lt. Comdr. Harry L. Hicks of *Atik.*

The three officers assembled in Andrews' office on

Church Street, and he gave them their personal orders verbally.

They were to sail from Portsmouth and then spread out, each to one area where enemy activity had *not* been reported. This was to be the shakedown cruise. They were to sail out just as if they were what they seemed to be, regularly commissioned patrol vessels. But then, out of sight of land, the crew was to remove from the ships the identifying numbers from the bows. The false bulkheads were to be drawn over the big guns. Depth-charge throwers were to be concealed. The ships were then to look like merchant men; *Eagle* would seem to be a trawler fishing out of Boston. The other two would be simple cargo vessels. *Atik,* for example, was loaded with a cargo of pulpwood that gave her a verisimilitude and also, hopefully, extra bouyancy in case she got into a fight with a U-boat.

Atik and *Asterion* would patrol in intensive-activity areas about 200 miles off the coast. They would pretend to be merchant ships until a submarine came to close quarters. If challenged by friendly ships or aircraft they were to use the old S.S. *Carolyn* and S.S. *Evelyn* names and call signs. But if they were challenged by enemy vessels, *Atik* was to identify herself as S.S. *Villa Franca,* a Portuguese merchantman with the call SSBT, and *Asterion* would become S.S. *Generalife,* Spanish registry, call EAOQ.

When it came time to return to port, the captains were to notify Huntington Morse or S. F. Helmbold of the Maritime Commission, and then they would be met at the port by Maritime Commission agents who would furnish them with all supplies. The captains would pay by check on the Riggs bank account.

Admiral Andrews looked at them appraisingly. If they got into trouble, by the way, they probably would not get any help. The situation was critical. Every available combatant ship and plane was employed to its absolute maximum capability for convoy and patrol duty. There were no spares to send after Q-ships.

The admiral paused. The briefing was over. The officers picked up their caps and made ready to leave.

"Oh, yes," said the admiral. There was one other thing. This was an extremely dangerous operation, and while it was impossible to make a "voluntary" mission of it—it would tip their hands—it should be made known to all officers and men that they could withdraw immediately if they chose. They were to be told no more than that.

And so the captains went back to their ships. They made the announcements, and no men withdrew. Most of them were like *Atik*'s Ens. Edwin M. Leonard. He once had been asked to serve on the staff of Admiral Wilcox, but he had declined and asked specifically for combat sea duty. This job was just what he wanted.

And as for secrecy, the mission of *Atik* and *Asterion* was unfortunately not as well kept a secret as Admiral King had expected it to be. How could it be? Hundreds of civilian workers in Portsmouth Naval Shipyard had been involved in the conversion of these ships. That they were building "Q-ships" was common knowledge in the Portsmouth boarding houses and bars. So the men of the Q-ships knew where they were going, all right.

They sailed, then, as ordered, on March 23, and once at sea, the hands turned to, to remove the telltale signs of naval vessels. They were ready for action but told to carry out the "shakedown" first. What they had not been told, however, was that they were completely expendable. The two ships were 30 years old and not suitable for patrol. Their present mission was about all they were good for, and Washington did not expect them to stay afloat for more than a month. So hurried had been these preparations that the officers and men were not quite sure what they were supposed to be doing. They knew nothing much about antisubmarine warfare. They knew only what the captains had managed to read about the manner in which Q-ships had operated in World War I.

And so, as Captain Hicks set out in *Atik*, he knew that he was supposed to be torpedoed, or that the submarine would surface and come in with its gun, or both. When this happened, one group of the crew was to "abandon ship," and the radio operator was to put out distress calls in the name of *Carolyn*. Then the concealed crewmen would wait until the U-boat came in to point-blank range, drop the camouflage bulkheads, and turn the batteries on the U-boat. If she dived, then they would go after her with depth charges. The changes in structure, and the pulpwood cargo were to offset any effects of the torpedoing.

On the second night out, *Asterion* had a submarine contact. The men were still building the screens for the concealment of the guns when the "pinging" of the sound gear began. Captain Legwen did not want to meet the enemy just then, so he took evasive action.

On the night of March 26, *Atik* was cruising about 300 miles east of Norfolk, and *Asterion* was some 250 miles south of her. Then, at 8:53 that night, *Atik* was torpedoed.

"SSS. . . . (chased by submarine). . . ."

"SOS . . . (I am in serious trouble). . . ."

"Latitude 36-00 N. Longitude 70-00 W, *Carolyn* burning forward. Not bad."

Two minutes went by; then another message came through the airwaves: "Torpedo attack, burning forward, require assistance."

These messages were received in New York, but as Admiral Andrews had warned, there were no ships to send. Down south, *Asterion* heard, and Captain Legwen turned north to assist his sister ship, although he knew his action was a debatable interpretation of his orders.

In New York, the attack did not even arouse much concern. There were so many of them, and so little could be done, and the duty officers knew nothing of the secret missions of these vessels. *Carolyn* was a small merchant ship caught by disaster, as far as the Eastern Sea Frontier's bullpen was concerned that night.

It was hours, then, before the word reached anyone who knew the truth about *Carolyn,* and by that time it was too late. It was a particularly nasty night at sea. Bombers, a tug, and a destroyer were sent out as dawn broke, but the weather drove the tug and destroyer so hard that the tug was finally sent back, and the destroyer used so much fuel fighting the storm that she had to break off search a few hours later.

Asterion came up to the position but found nothing. Freighters that had passed through the area reported they had seen no wreckage.

That was the end of it and of *Atik,* almost.

On April 9, the German radio broadcast a sinking report:

"The High Command said today that a Q-boat—a heavily armed ship disguised as an unarmed vessel—was among 13 vessels sunk off the American Atlantic coast and that it was sent to the bottom by a submarine only after a 'bitter battle.'

"The Q-boat," the communique said, "was of 3,000 tons and was sunk by a torpedo after a battle fought partly on the surface with artillery and partly beneath the water with bombs and torpedoes."

So Captain Hicks, who had been itching for action, had encountered his submarine. And he had been torpedoed, as he expected, and then the Q-ship crew had played out the role. The submarine had surfaced, fought with guns, and then, when the *Atik* had begun firing, had obviously submerged, and *Atik* had depth charged her.

But what had happened after that?

It seemed likely that the U-boat had managed to put another torpedo or more into the *Atik*, and she had broken up and sunk in spite of her buoyant cargo. That was the only sensible explanation, but even it was no more than conjecture, for the sea had swallowed *Atik*, Captain Hicks, his five officers, and 135 enlisted men.

Atik's was the first and last action of the U.S. Navy Q-ships with German U-boats. It was apparent that the Q-ship concept, which had worked so well in World War I, was an anachronism in World War II.

The Q-ships kept going, however. Once a plan was in effect, it had its own momentum, and *Asterion* continued in service, as did *Eagle*. Later, the U.S.S. *Big Horn* was employed as a Q-ship, but she and the others were lucky enough not to encounter a U-boat.

Lieutenant Commander Hicks was awarded the Navy Cross posthumously, but it was years before his family could even learn why, so secret were the operations of the Q-ships. Not until 1946 did the navy tell the story of what had happened to *Atik* that lonely night in the storm off Norfolk, when Captain Hicks had met his submarine.

14

FUMBLING

The U.S. naval authorities were in a quandary. Pushed by the British, they would have liked nothing better than to censor every account of the carnage that was occurring offshore, but the German radio boasted of the sinkings, and to maintain any sort of confidence in its credibility, the navy had to admit that ships were being sunk. No indication was given, however, of the degree of success of the U-boat campaign, which had all but paralyzed coastal shipping.

The newspapers carried sinking stories. They told how an explosion had shaken Atlantic City on March 27. A submarine had fired a torpedo at a ship and missed. The whole event was so close to shore that the torpedo ran in onto the beach and blew up.

A thoughtful reader would infer that the U-boats seemed to be having things pretty much their own way.

There were many stories of heroism at sea, such as that of the ship's helmsman who died conning his sinking tanker to keep the flames away from his mates as they struggled in the water.

Another story told how a pair of crewmen from a ship were picked up by the submarine that had sunk them and discovered the Germans had "full data" on their ship. (All that meant was that the U-boat captain had a Lloyd's registry of ships.)

The stories were fragmentary and sometimes incoherent, but a reader with a sense of place and time could gain an estimate of what was happening off the coast. There were too many different tales from too many different ports to conceal the fact that a large number of ships was being sunk. When one congressman suggested that the United States build wooden ships because they could be built quickly and would not sink when torpedoed (he said), then the avid reader might wonder.

But the public did not know even half the facts and could not sense the near desperation with which Andrews and his staff faced the task given them.

Admiral Andrews investigated every possibility that might bring more ships into his command. He asked the British about changing the cycle of east- and west-bound convoys to England. If they would just change from a six-day cycle to a seven-day cycle, it would release two groups of destroyers and corvettes for service off the American coast. But the British said that to change the cycle would deprive Britain of not less than 30,000 tons of imports per month. It simply could not be done. It would be like handing the Germans a half-dozen small steamers every month.

Because the U-boat attack pattern of February was repeated in March (heavy ship losses in the first and last ten days of the month with respite in between), Andrews suspected the U-boats were crossing the Atlantic in the south, holing up in Central American water, fueling there, and then moving north. He knew that the 500-ton boats would be hard put to cross and fight and return in a month. He made the mistake of underestimating the German discipline and effectiveness. Nor did he know that already he was facing the third wave of U-boats dispatched by Admiral Doenitz.

Andrews came to the conclusion that the Nazis were employing small tankers off the coast of South and Central America and using some deserted islands as bases. The suggestion was forwarded to Admiral King that such places ought to be searched. King sent it on to the Caribbean Sea Frontier, and many a small and innocent neutral ship was stopped and roughly handled by impatient searchers. But the sinkings went on.

The Germans were hitting the shipping in the south harder, but Cape Hatteras was still the favorite hunting ground of the U-boats in April 1942.

Admiral Andrews' constant nagging of higher authority seemed to produce results. To his destroyer "fleet" of three (*Jesse Roper, Noa,* and *Herbert*) were added *Hambleton, Hamilton, Emmons, Ellis,* and *Manley.* Suddenly, he had eight destroyers! But only for one week. On April 9, Admiral Andrews could muster for duty only *Herbert* and *Noa;* the others, given him on that temporary status, had been hurled off into mid-Atlantic for fleet duty.

But for the time that the Eastern Sea Frontier had this vastly increased patrol strength, the patrols were out constantly. With what results? That one week's activity was a fair indication of the effectiveness of the sort of defense that Admiral Andrews could mount even with eight destroyers at his call.

Hambleton and *Emmons,* for example, were immediately detailed to patrol from Wimble Shoals to Cape Lookout. They were ordered to report to the Eastern Sea Frontier regularly at eight in the morning and four in the afternoon. All contacts were to be reported immediately in plain language; no time was to be lost in coding and decoding while the U-boat listened and escaped.

On April 1, the two destroyers left Tompkinsville, Staten Island, for the shipping lanes. They reported nothing untoward that day. Next day, off the Virginia coast, they responded to a call from S.S. *Delsud,* which reported a submarine just south of her.

Hambleton was patrolling south of *Delsud,* so she took the call and sped north. As she came into sight of the merchant ship, *Delsud* let go with her deck gun. *Hambleton* evaded, identified herself, and the captain spoke in strong terms. *Hambleton* was the merchant ship's "U-boat."

Admiral Andrews warned the destroyers to look out for suspicious ships that might be secret tankers for the enemy. He had a report that six U-boats had entered the Caribbean in the last week of March, and he expected them along the U.S. coast momentarily.

After dark, On April 2, *Hambleton* and *Emmons* sighted two suspicious vessels. *Hambleton* stopped an innocent fishing boat for interrogation. *Emmons* hauled up a merchant ship and checked her papers.

Toward dawn, the destroyers were joined by a patrol bomber that seemed to zero in on an object, dropped a float light, which bobbed brightly on the surface of the sea, and then came in low to deliver a depth-charge attack. *Hambleton* hurried up, saw turbulence that might have been caused by a submerging U-boat, and delivered a depth-charge attack.

No U-boat revealed itself. The sound gear was totally silent. They had attacked the turbulence set up by the patrol bomber's attack.

That morning of April 3, the destroyers heard a message from the tanker *Esso Augusta*, "chased by a U-boat" 40 miles from the destroyers. *Emmons* detached and sped off to search while *Hambleton* continued to patrol. A few hours later, *Emmons* returned. There had been no U-boat.

At eleven o'clock that night, a U-boat was reported between Cape Lookout and Diamond Shoals. The destroyers sent up star shells and revealed a large U.S. tanker wallowing along.

On April 4, at one o'clock in the morning, the S.S. *Chester Sun* reported a submarine contact, but they did not discover the submarine. Four hours later, off Ocracoke, the S.S. *Phoenix* wirelessed that she was followed by a submarine. Again, search revealed nothing.

On April 8, at two o'clock in the morning, the destroyers were aroused to action by a bright light and explosion. S.S. *Bidwell* had just taken a torpedo.

The ships hurried to the scene but found no submarine. *Bidwell* was not sunk, and she managed to make Hampton Roads under her own power.

The destroyers continued on patrol. On April 6, *Hambleton* developed troubles with her port turbine.

On April 7, there was nothing to report. That day, the newspapers carried Secretary Knox's report of "increased effectiveness of the antisubmarine campaign."

On April 8: nothing.

On April 9: nothing. At the end of that day, the destroyers were recalled to Hampton Roads. Their temporary duty with the Eastern Sea Frontier had ended, and they had accomplished nothing except to use up fuel.

In his report on this patrol, the commander of Destroyer Division 19 complained that this use of destroyers was wasteful and self-defeating. It was virtually impossible for a destroyer to make contact with a submarine except by blind luck. Any alert U-boat commander would have his echo gear working and would hear a patrolling destroyer long before it came within attack range.

As far as the destroyer men were concerned, the system made no sense at all. There was no communication between the patrol craft and the air patrols. The talk in plain English on the airwaves could be a dead giveaway to U-boats. Worst of all, there were too many fingers in the pie. For example, in one contact, *Hambleton* had concurrent, and conflicting, orders from the Eastern Sea Frontier, the commander in chief, Fifth Naval District and Bermuda Naval Base.

When this report reached the Eastern Sea Frontier, Admiral Andrews read it and not only concurred but used it as the basis for a new assault on Admiral King.

"It is impossible to combat the menace with forces of inadequate strength," he said. What he needed was a fleet of 31 destroyers for convoy duty, not a handful of loaners to carry out a search plan that was so obviously futile. As he was sure Admiral King would agree, said Andrews, the search program violated two cardinal principles of war at sea: (1) concentration of force and (2) conservation of energy. Destroyers and patrol boats scattering all over the lot did no one any good, and the amount of energy they wasted was enormous.

The only real value of the patrol system was to give merchant seamen the feeling that something was being done to protect them. It was good that they did not really know how ineffectual the defense effort was.

Admiral King did not reply directly to Andrews' complaints. He did order the Eastern Sea Frontier to prepare for convoy. So the plan was drawn in detail. There was just one catch remaining: There were no convoy escorts.

But now those escorts were known to be coming. The British had promised the fleet of trawlers to assist the Americans in the battle against the U-boats. On the first day of April, the first of them had arrived in New York harbor. One of these was H.M.S. *Bedfordshire*. Her captain was Lt. R. B. Davis, Royal Naval Reserve. He had three other officers and 33 enlisted men serving under him.

Bedfordshire had been built in Middlesborough, England, in 1935 as a seagoing fisherman. At the beginning of the war, she had been commandeered like hundreds of others and made into an antisubmarine vessel. She was assigned to the western approaches to the British Isles.

As warships go, she was not very large: 900 tons, 170 feet long, and armed with a 4-inch deck gun in the bow and a .303 Lewis machine gun. But she carried nearly 100 depth charges, and by using two throwers and rails off the stern, she could lay down a pattern of ten charges. She was also equipped with ASDIC, the sounding device.

Her main deficiency was her lack of speed. She made only 12 knots. A U-boat could run rings around her on the surface.

On the way across the Atlantic, *Bedfordshire* came upon survivors of the Norwegian motor ship *Tyr,* which had been torpedoed and sunk off Nova Scotia. She picked them up and brought them into Halifax on March 11.

Bedfordshire was delayed there on orders. The *Queen of Bermuda,* a luxury liner, had been converted to an armed merchant cruiser, but in January, the *Queen* had run aground and made port limping badly. She had to be towed down to New York for repairs, and *Bedfordshire* and four other trawlers were held until she was ready to leave so they could protect her against U-boats on the way.

So it was April when the convoy was safely docked in the Brooklyn Navy Yard.

The Americans were shocked to see what they had gotten. All the trawlers were badly in need of refitting. As advertised, they had no tools at all, and they required high-grade anthracite coal to make them operate at even 12 knots.

But Admiral Andrews was in no position to be picky. They were ships, they could fight the submarines, and that was what he needed. At the moment he did not appreciate their greatest asset: the British crews who had already been fighting the U-boats for months and knew how to do it.

There was very little time for refitting. In less than two weeks, *Bedfordshire* and 13 other trawlers were in service along the coast.

All that could be done in April was to establish a half-convoy system, north and south. Ships coming north traveled in the daylight hours and ducked into harbor at night, where they could be guarded by the little patrol craft available to Admiral Andrews.

The ships would then sail early in the morning, forming up in columns, four to a column, with 600 yards between ships and 1,000 yards between columns. Any ship that traveled slower than 9 knots or faster than 13 had to sail independently, at much greater danger. During these daylight hours, the convoys were escorted by one slow escort in the lead, and three fast escorts on patrol. The escorts, of course, were not destroyers or corvettes, as they ought to have been, but 83-foot Coast Guard cutters and smaller craft. They used almost the entire ship resources of the Eastern Sea Frontier.

Forming up at the Florida strait, they traveled to Charleston and lay over at night. The next day, they made Cape Lookout, then the Chesapeake, then the Delaware. The convoy moved up to New York waters, to lie over a day or two. The convoy then traveled to Buzzard's Bay and through the Cape Cod canal and in Cape Cod bay made rendezvous with the British and Canadians, who had real escorts, and headed for Halifax. From there, they moved east in the big convoys bound for Britain.

In mid-April, Admiral King said he wanted convoys to operate regularly between Hampton Roads and Key West.

It would take five escort groups, said Admiral Andrews. It would steal all the craft of the Eastern Sea Frontier. There would be no rescue of sinking ships, no patrols.

In Washington, Admiral King said nothing.

At this critical time, everyone, it seemed, had a different idea of the proper course of action against the U-boats. The desperation of the situation was understood in shipping circles. Early in 1942, the oilmen had formed the Petroleum Industry War Council Committee. The committee surveyed sinkings, in January, February, and March, and announced that if the current rate of attrition continued, by the end of the year, 125 of the 300 tankers that served East Coast cities would be destroyed, and 3,000 lives would be lost. There would not be enough fuel for the war effort.

In Washington, Main Navy began to understand that the priorities might have to be rearranged.

15

"NO MORE TANKERS
WILL SAIL . . ."

In the desperate search for a method to combat the U-boats, many men offered plans. The commander of the Fifth Naval District suggested that the navy take over the tankers for the duration. Let them put naval officers and men aboard the ships and run them in the navy way. That would stop the sinking, he said.

Shell Oil Company asked to put its own Piper Cub planes on its own ships to search ahead in the most dangerous waters. When Admiral Andrews refused this request as impractical, Shell offered to establish its own shore-based air force, flying planes along the tanker routes. There was an indication of the shipping industry's faith in the ability of the U.S. Navy to protect them!

Someone suggested that the Civil Air Patrol be incorporated into the army. It seemed to be flying most of the search missions offshore, anyhow. The army air force wanted no part of that plan.

Admiral Andrews continued to pound at Washington for ships and planes. He secured promises for the future, and that was all.

In the first ten days of April, the U-boats took seven tankers. Those dire predictions of the Petroleum Industry War Council hung heavy in the air around Church Street.

So unsure were the defenders of the American coastal waters that they found themselves in danger of fighting one another. None were more uneasy than commanders of American submarines, for reasons that became clear when Fifth Naval District asked for the service of a submarine for ten days for maneuvers in Chesapeake Bay. The object was to teach pilots and antisubmarine warfare surface units something about U-boats in operation.

In New London, at the submarine base, *Mackerel* was chosen for the job. She was a modern fleet-class submarine, roughly equivalent in operation to a U-boat.

Mackerel just then was involved in antisubmarine exercises with the destroyer *Sapphire* off New London. When the exercises were ended, she and *Sapphire* headed back to base together, each of them flying a huge American ensign at the stern. It was evening, and dusk had settled down over the sea. The two ships moved along comfortably, then suddenly a P-38 twin-engined fighter-bomber zoomed down over the submarine and dropped four depth bombs. They straddled *Mackerel* and might have sunk her had the pilot been more experienced. But the bombs were dropped at a bad angle; they ricocheted and bounced away from the submarine.

The P-38 circled. The submarine blinked a challenge. The P-38 ignored the challenge and then flew away in the direction of Quonset Naval Air Station.

Mackerel and *Sapphire* headed back to New London, where the captains indignantly told their story. The fighter and bomber bases of all commands were combed that day, but no one knew of a P-38 that had dropped any bombs anywhere. New London never discovered the identity of the culprit.

With a certain justified uneasiness, on April 12, *Mackerel* set off from New London for Norfolk. A hundred miles off Cape Charles, *Mackerel* encountered the patrol boat *Legare,* just as *Legare* sighted the submarine. Both ships went to general quarters. *Legare* was ready to start firing, but her captain sent the challenge first. He was surprised when *Mackerel* answered correctly.

They conferred then, submarine and ship captains, and *Mackerel*'s commander learned that although her sailing instructions had been clear, no information had been sent out from New London to the Eastern Sea Frontier about the passage of the submarine. That meant she was in danger every minute from every patrol plane and vessel. Obviously, this was a difficult state of affairs. *Mackerel* could dive and make the rest of the trip submerged. but she would travel then at around 8 knots and would be so late in reaching Norfolk that Fifth Naval District would be unhappy.

The captain of *Mackerel* asked the captain of *Legare* to escort the submarine as far as Cape Henry, and they set out together as night fell.

At 11:15, the submarine changed course. The officer of the watch on *Legare* saw and ordered the escort's course changed, too. The submarine changed course again, and so did *Legare*. Just as she swung around, a torpedo came streaking down her port beam, missing the ship by no more than 20 yards.

Looking through their glasses, the men on the bridge of *Legare* swore that *Mackerel* had fired a torpedo at them.

The captain of *Mackerel* had quite a different story.

He said that at the time in question, he had sighted a submarine, and it fired a torpedo at him. (That was the torpedo, said *Mackerel*, that had narrowly missed *Legare*.) *Mackerel* had replied with two torpedoes against the U-boat, but the U-boat had then disappeared.

Whatever the answer, *Legare* wanted no more of this treatment, and she sped back to her patrol area, leaving *Mackerel* to shift for herself.

Mackerel moved on south. At five o'clock the next morning, she sighted another "U-boat" on the surface and fired another torpedo. It missed, and the "U-boat" sped away.

Mackerel headed for Hampton Roads. She encountered the patrol vessel *Tourmaline* and very nearly had another "U-boat." But the two recognized one another in time.

The *Mackerel-Legare* incident simmered through the various commands until it came finally to Admiral Andrews' desk. He studied the evidence, particularly the statements of those on the bridge of the patrol craft who said they saw the torpedo come from the American submarine. Andrews concurred: Somehow *Mackerel*'s captain had become so disoriented that he had fired on at least one American ship, believing it to be an enemy U-boat.

Mackerel participated in the exercises in Chesapeake Bay without further incident. But on the way back to New

London, she came across the American tanker *El Lago,* and the tanker captain, believing he saw a U-boat, opened fire. Once more, *Mackerel* barely escaped destruction. It was a wary, weary submarine crew that moored the boat at New London. But since no harm had really been done, save to the morale of the men of *Mackerel,* the incident passed into the files of the Eastern Sea Frontier and was forgotten.

The whole series of incidents could have been avoided if Andrews had been able to send a proper escort to accompany *Mackerel* to Hampton Roads. The admiral threw down the gauntlet to Admiral King: He *must* have more destroyers, or King *must* stop the sailing of tankers up the North American coast until such time as Andrews could protect them. They could not stand the loss of a ship a day.

Admiral King took the situation under advisement, along with several new, disturbing reports of misadventures to tankers that had attempted to run the U-boat gauntlet up the coast. One of these was S.S. *Victoria,* a 7,000-ton Argentine tanker, a neutral, for Argentina's President Juan Peron was as close to a friend as the Germans had in the Western Hemisphere.

Victoria was bound for New York, with an Englishman along, to check the performance of her new engines. The Argentine captain was worried about having an Englishman aboard, but the big blue and white flags painted so prominently on the sides of the ship should assure the U-boat commanders that the ship belonged to a nation that was not unfriendly to Germany. The captain's concern was to maintain the careful neutrality that President Peron had instituted.

The captain was punctilious about his neutrality, so much so that when the radio operator heard a distress call 10 degrees north of the equator, he refused to respond. The call was only 60 miles away, said the operator. That was not the point, said the captain.

The English engineer pleaded the cause of charity.

The first mate pleaded that they were only a day's steaming away from the point of call.

The captain was obdurate. For three days, "Sparks" listened to the distress calls. Finally, the signals died out.

On April 17, *Victoria* was in the sealane 300 miles off the American coast, east of Cape Hatteras. She was bound on a course of 311 degrees at 8.5 knots. The wind was brisk and blowing from the northwest. The skies were clear.

After a little calculation, the captain came to the bridge at 6:45 that evening and then gave a message to the radio operator to send to the New York agents. *Victoria* would arrive in New York harbor on April 20.

Hardly had the captain given the message when he was jolted by an explosion that shook the ship. Quickly, the word was passed: A torpedo had struck *Victoria* on the port beam between Number 1 and Number 2 holds.

The captain called for the general alarm, and in the radio shack, the operators began sending out an S O S call. The identity flags, showing that the ship was neutral were run up fore and aft.

The S O S was acknowledged by a shore station. (*Victoria*'s operators did not catch the identity.) Then they waited. The ship went dead in the water, the tanker drifting slightly, the blue and white flag of Argentina plain against her sides.

At 7:50, the captain's hopes that it had all been a ghastly mistake were shattered by another torpedo, which flared a bright yellow as it struck.

The danger of fire was with them now. The captain saw the flames and ordered his men to abandon ship.

In the port boat, the falls jammed as it went down, and three men spilled out into the sea like peas falling from an opened pod. Their mates pulled them to safety against the stopped ship.

The chief officer, the British engineer, and 19 men clambered into this boat and soon were away. The captain, the other officers, and the remainder of the crew got into the starboard lifeboat and rowed away. Soon the boats were out of sight of one another.

On April 17, the U.S.S. *Owl,* an old mine sweeper, was en route from New York to Bermuda, engaged in the task of towing an oil barge to the naval operating base leased from Britain. She was 300 miles off Cape Hatteras, making 10 knots. A message from the naval operating base (for it was this shore station that had heard the S O S, luckily for

Victoria) informed her that the tanker was in distress and about 40 miles from the minesweeper.

Owl turned and headed for the position. Two hours after midnight, her lookouts saw lights ahead. The ship was placed at general quarters.

Was it a U-boat?

No, it was a tanker, low in the water.

The mine sweeper, still pulling her tow, circled slowly around the tanker until dawn. As the gray lightened, the men could see that she was on an even keel but had two holes in her port side. The torpedoes had been set for shallow run, and apparently they had done little damage below.

The captain of *Owl* was certain the tanker was salvageable and so informed Bermuda. He ordered the tow line tripped, and the barge was set adrift. At eight o'clock in the morning, *Owl* put an emergency crew of seven men aboard the tanker, under the executive officer.

After a look around, they decided they could start the diesels. The rudder was all right. The ship seemed seaworthy.

At 8:18, they started up. But the electrical system had been damaged by a torpedo, and a circuit breaker failed. The chief petty officer, who could fix it, was aboard *Owl*. The weather was roughing up, and they could not transfer him for hours. It was midafternoon of April 18 before they got the chief aboard.

When Bermuda had the message that the tanker was salvageable, the station dispatched the destroyer *Sagamore*.

Meanwhile, the steamer *Empire Dryden* had found and rescued the crew of the port boat of *Victoria* and brought them to *Owl*.

The electrical expert found that he could not start the engines, so *Owl* had to come alongside and use her compressor. It was nearly midday on April 29 by the time she got going again.

Late that afternoon, the destroyer *Nicholson* came up with the captain and remainder of the crew of *Victoria*, whom they had rescued that morning. By evening, she was on her way again to New York, escorted by U.S.S. *Sagamore*, a one-ship convoy.

For there would be no more tankers coming up the coast

alone. Since the U-boats were now trying to sink even neutral vessels off the American shore, something had to be done. Admiral King approved Admiral Andrews' request for "action." Tanker sailings north of the Florida straits were prohibited until further notice.

16
THE FIRST U-BOAT

The U-boats had approached the U.S. coast in January with care, but in the months since, seeing the childishness of the American defenses, they had grown careless. In April, U-boats attacked on the surface even in daylight hours; some captains ventured into shallow water. After three months' experience, they were fairly certain there would be no surveillance.

The North American cruise was regarded as the best possible duty for a U-boat captain to make his reputation. So when Kapitaenleutnant Eberhard Greger's *U-85* was assigned to North American waters on her fourth war cruise, Greger and his men were envied in the U-boat fleet.

U-85 sailed in the third week of March, at night, to take advantage of the darkness that protected the U-boats in the Bay of Biscay from the growing number of British search planes and destroyers.

For two days, Greger kept the U-boat submerged. Then, out past the patrol zone, *U-85* surfaced and began to travel at high speed. For three days, the crew enjoyed such fine weather that the men could sunbathe on deck. The sea was as smooth as a table. But on the fourth day, a spring Atlantic storm struck, and the submarine began to plow through heavy seas. The pitching unseated several torpedoes, and one aft damaged part of the electrical motor system.

The damage was not serious enough to cause Greger to abandon the cruise. *U-85*'s crew made repairs and continued toward the U.S. coast. On April 4, Greger announced to the crew that they were in the zone: "Six hundred and sixty miles from Washington" is how he put it.

U-85 reached her station two days later. And on April 10, she found a steamer and sank her with two torpedoes.

Captain Greger was eager to sink ships. When he did not find more at the 100-fathom curve, he decided to go into shallower water. On April 11, *U-85* was off the entrance to Chesapeake Bay in 164 feet of water, less than 30 fathoms. She stayed submerged. The crew heard the noises of three ships going by, but Captain Greger did not even come to periscope depth. He had second thoughts about the defense possibilities up there. *U-85* headed north into deeper water. On April 13, she was near Wimble Shoals. She came to the surface that night south of Bodie Island.

That night, the destroyer *Roper* was assigned to the search area off Wimble Shoals. Just after midnight, *Roper*'s radar operator made a contact with an object at 2,700 yards. Almost on the heels of his report came one from the sonar operator, who heard propellers. From the bow came a report from a lookout who had seen the wake of a vessel ahead of them.

Roper had been cruising at 18 knots. The captain, Lt. Comdr. H. W. Howe, ordered the speed increased to 20 knots. The klaxon sounded general quarters. The gunnery officer sent his crews to the machine guns and the 3-inch battery. Torpedoes were made ready. The depth-charge crews stood by the Y guns. The executive officer hastened to the bridge.

Whatever the vessel was out front, it was trying to get away. In recent weeks, the Eastern Sea Frontier had warned against small craft outside their normal area under abnormal conditions, behaving in strange ways. Admiral Andrews and his men continued to suspect that the German U-boats offshore were receiving aid and even supplies from enemy agents and sympathizers within the area under Andrews' command.

Captain Howe, then, was determined to check out this strange vessel.

The quarry changed course suddenly, turning hard a-port. *Roper* turned with her. The other turned to starboard almost immediately. Like a terrier, the destroyer swung hard over.

Port again, starboard again; it was apparent that the other vessel was trying desperately to get away.

Roper was making maximum speed and slowly closing on the other craft.

Then, off the starboard quarter, came the cry "Torpedo."

In a few moments, the torpedo crossed the wake of the ship, closer than anyone liked to consider.

Three hundred yards farther on, the captain ordered the *Roper* to turn hard to starboard, and as he did so, the 24-inch searchlight beam stabbed an object ahead of them.

It was a U-boat.

Captain Greger now began the frantic search of the trapped for an avenue of escape. His one advantage was the smaller turning circle of the submarine, which enabled him to turn inside the destroyer. With any luck, he could gain enough advantage to give him the few moments he would need to submerge.

Turn, turn, turn. *U-85* waited for *Roper* to make a mistake.

But *Roper*'s captain made no mistake. With each turn, Howe's ship came a little closer to the U-boat, whose gun crews were now on deck.

On order, the number 1 machine gun began to fire on the U-boat. At this close range, the machine gun cut down the gun crew. More men poured out of the conning tower.

The crew of number 5 3-inch found the range and got a hit on the conning tower. Soon the U-boat began to fill with water and sink. Germans were coming up, fast.

Captain Howe ordered the torpedo officer to get ready to torpedo the submarine, but as he turned for a run, the U-boat disappeared beneath the surface, leaving 40 men struggling in the water where she had been.

Now the captain of *Roper* had to make a hard decision. Should he stop and pick up survivors?

There might be another U-boat in the area, just waiting for him to stop. That was a tactical consideration.

Another concern that was on the minds of the men of *Roper* were tales they had heard of U-boat warfare in the Atlantic, stories of merchant seamen machine-gunned in their boats.

Roper steamed through the men struggling in the water. She did not stop. She did not slow. She dropped 11 depth charges in the debris where she saw the oil slick.

There would be no survivors.

Roper moved in the area until seven o'clock in the morning, when, in the light of day, she was joined by two patrol planes that buzzed the area. One of them dropped smoke floats and called attention to many bodies floating in the water.

Roper moved in among the bodies, slowed, and stopped. Boats were sent to pick up the bodies and search them for material possibly useful to Naval Intelligence. Twenty-nine bodies were recovered. Six of them were wearing escape lungs, and two had the tubing in their mouths.

Two other bodies were in such poor condition (after the depth charging) that they were allowed to sink back into the sea after cursory search of their clothing.

The destroyer men found enough material to reconstruct part of the story of *U-85*. In violation of orders Seamen Ungethüm and Degenkalf had kept diaries. Apparently aware of their constant brush with death, they both had the little books on their persons at the end. And from them came bits and pieces of the story of *U-85* and her four war cruises. One crewman had saved a home-town newspaper, the *Offenburger Tageblatt*.

And that was almost all. Two of the British trawlers came up to assist *Roper*. One of the trawlers was *Bedfordshire*. She stayed in that area through April 22. The navy had decided the water was shallow enough to attempt to recover intelligence material by diving to the wreck of *U-85*. Tugs and a tender and divers were sent to the scene, and *Bedfordshire* remained on guard as the operations were carried out. The divers recovered little.

The story of the sinking of *U-85* brought a wave of enthusiasm to the beleaguered defenders of the Eastern seaboard. But in England, where the view was tempered by experience, there was the chilly realization that in more than four months of war, the Americans had just managed their first U-boat, and that almost entirely by chance.

17

THE END OF
H.M.S. *BEDFORDSHIRE*

When, at the end of April, Admiral Doenitz learned that the tankers had stopped coming up the East Coast of the United States, he felt it was time to change his plans.

Doenitz's U-boats were doing so well that he wanted no letup. By the end of the month, with only the loss of *U-85*, he claimed to have sunk 198 ships (a total of 1,150,675 tons) in American waters. Harry Hopkins had cabled President Roosevelt from London with Winston Churchill's observation that the Germans were sinking Allied ships faster than the Allies could build them.

To keep that happening, Doenitz decided to send more U-boats to the Western Hemisphere. It was possible because U-boat production had been increased in view of Doenitz's successes. And Doenitz now had what Admiral Andrews had most feared: a small tanker to serve the U-boats in American waters.

The Eastern Sea Frontier would have been more alarmed had Andrews known that the tanker was also a submarine, known affectionately among the U-boat commanders as "the milk cow."

First of these was *U-459*, a 1,700-ton U-boat that carried no weapons but could deliver 700 tons of fuel oil on the western side of the Atlantic. This meant she could fuel a dozen operational U-boats on station, enabling them to double their fighting periods. On April 22, when *U-459* met *U-108* 500 miles northeast of Bermuda and refueled her, the sea war off the U.S. shore became twice as deadly as it had been in the month previous. And besides this increased capability, Doenitz had assigned 18 U-boats to station between northern Canada and Key West and nine more in the Caribbean.

But Doenitz's plans met one snag. For when the full moon came at the end of April, and the fueled U-boats were moving into position off Hatteras and elsewhere, there were no ships to sink.

The seventh war cruise of *U-558* told the story.

Kapitaenleutnant Gunther Krech sailed *U-558* out from Brest on April 12, headed for the happy American hunting grounds. Krech was already a legendary figure in the German submarine service. He had trained under Otto Schepke, who was one of Germany's three greatest U-boat captains. He had assumed command of *U-558* when she was commissioned in January 1941.

Krech fostered the legends. He carried with him to sea a small aquarium full of fish he named for the heads of state of Germany's enemies. Winston Churchill was a small pirate fish. He died on the third war patrol and was pickled in alcohol in a vial, with bawdy references to Churchill's drinking habits. The vial was suspended from a lamp in the wardroom.

In Krech's orders were instructions for him to meet "the Milch Cow" off Bermuda and take on extra fuel to replace that consumed in the crossing. The refueling took place on April 29. *U-558* was then equipped to move to the North American station and remain until June 21.

As May began, *U-558* patrolled off Bermuda but encountered no vessels. The U-boat captains had been told the best hunting ground of all was off Cape Hatteras, so Krech took the U-boat there, and on May 5 he was cruising between Hatteras and Cape Lookout. For three days, he saw nothing.

At 1:15 on the afternoon of May 8, the U-boat was lying on the surface when Captain Krech saw a small convoy of seven tankers and cargo ships. They were escorted by three warships, which was something new. But Krech's early war cruises had been against the hardy British, and he was prepared to fight warships as well as sink cargo vessels.

He decided to run on the surface around the convoy and catch it as it rounded Cape Lookout. The convoy was moving at 8 knots along the 25-meter depth line. The water was too shallow for him to try a daylight attack. The sinking of *U-85* in shallow water had been a lesson to the U-boats that even the hapless Americans were dangerous if a captain became foolhardy.

So it was to be a night attack.

Somehow, however, in making the run around the convoy, Kresch lost contact with the quarry. He began to search.

On May 9, he was still searching, moving south on the surface in the direction the ships had gone.

That evening, the men of the U-boat had a scare. A patrol plane came by close, but in the dusk, the low silhouette and the gray of the submarine's hull saved them; the plane did not see them.

That night, Krech had to admit ruefully to his hard taskmaster Doenitz that he had lost contact with the convoy.

On the night of May 10, *U-558* was searching for a new target, southeast of Cape Lookout. The skies were gray and the visibility good.

But there were no ships.

At 1:30 in the afternoon, while carrying out a training dive, the man on the sound gear sang out: He had a contact astern.

Krech took the boat to periscope depth and swung the tube around. He saw two patrol vessels, and he heard the distinctive pinging of the British Asdic. One of the vessels turned and came straight for the submarine. Down went the periscope, and the U-boat dived for the seabed.

The patrol boats were two of the trawlers on assignment to the Eastern Sea Frontier, and one of them was H.M.S. *Bedfordshire*.

They came near the stilled U-boat, but they did not find it. Krech stayed down for hours, until he heard the sounds of detonating depth charges far away and propellers in the distance.

It was five and a half hours before he brought the U-boat up. In the setting sun, he saw through the periscope silhouettes of the two patrol vessels on the horizon.

U-558 stayed at periscope depth for another 45 minutes and then surfaced. She began to run south at 18 knots, following the coastline.

Then, at 10:07, out of the darkness appeared the *Bed-*

fordshire once again. She was moving at 6 knots. Captain Krech decided to get rid of her. He had been at sea for a month and had sunk nothing at all. A warship, even a small one, was better than nothing.

Krech maneuvered and fired two torpedoes. They missed, but the officer conning *Bedfordshire* did not even see them. Krech decided it was safe to try again. This time, Krech moved in to within 1,800 yards of the trawler and fired another torpedo, from periscope depth. It struck *Bedfordshire* square amidships. Her stern rose high out of the water for a moment. Then she plunged straight under the surface.

Krech snapped the handles on the periscope and brought it down. Whatever else happened, the cruise was not a total failure.

That was the end of *Bedfordshire*. Even in death, however, this little British trawler had an impact on the war at sea far greater than her size would indicate.

On the morning of May 14, the Coast Guard Chief Boatswain's Mate Arnold Tolson and a companion set out from Ocracoke Station to look over the beach-patrol route. Tolson was showing the new man the route he would take when he later went on duty alone. At six o'clock, they got into a Coast Guard truck, drove to the beach, and headed off toward Hatteras inlet. They would patrol half the way up the beach since the Hatteras Coast Guard station patrolled down to the point where their route ended.

An hour later, they were at the end of the beach, the wide deserted stretch of sand, some of it still discolored by the scum of oil that reminded anyone who saw it of war.

Tolson spotted something in the water. It appeared to be a swimmer, his arms flailing about. But how could it be a swimmer? There was nothing here, nothing at all on the dunes but the ponies of the wild herd that sometimes thundered up and down the beach.

They came closer. Tolson saw the object was a body. He stopped the truck, jumped out, took off his shoes and socks, and waded out into the white water. With the help of his companion, he dragged the body into the back of the truck, covered it with canvas, and headed back to the Ocracoke Coast Guard Station. Tolson had lived in this area all his life; he was a native of nearby Buxton and the Outer Banks, and this was his first body. He was shaken.

As they came to the village of Ocracoke, Elwood Austin excitedly flagged them down. Austin had been fishing on the point with his wife, and he had seen another body in the surf. The Coast Guardsmen turned the truck around and went down to the beach, two miles farther to the point. There they found the second body. They took both to the Coast Guard station at Ocracoke village and turned them over to Chief Homer Gray.

The two bodies were taken to the back of the station, laid carefully in canvas, and Gray telephoned naval headquarters at Morehead City.

Soon a marine amphibian aircraft arrived from Cherry Point to pick up the bodies. The pilot, Naval Intelligence Investigator Aycock Brown, recognized one body as that of a man he knew, Sub-Lt. Thomas Cunningham of the Royal Navy.

The other was that of telegraphist Stanley Craig.

They searched the bodies and found a copy of the Morehead City newspaper in Cunningham's pocket and a bankbook on a Morehead City bank.

Dr. Charles Swindell came to examine the bodies. The cause of death was either a concussion or drowning, he said, or perhaps both.

The men worried about the problem of procuring coffins, for the war had brought shortages of everything, including lumber. But the Coast Guard produced a pair of long boxes that had been found on the shores of Silver Lake. Actually, the boxes were a local invention for duck hunting. Hunters put them in the water and lay in them, their decoys scattered on both sides. Then, when the ducks came in, they lifted their guns.

But these portable blinds were abandoned, or so said the Ocracoke postmaster, who was the local authority in such moral matters. They certainly might be used as coffins.

Consulting naval regulations, the little band learned that there was no objection to giving the recovered bodies a Christian burial, and they might be buried in private ground. The Williams family, which had its own cemetery on the island, donated two lots next to their own.

No priest or minister was available that day, so Brown

asked Amasa Fulcher, a lay preacher of the Methodist persuasion, to do the service.

That evening, the dead were wrapped in white sheets and blue navy blankets and placed in the coffins. From all around the island, men had assembled the Coast Guardsmen, and they arrived dressed in their best uniforms.

Back in the days when *Bedfordshire* was a happy, living ship, Cunningham had given Aycock Brown several British flags. Brown now produced two of these and draped the makeshift coffins with them.

The uniformed men silently carried the coffins to the site where others had spent the afternoon digging the graves. The Outer Banksmen stood solemn as Amasa Fulcher conducted the brief burial service. Then they all sang a hymn without accompaniment.

When the simple funeral service was over, the men returned to their duties. Aycock Brown called navy headquarters to report on the deaths of the two men from the *Bedfordshire*. He was greeted by incredulity.

There had been no distress call or any indication that *Bedfordshire* was sunk, said the navy. How did he know the identities of these men? was the question.

Brown explained that he knew young Cunningham personally, and then there were the papers on the bodies.

The navy was stubborn. Perhaps the men had fallen overboard. The records showed *Bedfordshire* on station on May 11, and as far as the navy was concerned, she was still on station. The record keepers were not convinced that they might be wrong. They continued to carry *Bedfordshire* "on station" for another 48 hours, until Brown appeared with the Cunningham papers. Then the British trawler was listed as "missing in action and probably sunk."

Ocracoke had much to talk about.

Wahab Howard, a local businessman, spoke to his cousin Harvey Wahab, a Coast Guardsman, about the deaths, and when Cunningham was identified (he had a black beard and mustache), Howard said he knew the man well and had conversed with him on several occasions.

A 19-year-old boy, Jack Willis, recalled that he had seen the British officer in the drug store, just a few days earlier playfully trying out an electric razor on his magnificent beard.

All who had any connection with *Bedfordshire* talked about her to their friends. The war was suddenly close and deadly.

A week later, while cruising aboard Ocracoke station's 63-foot Coast Guard cutter *63-067,* Arnold Tolson spotted two bodies in the water 5 miles northeast of Ocracoke Inlet. They were dressed in the dark-blue turtleneck sweaters that the British trawler men usually wore. The bodies were in bad condition after 10 days of immersion, and they bore no identification. But Chief Tolson was certain they were men from the crew of *Bedfordshire* and brought them ashore for burial next to the others.

This time there were no portable duck blinds for coffins. A call went out around the community for lumber. One man, who had laid in a supply to build a new outhouse, said he would give it up. The T. A. Loving construction company also had lumber; it was building some naval facilities on Ocracoke. So suitable lumber was found as well as the hammers and nails, and two simple coffins were built for the unknowns.

They were buried as had been the others, and in lots right next to them.

Brown undertook the settlement of the affairs of the British sailors he had known, if only slightly. He went to the First Citizens Bank and Trust Company of Morehead City with the bankbook. He found the bank had no fewer than three officers' accounts plus a wardroom account for the ship. The records were turned over to the navy and forwarded to the British embassy in Washington.

A few days after the sinking, one of *Bedfordshire*'s lifeboats came ashore at Portsmouth Island, and two more bodies washed up on the beaches. Seaman Alfred Dryden was buried with full military honors in the presence of a contingent from the other trawlers in the Baptist Cemetery at Creeds, Virginia. This place had been selected as the "official" burying place for the British sailors who lost their lives so far from home.

And so the story of *Bedfordshire* ended on the beaches of America, 5,000 miles from beleagured Britain, but there doing a job that was essential to the survival of England and her allies.

H.M.S. *Bedfordshire*'s service had brought home the hellishness of the war to many a person on shore, and she had helped cement relations between American and British navies. She had also shown that the use of even trained officers and men did not make antisubmarine patrol by single craft effective in the war against the U-boats.

18
HOW NOT TO FIGHT A U-BOAT

The best U-boat pickings were found along the coast of Florida, close inshore.

During May, people driving their cars along the beach roads north and south of Miami deluged the authorities at Morison Field in West Palm Beach with telephone calls: They had seen submarines on the surface in daylight hours.

These were not crackpot calls: The submarines were there. But each call had to be relayed to Washington and from there into the "chain of command." The red tape was so tangled that by the time a plane or ship appeared at the point indicated, the submarine was always gone.

The daring of the U-boats was amazing. On May 6, near Jupiter Inlet, a U-boat torpedoed a freighter, *Amazon*, in broad daylight just offshore. She sank in only 13 fathoms of water. That same day, the U-boat sank the tanker *Halsey* in the same area. She was so close inshore that the tips of her masts stuck up above the surface, although her hull was on the bottom. And her cargo of gasoline, fuel oil, and naphtha drifted in to turn the beach black.

Two days later, a U-boat sank the freighter *Ohioan* nearby, then the Cities Service tanker *Empire*, which broke in two and spilled 92,000 more barrels of oil almost on the shore. Then, on May 13, the tanker *Potero del Llano* was blown apart just here.

The Miami-Palm Beach area was getting its share of the war.

Mrs. Grady Stevens, night supervisor of the Good Samaritan Hospital in West Palm Beach, handled the emergency room, too. Nearly every night, the rescued came in. Sometimes there were only one or two. Sometimes there were 50 men. Some were burned, some were wounded, some were suffering from shock. All of them were filthy, usually with oil that ruined sheets and stained the cots and blankets.

The worst night Grady could remember was the night the U-boats sank a Danish tanker. She flared, and the men who escaped had to swim to safety through fire. Those who made it were almost all horribly burned.

To fight this onslaught in the South, the Americans decided they had to adopt the convoy system. For the first time it was possible, for Andrews had aircraft now and at least some of the destroyers and other ships he had been calling for. The planes would carry most of the responsibility. There were enough of them at Langley Field, Norfolk, Elizabeth City, Cherry Point, Wilmington, Charleston, the Banana River in Central Florida, and Miami to protect ships from Hampton Roads to Key West.

Besides the planes, Admiral Andrews had assembled six groups of surface vessels. Each consisted of two destroyers, a corvette (from the British), two patrol craft, and two trawlers (also from the British).

On May 14, the convoy from New York to the Delaware Capes was ready. KS-500 was the name. It set out on May 14. The next day, May 15, KN-100 started north from Key West.

In these first two convoys, all kinds of difficulties developed. The masters did not know the merchant signals and were often confused. The naval men had to send visual messages constantly when the flag system failed to produce results.

Furthermore, the masters failed to respond to the commodores when they issued orders, the vice-commodore of the northbound convoy did not join up until they were off Miami, and then four vessels showed up that had not appeared on any orders. All the way north, ships dropped off whenever they felt like making a port of call.

Yet, somehow, the charges were delivered, north and south, and not a ship was lost from either convoy. It was the end result for more than five months of work.

The system was still tenuous. On May 16, at six in the morning, the ships *Bluefields*, *Schickshinny*, and *C. O. Stillman* left New York heading for Delaware Bay to join convoy KS-502, which would assemble them at Hampton Roads and head south.

Beneath an umbrella of planes and shepherded by several Coast Guard cutters, they moved toward Delaware Bay. By nightfall, they were inside and in the canal en route to Chesapeake Bay. Next morning, they were in the bay, and they made Lynnhaven Roads at five o'clock on the afternoon of May 17, having traveled by daylight, largely through inside protected waters.

The ships were gathering at Hampton Roads, and by the nineteenth, eleven of them had assembled. The commodore was riding in the *M. F. Elliott,* and he had some difficult decisions to make that related to the whole convoy. One concerned the Brazilian freighter, *Mogy.* She made only 8 knots, which was really too slow a speed for the rest of the ships assembled. No one aboard *Mogy* spoke a word of English, and she had none of the publications that others considered necessary to navigate in war-drenched waters. In other words, *Mogy* was very likely to become a liability on the way.

The commodore considered carefully, but he had all the usual problems of command. *Mogy* carried a cargo that was valuable to the war effort, no matter her speed or the language problems.

The commodore decided to take her, anyway.

As he considered, the escorts were assembling. The destroyer *McCormick* came down from New York and joined the destroyer *Ellis.* They also had in company H.M.S. *Cape Warwick* and H.M.S. *Coventry City,* a pair of those British trawlers. The Coast Guard cutter *Dione* was assigned to this convoy. So were the little *PC-68* and *PC-462.*

On the night of May 19, all the captains of the ships— merchantmen and warships—met on the *McCormick* for a presailing conference. There they went over the rules about darkening ship at dusk, staying in line and in column, and maintaining speed. The navy men warned about enemy submarines and told them of the submarine menace that existed particularly off the Virginia Capes and the Florida Straits.

Then the captains went back to their ships and waited for morning to come.

At 6:22 in the morning, they got under way from Lynnhaven Roads, and two hours later, they were south of the Chesapeake entrance buoy.

On May 21, they were off the North Carolina coast, well inshore. They were taking no chances with deep water where the submarines lay.

Mogy slowed them down dreadfully. But she posed a minor problem compared to *Bluefields*. That ship was carrying a cargo of kapok, burlap, and paper. Somehow she caught fire, and when *Ellis* rushed up at the sign of smoke, the captain informed him that the ship had only one fire hose. So *Ellis* came to the rescue. Her captain ordered the captain of *Bluefields* to move the ship so that the wind was on her beam. He brought up six hoses from *Ellis* and soon had the fire out.

But *Bluefields* could not continue in the convoy. *Coventry City* was detached and escorted the freighter into Beaufort, South Carolina, for survey and repair.

They weren't sorry to lose her. She had turned out to be a straggler, anyhow.

On the evening of May 21, the convoy was off Southport, North Carolina.

The next day, they were moving south when *Dione* and *PC-462* made contact with a submarine. It came at about noon. They attacked and dropped 18 depth charges. They discovered oil and bubbles but nothing more. It was a neat trick of some U-boat commanders to locate wrecks and hide by them. If this U-boat commander did so, he did it well. They could not find him, and after three hours, they moved hastily south to join the convoy.

What they had done, of course, was bad antisubmarine warfare technique. By chasing submarines and staying with the hunt, they left the convoy very weak for hours, and this was how ships got sunk. It would be called to their attention later.

On the twenty-third, the convoy was off Fernandina and straggling. The destroyers ran about trying to push them back together, but it was a thankless task.

On the twenty-fourth, they made Cape Canaveral and came under the air blanket of the Banana River planes. On the last day, they reached Alligator Reef at the end of the Florida straits at six o'clock in the evening, and the convoy was over. The 17 ships would sail unaccompanied through the straits to Rebecca Shoals without help. That was the way it had to be. This time, they all made it safely. The convoy system was beginning to work. KS-502 had come down through waters where at least seven U-boats were working, and they had not lost a ship.

But that was pure, blind luck.

There were plenty of U-boats about, and the carnage was fearful, for at the end of four months of war, the Americans still did not know how to fight U-boats.

The information was available since before the beginning. When war came in 1939, the Royal Navy approached the struggle with its routine sense of duty. Quickly, the British standardized Asdic (sound) operating procedures and put all the information into a pamphlet. Gaining experience, they produced an antisubmarine-warfare manual. Monthly, the antisubmarine-warfare units made reports, and with each new development in antisubmarine tactics, they brought the body of information up to date. This material was transmitted to various antisubmarine warfare schools in the United Kingdom, so that when a new man joined a crew, he knew, at least theoretically, all that the old hands at sea had learned by experience.

The U.S. naval attachés in London were soon privy to all this confidential and even secret material, and they carefully laid it out for Washington in reports, beginning in 1939. But in Washington, the reports were filed away in 1939, 1940, and 1941, and the U.S. Navy traveled along its old course. The best-informed man in the U.S. fleet on antisubmarine warfare was a chief petty officer. He was also nearly the only informed person.

It was not until February 7, 1942, that Admiral King finally established the Anti-Submarine Warfare Unit of the Atlantic Fleet, with Capt. W. D. Baker as officer in charge. It was a paper command, with headquarters at 150 Causeway Street in Boston. Baker's task was simple: to start at the beginning and do everything.

That's where the American navy was months after war began. There was no manual for sound operators. There was no manual for destroyer skippers. Radar operators functioned in the best way they knew how, without a standard.

Baker quickly delved into the reports from London. He discovered that the British had developed devices called "attack teachers" that simulated problems. Every British operating base had them. They were on hand at Halifa, Iceland, Londonderry, and Greenock, and these were the bases to which American escort vessels sailed in protecting the convoys to Britain. So some U.S. destroyer men had begun to learn the ropes from the British, courtesy of the Royal Navy.

But qualified men were very few. The British were transferring corvettes and others vessels to the Americans. When the first batch of officers and men of the U.S. Navy showed up to pick up their vessels at the station H.M.S. *Osprey,* on the western shore of England, the British were appalled to learn that the Americans did not know how to use the ships. They undertook to teach them.

Captain Baker had to procure a large number of attack teachers in a short time, set up antisubmarine-warfare bases to train American sailors, bring in those few experienced men, and get the program going before the Germans managed to sink so many ships that the war would end.

Within a month, he had the program working. One of his first tasks was to show the attack teachers to American manufacturers and get contracts to build enough of these machines to go around. He made contracts with General Electric, Sangamo, and Submarine Signal Company.

He began production of an antisubmarine-warfare manual and set up a system for the analysis of all action reports from the Atlantic Fleet so the men could learn from their mistakes.

In April, Baker moved down to Washington as antisubmarine-warfare commander of the whole navy. On the way down, he stopped in New York to see Admiral Andrews, and they discussed the problem. Two weeks later, Andrews' men were in Washington setting up a system, and by the first of the month, the Eastern Sea Frontier had its own organization. Comdr. R. W. Hungerford was entrusted with the task. He was a destroyer man, just off the convoy run. He would bring in navy and army air force officers and establish training-base plans for each naval district.

The naval districts would each establish a school and

then work with action reports from the ships and train the men.

It was all there, in the plans, by May 1. Washington would supervise all. Washington would keep in touch with the British and track the submarines as they moved across the Atlantic. Washington would work with London to keep up to date and produce manuals for merchant captains and cut down the time of transmission of information from hours to minutes. But right now, it was still all plans, and plans did not fight submarines. The civilians who spotted submarines just off the Florida coast continued to call the authorities excitedly to make their reports. The authorities at the naval air station continued to call Washington to get permission to send a plane to investigate. The submarines continued to move along the coast, contemptuous of the defenses.

On May 2, the state of the defenses was tested and proved.

On that day, the U.S.S. *Broome* was on patrol 100 miles off Cape Fear. It was Sunday, a beautiful spring day, with a light southwest wind that barely rippled the water. The clouds hung wispy above, and the sun was bright and warm. *Broome* was heading southeast at 22 knots on one leg of a patrol pattern.

At 10:23, the sound man reported a contact at 2,300 yards. It seemed tenuous. It was two minutes before he reported again; the contact was now at 1,400 yards and moving.

Broome belatedly came to general quarters at 10:28. The sound contact was now only 180 yards off the bow. Then the contact was lost.

Broome dropped a smoke bomb to mark the place and went on searching.

Fifteen minutes later, she returned to the smoke bomb and dropped a full pattern of nine charges. Oil appeared on the surface, and so did air bubbles. The sound man reported propeller noises, and as they tracked them, the captain saw that a submarine beneath the surface was moving inside his turning circle.

At 11:34, a periscope appeared off the starboard beam. *Broome* began racing forward, firing the 20-mm. guns and the 3-inch.

Seven minutes later, she moved back and forth, attacking. At two o'clock in the afternoon, the sound man heard two underwater explosions. In 16 attacks, *Broome* fired 20 depth charges. Then, up from the depths, bobbed a piece of wood. That was all.

The captain of *Broome* had kept his base informed, and at 2:35 that afternoon, up came two British trawlers, *Le Tigre* and *Cape Warwick*, manned by trained destroyer men of the British Royal Navy. They took over, but by this time the sea was silent, and no more was seen of the U-boat.

Back at base, *Broome*'s captain was commended by the antisubmarine-warfare unit of the Eastern Sea Frontier. She had been a little slow, but she had stuck with the target. Her captain had shown good sense and good tactics.

But, praise or no praise, *Broome* had failed. She had come upon a U-boat in water so shallow (120 feet) that it seemed impossible for it to get away, yet the U-boat had slipped through.

As the antisubmarine-warfare men knew, if *Le Tigre* and *Cape Warwick* had gotten there first, the story would have been quite different.

19

THE SECOND U-BOAT

On May 3, the U.S. destroyer *MacLeish* went out to sea on patrol along with *PC-496*. They made a "contact" at 8:45 in the morning and then were joined by a PBY patrol bomber that "saw" the submarine and dropped two depth charges. *MacLeish* almost immediately attacked with 25 depth charges. A B-25 army bomber came by and dropped four depth charges. *MacLeish* threw two more patterns, totaling 14 depth charges. But if there was a U-boat at all, and that is doubtful, it got away. The reason: inexperience. Men of *MacLeish* then observed, at one point, "a distinct, light-green discoloration below the surface." As any old antisubmarine-warfare man could have told them, it came when a depth charge exploded in shallow water.

Still, the Americans were learning. Equally important, they were beginning to be able to concentrate formidable air and sea forces against U-boats. Even when badly organized, two ships and two aircraft represented strong force.

Admiral Andrews' new measures, convoy and controlled ship movement, began to have more effect in May than he or his officers then knew. Eleven of Doenitz's submarines stood off the U.S. coast along the 100-fathom line, from Charleston to Portland, and their captains began to grow restless in the paucity of shipping that came their way.

Restlessness made the U-boat captains overeager. They were ready to attack any target. Early in May, *U-352* was on war patrol just off Hatteras. Back in Lorient, Kapitaenleutnant Hellmut Rathke had heard how easy the sinkings were. He had been told that American defenses were nonexistent. But now Rathke's experience was not bearing out this story. One day, *U-352* had to dive to hide from a patrol plane that came sniffing about suspiciously. Two days later, a patrol plane came upon her on the surface, and as the U-boat went down, the plane dropped two depth charges that exploded dangerously close. It was a narrow escape.

That night, Rathke heard from Doenitz. Agents had reported a convoy would soon be sailing north from Norfolk, and Rathke was to watch for it.

He did. He waited through May 5, and for four more days. He waited for a convoy that never came.

Late on the afternoon of May 9, Rathke was so impatient that when he sighted a vessel through the periscope, he decided to attack even though the ship was small and, under ideal conditions, would not have been worth the effort.

The vessel sighted by *U-352* was, in fact, the U.S. Coast Guard cutter *Icarus*. She was en route from New York to Key West. As Rathke watched through his periscope, the sound-gear operator aboard *Icarus* noted what he thought was a contact 1,900 yards off the port bow. But it was so "mushy" he did not report to the bridge. He knew there had been several sinkings in this area, and he suspected that he had a fix on a wreck.

Five minutes later, the "contact" was much sharper. This time, the operator was aroused. The "contact" was moving abaft the beam of the ship. He called the captain, Lt. Comdr. Maurice Jester.

Just then, at 4:28, the captain and crew of *Icarus* were startled by an explosion under water, 200 yards off the port quarter. It blew a geyser high in the air. Rathke had fired a torpedo, and it had misfired.

Icarus heeled, put on speed, and laid a pattern of five depth charges over the spot where the contact indicated the submarine lay. It was done within two minutes.

The cutter moved off, turned, and came back, tracking, with sound gear. Fourteen minutes after the first depth charging, *Icarus* laid a V-pattern of three more charges. This time, the explosions were followed by a series of air bubbles. *Icarus* dropped another charge on the bubbles.

One minute later, the dark hull of the U-boat broke water. The depth charges had done their work.

Icarus' men were at the machine guns, and the captain maneuvered to bring the 3-inch gun into play. At 1,000 yards, the gun opened fire.

The first shell was short but effective. Luckily, it ricocheted off the water and burst through the conning tower, taking the arm off one man and the leg off another.

The second round missed, but the next six rounds were on target. The U-boat began to sink.

Captain Rathke ordered his men to abandon ship. Six minutes after she came to the surface, *U-352* went down. The captain of *Icarus* marked the spot: 34′25″ N, 76′35″ W.

In spite of the men struggling in the water, *Icarus* moved in and dropped one more depth charge on the sinking U-boat. *U-352* went to the bottom in 120 feet of water, taking 12 men, including an engineering petty officer who, until the very last, was shouting that they were crazy to abandon ship and surrender when they could escape on the surface.

Icarus stood off then while the Germans struggled in the water. Captain Rathke moved in the water among his men, helping them. He fixed a tourniquet on the stump of the man whose leg had been blown off. He cautioned the men that when they were rescued, they were to say nothing. Then they waited and looked at their enemies circling them.

As the U-boat sank, Lieutenant Commander Jester sent a message in plain English to Norfolk base.

"Have sunk submarine. 30 to 40 men in water. Shall *Icarus* pick up any of them?"

There was no answer.

He sent the same message to Charleston two minutes later.

No answer.

Six minutes later, he asked Charleston if there was a message for him.

The answer was no.

Eight minutes after that, he sent the message to Sixth Naval District headquarters.

Seven minutes later, he repeated the message to Sixth Naval District.

Finally, 35 minutes after the sinking, the Germans still

treading water, Sixth Naval District told *Icarus* to pick up the survivors and bring them to Charleston.

Gingerly, the sailors moved to rescue the awesome enemies who had invaded their shores. They searched all the men at the gangway, as if they might have some explosives or weapons on them with which they would try to take over the ship and sail away to Germany. They sent the 30 able-bodied men to the crew's quarters forward under heavy guard. Two wounded were taken to the crew's head. The man whose leg had been blown off was laid in a litter on deck and wrapped in blankets. He was not much of a danger, the men of *Icarus* decided.

Up forward, Captain Rathke exerted the discipline for which the U-boat service was famous: The men would say nothing, he warned them. There would be no talking, and what had to be said would be said by him.

Icarus headed toward Charleston.

That evening, the Germans were fed after the crew had their supper, and the wounded were treated. The man whose arm had been severed was in terrible pain, and although he said he spoke no English, as the pain increased, he asked in perfectly plain English that somebody shoot him to put him out of his misery.

The man whose leg was off was in much worse shape. They gave him Adrenalin and sedatives, but nothing helped. He died just before midnight.

Icarus reached Charleston; Naval Intelligence officers separated captain and crew and officers from men and tried to question them, but Rathke had been with his men long enough in the forward compartment of *Icarus* to indoctrinate them on procedures as prisoners. None of them would talk.

Naval Intelligence was furious, and a few days later the whole Eastern seaboard defense establishment had instructions that when U-boat crews were captured, the captains and officers were to be segregated from the crews *immediately.*

As it was, very little was learned about *U-352*, and most of that far too late to do any good. For in the red tape and confusion of the battle offshore, investigation of the sinking was delayed.

A British-American salvage force had been dispatched

promptly to Morehead City, North Carolina, to raise the wreck for Naval Intelligence, but on May 21, this little force blundered into the path of another submarine and attacked with depth charges. But the second submarine got away.

Two days later, the vessels found the spot where the submarine had gone down and put a grappling hook on her. The next day, a diver went down and identified the bow as that of a U-boat. The salvage work began.

But the tugs and tender were bedeviled by every conceivable difficulty. Cables snapped. They had engine trouble. Anchors dragged. They kept at work for a week, but then the navy called them off to other tasks. *U-352* was left on the bottom with her secrets.

Three months later, another try was made. This time, a navy diver found the wreckage, attached a cable and hook to a part of it, and a 20-foot section of the upper deck grating came to the surface.

Divers went down again the next day to try to get cables around the whole hull and bring it up. But down there they discovered five unexploded depth charges around the wreckage. This new danger, plus strong currents that had hampered the first effort, caused the navy to abandon the salvage.

The naval authorities remained puzzled by the reason *U-352* had allowed herself to be trapped in such shallow water. The answer was simple enough: The Americans did not understand how much contempt the Germans still had for the American defenses.

20

THE JUGGLING ACT

Admiral Andrews and his staff were like circus jugglers trying to keep a hundred balls in the air at once. On May 21, at 8:11 in the morning, a Civil Air Patrol plane claimed to have sighted a submarine at 30°10′ N, 81°07′ W. When the plane moved to investigate, the pilot said the submarine submerged.

An hour later came an SSS call from the S.S. *Plow City*, a 3,200-ton cargo ship at 38°48′ N, 68°30′ W. The SSS continued, but there was nothing anyone could do. There were no planes to send and no ships to dispatch to get there in time. Early in the afternoon, S.S. *Plow City* was torpedoed.

At 10:30 came a report that the *City of Birmingham* had picked up 25 survivors of the British cargo ship *Empire Dryden*, which had been torpedoed on April 19. The men had been in the boats for a month. Now they were one day out of Savannah and safety.

At noon, a Coast Guard patrol plane from Elizabeth City dropped depth charges on rising oil bubbles at 34°40′ N, 75°45′ W. Since nothing happened, the pilot sent a second message. It must have been a sunken wreck, he said. But the Eastern Sea Frontier, which plotted every ship that went down, had no record of any wreck at that position or even very close to it.

At 12:40, a shore station caught a report from a station calling itself HBDL about a floating mine offshore at 37°48′ N, 57°21′ W. But there was no entity in the book with the call letters HBDL.

At 2:45 in the afternoon, the Coast Guard reported a plane had seen a "submarine" at 27°10′ N, 79°52′ W. The destroyer *Vigilant* confirmed it shortly afterward; she had a contact at those coordinates.

At 2:50, an army plane reported in: The pilot had seen a freighter burning not far from Morehead City. (That was *Bluefields* of convoy KS-502.) A destroyer was standing by, pumping water into her. Three hours later, another plane reported the fire was out and the ship was moving into Morehead City.

At 3:30, an army bomber attacked "a submarine."

At 3:45 came a report of survivors who had just arrived on the S.S. *George Washington*. They included men from the British tanker *Athel Empress*, sunk April 29, and the Dutch tanker S.S. *Amsterdam*, sunk April 16.

At 3:50, a plane sighted an empty life raft at 37°50′ N, 75°15′ W.

At five o'clock that afternoon, a plane from the 104th observation squadron reported "a submarine" had just submerged at 39°00′ N, 74°40′ W. The submarine was traveling on a northwest course. At 5:50, navy bombers believed they had found the U-boat, and one dropped a depth charge. A Coast Guard cutter came up and continued to search for the submarine.

At 6:40 that evening, while many people in Jacksonville were sitting down to supper, the naval base reported that one of its PBY patrol bombers was missing. The plane had left that morning for Norfolk and had not been heard from since. It was more than 12 hours out.

The army reported at 7:30 that "a submarine" had been sighted due south of Pigeon Key bank buoy. It surfaced five miles offshore and stayed up for about two minutes before submerging and heading south by east. The plane's pilot believed it was preparing to attack a large barge and tug that could be seen in that direction.

A few minutes later, another army plane reported seeing two patrol craft off Miami dropping depth charges.

Twenty minutes later came a report of a collision between S.S. *Samuel Bokke* and the H.M.S. *Worthington*, a British destroyer, off the east end of the Cape Cod Canal.

The destroyer was badly damaged, and two crewmen had been knocked overboard and were missing.

Later came a report that a suspicious long black vessel was seen south of Martha's Vineyard. Newport sent out patrol craft to investigate.

And so the night passed by. The next morning, at 7:30, a

U-boat was sighted by U.S. cargo ship *Curaca* at 28°50′ N, 91°40′ W.

Another day was beginning, another day of reports, patrols, sightings, suspicions, and above all, sinking of precious ships.

Now came a new complication: There simply were not the resources available for the defense of coastal waters because of the tremendous drain on naval resources in the Pacific. The battle of the Coral Sea had been fought, a Japanese victory that was to prove more or less Pyrrhic. The Japanese were still moving, heading for Midway and the Aleutians in what they hoped would be the decisive Pacific battle. From Pearl Harbor, Admiral Nimitz was pleading for ships, guns, ammunitions, men, planes, everything he could get. And, of course, every destroyer and every plane that was sent West meant one less for the defense of the American coast against the U-boats.

A direct result of these demands was a request from Admiral King that Andrews release convoy and patrol craft in view of Nimitz's needs and King's attempt to supply them.

Let Andrews strip all local defense forces of everything that would stay upright in the open sea, said King.

Andrews spent a week investigating. Then he reported back to the commander-in-chief; he had already stripped. There was not a single seaworthy boat to be found up and down the U.S. East Coast that was not now employed.

The needs of the East must be matched against those of the West. Admiral Nimitz in the Pacific was about to face most of the Japanese navy at Midway, and he needed every ship he could get. Obviously, Nimitz had priority. Even little patrol craft were sent to the Pacific. The converted yacht U.S.S. *Cythera* was dispatched from Norfolk on the first of the month to Panama, en route to Hawaii.

She did not get far. The next morning, off the South Carolina coast, *Cythera* was torpedoed. And then came one of those strange incidents of warfare that are so often lost in history.

Seaman James M. Brown was standing watch on the bow of *Cythera*. That's what saved him, for when the torpedo struck the little vessel, the craft simply disintegrated. Of the crew of 70 officers and men, only Brown and a pharmacist's mate, who was standing watch on the bridge, were saved.

Doenitz had strict rules against picking up any survivors, but the captain of this submarine was, in his way, humane. He saw the survivors struggling in the water, surfaced, and picked them up. He was just on his way back to Germany; the torpedo had been "wasted" on a patrol craft because he wanted to get going home. And so the two Americans were taken aboard and carried across the Atlantic to St. Nazaire. There they were sent to a camp populated largely by British naval prisoners, the first American naval defenders to become prisoners of war.

Andrews could not help Nimitz further. He was already depending far too heavily on air patrol in his own area, and U.S. air patrol at this stage of the war was not often reliable.

At 9:37, on the morning of May 15, Coast Guard plane OS2U No. 5771 left Elizabeth City on a routine patrol in broken clouds with good visibility. The sea was choppy, with a 30-knot southeast wind, so it was hard to keep a lookout for periscopes.

Yet, at 12:30, the pilot sighted a feather wake 12 miles off, about 30 miles from the coast. He put down his glasses to make a turn and lost the wake. But he had the good sense to keep going and looking; having flown about 5 miles, he identified the wake as a U-boat and caught it once more.

He flew in close, and his radioman concurred in what he saw. He also showed the good sense not to fly too close and to throttle back to quarter speed; in that way, he came to within a mile and a half of the U-boat before he was spotted.

The pilot identified the submarine as an Italian of the *Enrico Tazzoli* type, 250 feet long. (There were no Italian submarines in U.S. waters.) A dozen men were on deck, he said, but as they saw the plane come out of the broken cloud, they began pouring down the conning tower. As the hatch slammed, two were left on deck, one clinging to the conning tower and the other scrambling toward the stern. The submarine crash dived, and the plane leveled off 50 feet above the water. The pilot dropped two depth bombs set to explode at 50 feet, placing them 150 feet ahead of the submarine.

The bombs exploded, but they did not flush a submarine.

The pilot sent messages back to his base to tell the story and bring help. Soon he spotted a piece of dark-gray wood on the surface and presumed that it came from the submarine. He also saw an oil slick about where he had dropped the depth bombs.

At 1:30, the pilot was still circling the area. Then he was relieved by a pair of Coast Guard planes. Four hours later, the airship K4 arrived, dispatched by the Eastern Sea Frontier. The airship dropped a buoy at the place where the wood had come up; the oil slick was still there.

The next morning, the destroyer *Ellis* left Norfolk and headed for the scene, guided by Coast Guard planes. The oil slick persisted. *Ellis* came in, made two runs, and dropped eight charges. More oil came up.

She made another attack, with depth charges set at 200 feet. It was followed by an underwater explosion, and bubbles came to the top, plus a timber 16 feet long, painted black.

The submarine hunt had interested everyone in the area; the next morning, the commanding officer of the Elizabeth City air base came out to circle the area. He saw pillows, life belts, and other debris on the surface of the water. He came in lower and saw cartons, a canvas chair, papers, and the body of a man in a white uniform wearing a life belt.

Excited, he flew four miles up the coast where a convoy was moving along and dropped a message on the deck of a corvette to check out the body. He flew back and dropped a buoy near the body, and later he saw the corvettes trying to pick up the body.

The excitement continued until the reports all were gathered together on the desk of Admiral Andrews. He then informed all concerned that they had been bombing the wreck of the S.S. *Duarque,* a steamer that was sunk there on February 16. The timber, the debris, the dead body, were all blown up from the wreck. The mathematicians calculated: As for the submarine, assuming there really had been one, the charges dropped by the first plane and set at 50 feet would have exploded well forward of her bow and could not have done any damage. Nor were there any other reports of Italian submarines off the American coast.

21
A MATTER OF INFORMATION

The daylight or half-convoy system seemed to have solved all the problems of defense along the Eastern Sea Frontier, and some of the defenders began to congratulate themselves on having eliminated the U-boat menace. The number of sinkings was down, but Naval Intelligence knew that the real reason was Doenitz's dispatch of most of the U-boats to the Caribbean and Florida waters.

The result was an unreal quiet in the north. On May 30, a large convoy, headed south from New York to Delaware, was protected from harm by her escorts but by only one airship, ZNP-K-7. But all day long, the airship floated over the convoy and saw nothing at all, and that evening, when the ships arrived off Overfalls lightship at dusk, they met a northbound convoy whose experience had been almost precisely the same.

The two convoys stopped here for the night. They waited at the lightship for pilots to come out and take them into the safe inshore waters.

They waited, and they waited. Thirty ships lay drifting about, barely keeping way, in danger of collision, in danger of submarine attack beyond the ability of the escorts to protect them, while one single small launch went scurrying about, carrying pilots to one ship after another.

The convoy captains complained about the danger, but eight days later, the situation was as bad as ever. H.M.S. *Arctic Explorer* (one of the trawlers) was escorting a convoy up the coast, and her British captain, wise in the ways of war, saw with dismay his ships stranded just outside a port entrance for three hours, perfect targets for U-boats. He reported the matter to Admiral Andrews, and

Andrews chided those involved, but nothing much happened. Andrews had finally gotten enough ships together to make a defense, but he still had to perfect an organization.

One problem was an official overconfidence at the Washington level that distorted the reality of the war at sea. In Washington, on June 10, Secretary Knox gave another of his press conferences, at which he spoke vaguely of the "progress" being made in combating the submarines. Across town, on Capitol Hill, Senator Harry Truman came much closer to the point when he warned the public that the navy did not have enough ships to protect both oceans. And sandwiched between was a United Press report that day that gave the truth, although in a careful, low-key way: "The latest sinking (of two New England fishing vessels) brought to 266 the total of vessels lost in the Western Atlantic area by axis submarine action since mid-January." There were other tales in the news, all carefully edited, for Winston Churchill's warnings had finally struck home, and care was being taken not to give information to the enemy about sinkings.

But one result of this program was a curious hiatus, a breakdown in caution on the part of the defenders.

Merchant captains complained that the navy people did not hold presailing conferences to tell the civilians what was expected of them. They also said the navy patrol craft stopped them wherever they pleased, without regard to safety.

The naval commanders complained that the merchantmen did not follow directions. The commodores of convoys (most of them retired officers or naval reserve officers) complained that the merchant captains did not understand the signals they gave and did not follow them if they did understand. Too many ships failed to keep up, and the faster ships were like little children in the playground, running ahead of the convoys to get into port and get the pilots before anyone else.

The convoy system was complicated by the expectation of British and Canadian officials that the U.S. convoys would be as efficient as their own. A series of meetings, attended by American, British, and Canadian officers, tried to deal with difficulties and differences, but the Americans were still far behind in managing safety precautions, and as the sinkings decreased, so did safety. During the first week of June, the 9,000-ton tanker *F. W. Abrams* sailed from Aruba for New York with 90,000 barrels of oil. She was routed north by a British naval officer at Orangestad, who had no information about the area the U.S. Navy had recently mined off Cape Hatteras. Admiral Andrews, on May 20, had issued a warning to mariners, but the message had not gotten so far; at least the captain of *F. W. Abrams* was told nothing. He was informed only that if he arrived at Cape Lookout, he was not to try to enter without escort. But there could have been any number of reasons for that, including one merchant captains always suspected, the arrogance of the navy.

On June 10, *F. W. Abrams* arrived at Cape Lookout just after four o'clock in the afternoon. The captain signaled for instructions, and Coast Guard cutter *Number 484* came out to escort the tanker into harbor and led her to a berth. No information was passed about local conditions.

Next morning the day broke dark and heavy. A fierce rain pelted the ship and a strong wind blew her taut against the cables. At dawn, the tanker was led out of her berth by Coast Guard cutter *Number 484*. As they began to move, the captain of the cutter warned the captain of the *Abrams* that he must stay close and not lose the guide ship. He did not say why.

Tanker and escort headed out into rain that grew steadily worse until it blinded the captain of the tanker. He and the helmsman lost track of the cutter ahead. It disappeared in the murk and never came out.

In this blinding rain, with no visibility, there was nothing to do but anchor or creep on. With no known dangers ahead, the captain decided to sail on.

The ship moved slowly ahead for 20 minutes. Then, at 6:40, an explosion shook the *F. W. Abrams*. The captain believed the ship had been torpedoed. When no submarine appeared, he decided to drop anchor and wait for help. The windlass pawls were loosened and the anchor dropped, but the cable caught in a pawl and stuck fast. The anchor hung, suspended, halfway to the bottom, and the ship began to drift.

For half an hour, she drifted aimlessly. At 7:17, another

"torpedo" slammed into her starboard side. This time, the damage was more serious. Water began coming into the pump room through the twisted plates. Twenty minutes later came a third explosion, and the captain decided this one was fatal. He ordered the crew to abandon ship, and they did. The *F. W. Abrams* sank very quickly.

After the first explosion, the captain had ordered the radio operator to stay in touch with the shore, and the operator had reported each "torpedo" to the shore station at Cape Hatteras. *F. W. Abrams* was under "submarine attack," and the shore operator began calling up naval vessels for assistance.

Coast Guard cutter *Number 484* answered, and the operator learned that she had lost her charge in the rain. Asked why, the captain of the cutter said *Abrams* had refused to follow directions and had not answered blinker signals.

When the cutter reached shore later in the morning, operations and intelligence began to ask questions. A slightly different story came out.

The mate on watch of the cutter did not know the course. The captain of the tanker said the cutter was supposed to be 135 degrees, but the first mate said it was 100 degrees, and the heimsman said it was 90 degrees.

Some crewmen of the tanker insisted that they had seen torpedo wakes.

Of course, what had happened was that the *F. W. Abrams* had blundered into the Hatteras minefield, whose existence the captain did not even suspect, and the ship had been sunk by American mines.

The failure was a failure in communications. It was the navy's failure, a matter that was not reported at Secretary Knox's press conference. In fact, the story was never told to the public at all.

22

THE MISADVENTURE OF *YP-389*

The convoy system worked better than the mine system, to be sure, but its deficiencies were still serious. On June 14, a convoy of six merchant vessels left Halifax for Boston on the first leg of a journey south. No one could say the ships were not well protected; they had two escorts out ahead of them, one on each side, and one patrolling their rear.

The ships were arranged in two columns of three ships each. S.S. *Cathcart* led one column, with *Port Nicholson* and *Pan York* behind. The other column was led by S.S. *Malcrest*, with *Norlago* and *Cherokee* behind.

What *Cherokee* was doing in that convoy was hard to understand. She was a fast freighter, easily capable of 16 knots. She had been cut out of a fast convoy earlier for some administrative reason after she had come down safely from Iceland, bearing 41 army enlisted men, four Russian naval officers, and an army air force pilot, all bound for the United States.

The convoy steamed steadily southward. From the beginning, *Cherokee* had trouble trying to go slow enough to keep in line. At 11:25, on the night of June 15, *Port Nicholson* was hit by two torpedoes on the starboard side. Immediately, she began sending distress signals (in the clear) and put up flares that illuminated the little fleet as brightly as if it were day.

The crew of *Port Nicholson* abandoned ship, although she did not appear to be sinking. She drifted, unmanned, and one of the escorts was detached to circle and protect her.

Toward morning, the captain and chief officer of *Port Nicholson* decided to return to the ship; in the panic, they

150

had forgotten to pick up the ship's records. They went aboard, and then the men of the escort heard a "popping" as the bulkheads broke, and the *Port Nicholson* went down like a broken bottle, carrying the two officers to death.

Meanwhile, *Cherokee,* the fast transport, had turned sharply to starboard to present her bow to the U-boat when she saw the other ship hit. Out of column, she moved on for 10 minutes, and then she took two torpedoes and sank almost immediately with half her crew. When the convoy reached New York, the authorities questioned all the participants who were still alive.

The men of the escorts said they believed the convoy had run into a "nest of submarines." How those U-boats found the convoy was a great mystery to the navy men.

But as Naval Intelligence began checking out the stories, it became apparent that the convoy had virtually asked to be torpedoed. The whole port of Halifax knew the names of the ships, their departure date and time, the strength of the escorts, and their destination. Furthermore, when the first ship had been hit and sent up the flares, she was inviting the U-boats to destroy all the others. Then *Cherokee* had turned out of line, making it impossible for the escorts to protect her.

The Americans had a good deal to learn about convoys and security.

They also had something to learn about how to manage the small emergency craft they had been forced to enlist into the navy in these trying months.

One such was *YP-389.* She had begun life as a Boston trawler, and as such, she was admirable. But when it had come time for Admiral Andrews to scour the harbors of the East Coast for anything that could be put to sea, and she was chosen as a patrol craft, she left much to be desired in the new job.

Her hull was steel, but she carried no degaussing (demagnetizing) equipment, which meant she was constantly in danger of attracting magnetic mines. She had no sound gear. She supposedly made 9 knots, and her captain swore that she could do 10 with a following wind, but for practical cruising purposes, she made 6.

She carried one 3-inch gun and two .30-caliber machine guns. She also mounted four depth charges in the racks. A normal depth-charge pattern for a patrol boat was eight. But *YP-389* had no storage space at all for depth charges.

As for amenities, she had a cramped galley and a tiny mess room, a single head, and no showers or even air vents for the men's quarters. She was meant to stay at sea for only a few days with a crew of three or four. She was a fishing boat turned warrior, and the dozen men who sailed aboard her had to be prepared for hardship.

Just before the first of June, she and a sister ship were detailed to Cape Hatteras to patrol those troublesome mine-fields. *YP-389* got as far as Staten Island, where the captain decided she could not go farther without some basic repairs. He stopped at Tompkinsville, and the ship was put into Sullivan's dockyard for a bottom painting with anti-fouling paint and the addition of a fresh water tank that was sorely needed. While they were at work, the dockyard men installed blackout ventilation systems in the engine room and galley.

YP-389 was out of drydock in a few days, and she was then sent to convoy-protection duty on the Norfolk run. In his great need, Admiral Andrews was using her thus while moving her south. But *YP-389* was not a convoy escort. She could not even keep up with the 8-knot convoy to which she was assigned.

At Norfolk, when she finally arrived, the captain asked to put her into drydock again for more necessary repairs. But this was an operating naval base. *YP-389* seemed anything but a naval vessel, and her captain did not know the ropes of dealing with navy dockyard people. His repairs remained undone.

Six days later, *YP-389* was ordered to Morehead City, and the captain was told he could take his repair orders there.

The ship sailed to Morehead City. There the engines did get the overhaul they needed. *YP-389* went on her first patrol. Five days at sea knocked many parts on the ship loose, but that was to be expected. What was not expected was that when the captain called for gunnery practice, the 3-inch gun failed to fire.

The gunners literally took the gun apart. It was no use. The 3-inch simply would not work.

Back at Morehead City, *YP-389* was put in dock for

more repairs, and these were duly made. In the course of them, the chief gunner's mate at the repair facility reported that the 3-inch gun would not fire because the firing spring was broken. He said another spring had to be ordered, and it would be.

But before the order was filled, the patrol craft was ordered to duty. The captain reported that *YP-389*'s 3-inch gun would not fire, but this information got misplaced and did not reach the operations office.

And so, on June 18, *YP-389* was provisioned and otherwise ready to sail. She was ordered outside to keep the ships from running afoul of those mines off Cape Hatteras and, with her armament, to patrol for U-boats.

The captain of a patrol craft, like any other naval officer, followed his orders no matter how much he might disagree with them. That evening, *YP-389* sailed. Soon she was 5 miles west of Diamond Shoals, moving east. There was no moon, and the air was warm and quiet. She was traveling at her 6 knots, with lookouts on both bridge wings, at the wheel, and on the flying bridge. There was also a lookout on the stern. The captain of *YP-389* was a careful man.

At 11:45 that night, the signalman on the bridge saw what he believed to be a flare off in the distance. The other bridge-wing lookout disputed the claim. It was a falling star, he said.

In any event, it seemed nothing to worry about, so *YP-389* stayed on course, completed the leg of her patrol, and reversed direction, following orders.

It was midnight, and all was quiet.

At 2:45 in the morning, the general alarm bell's racket shattered the quiet. The executive officer and the chief engineer were awakened from sound sleep. They came on deck to find the captain there already, and just as they arrived, they were greeted by a hail of tracers from an unseen machine gun somewhere out there in the darkness.

In response to the call to general quarters, the men came running up from the crew's quarters forward and out on deck, just in time to catch a 3-inch shell that struck right at the hatch. The first man out of the forecastle was killed, and the next three were injured.

The captain radioed Ocracoke Coast Guard station, and

Ocracoke sent out a radiogram to all ships and aircraft in the vicinity. –

Help was on the way.

But if it was to be effective, help had to be there right at that moment, and it was not.

The U-boat, for the captain by this time knew his enemy, was attempting to close with the patrol craft. There was no point in even trying to train that inoperable 3-inch gun on the submarine.

The men began firing the .30-caliber machine guns, a procedure akin to attacking a whale with an air gun. Worse, the tracers in the .30-caliber ammunition gave the gun positions away.

The captain tried to take evasive action, but at 6 knots, the attempt to evade an enemy with almost three times their speed was obviously futile. Steadily, the shadow "out there" grew larger, and the angle of the guns grew broader.

Twice the captain ordered depth charges dropped, hoping to frighten the U-boat away even though it was almost impossible to damage a submarine thus.

The U-boat kept closing the range.

The enemy's deck gun fired regularly. One shell set off the CO_2 fire-control system in the patrol craft's engine room and flooded the compartment with fumes. The men below were forced up on deck.

In an hour, the U-boat was visible, firing with her deck gun and machine guns at 200 yards. That was virtually point-blank range, and the Germans could hardly miss. The shells set the patrol boat's chart room afire, and then the stern began to blaze.

The captain knew that the little trawler could not stand the punishment much longer. He ordered his men to abandon ship.

The life rafts had been shot away in the unequal battle, and to go into the starboard boats would be to put themselves right under the guns of their enemies. So the men of *YP-389* slipped over the opposite side, each wearing a life vest, and the captain kept the helm to protect them as much as he could from the U-boat until the last man was off the deck. Then the captain slid over himself, gathered his men around him, and kept them together for four hours as their ship sank, and they were left afloat. The U-boat either missed them in the darkness or had no interest in the waifs of the sea, and they were undisturbed in their fear and misery.

After daybreak, two Coast Guard cutters came up and rescued the men of *YP-389*. It was eight o'clock on the morning of June 19. *YP-389*'s short life was ended, further proof of Admiral Andrews' contention that he could not fight U-boats without real warships.

23

THIS HARBOR IS MINED!

Army intelligence agents on the European mainland had been reporting regularly about German plans to mine the western coast of the Atlantic, and one particular agent, whose reports had been detailed and accurate in the past, sent in an overlay that showed the ports and places. The mining had been scheduled in March, the agent said, but for some reason had been postponed.

When May came and went, and there was no indication of German mining, instead of relaxing, Admiral Andrews' staff became more nervous. But what could be done? All they could do was study intelligence reports, caution the naval vessels in the command to be wary, and wait.

Early in June, reports from Washington indicated that the Germans were in possession of a new magnetic acoustic mine. It was designed to be drawn magnetically toward a steel ship bottom and would explode long before it touched, actuated by the acoustical device.

On June 10 came an alert from Santiago, Chile: An official of the C.S.A.V. steamship line said the Nazi ambassador had informed the Chilean foreign minister that he ought to keep all Chilean ships out of New York harbor. The Reich's navy had mined these waters, the German official declared.

Two days later, Admiral Andrews had confirmation of the seriousness with which Chile took the story: The C.S.A.V. line announced a change in its American terminal; no longer would Chilean ships dock at New York. They would come no farther north than New Orleans.

The day after that report, Admiral Andrews had intelligence that German U-boats were loading mines in their

French submarine bases, and these were destined for American waters.

Admiral Andrews, as a student of naval history, could recall only too clearly what the Germans had done off the U.S. coast in 1918.

In that year, German submarines had laid 57 mines between Fire Island and Wimble Shoals. The mines had been put down, in groups of six or seven, in the most logical places. Cape Henlopen was mined. So was the entrance to Delaware Bay. Mines were sown at the entrance to Chesapeake Bay.

The result in World War I was the sinking or damaging of seven merchant ships, one light cruiser, and a battleship.

If the Kaiser's men could do that in 1918 with the primitive U-boats at their disposal, then what could Hitler do a quarter century later with improved submarines and improved mines?

On June 15, early in the day, Convoy KN-109 was heading for Norfolk out past the 100-fathom curve. The convoy commodore sat down and prepared a message for Norfolk naval base. The convoy would reach the Chesapeake at around five o'clock that evening, he reported. He expected, then, to have pilot boats and patrol craft out to meet him.

In fact, the convoy was 10 minutes early off Cape Henry. The dozen merchant ships and six escorts appeared, but if they expected a warm greeting, they were disappointed. No patrol craft came out to meet them. Two pilot boats lay near the Cape Henry sea buoy, but only one of them seemed to be moving. There had been no improvement in harbor practices since the sinking of *F. W. Abrams*.

The commodore of Convoy KN-109 was riding in *Empire Sapphire*, and he ordered a pilot to come aboard that vessel and take her into Lynnhaven Roads.

The sailors on the ship could see the bright costumes and umbrellas of the bathers on Virginia Beach that day, and from the beach, those bathers with good eyesight could watch the maneuverings of the convoy as she headed in. The ships were only 6 miles away, at most.

Empire Sapphire headed toward the haven, past the red and white whistle buoy that had earlier marked the entrance to Chesapeake Bay but now marked the channel through the American minefields.

At five minutes to five, the ships began moving through.

Seven minutes later, an explosion rocked the tanker *Robert C. Tuttle*, the fifth ship in line. She listed to starboard and fell out of column. She had been struck at Number 2 oil tank, the first officer reported, and the engine room was flooded. She stopped.

Twelve minutes later, the ship was sinking.

In the confusion and panic that accompanied the loud noise of the explosion, the tanker *Esso Augusta* broke out of column, hoisted zigzag signals, sounded general quarters, and ordered full speed. She headed inshore to safety on her own.

Eight minutes later, she struck a mine.

H.M.S. *Lady Elsa,* one of the British trawlers, tried to tow *Esso Augusta* into Hampton Roads, but the trawler was too small for the task. The tow line parted three times, and finally *Lady Elsa* abandoned the attempt.

Esso Augusta, then, radioed the shore for help.

Soon planes were overhead, searching for the "submarine," for, of course, that was what everyone in the area thought had attacked both ships.

The destroyer *Bainbridge* came rushing out, made an apparent contact, and dropped a pattern of eight depth charges. They began to explode: one, two, three, four, five, six, seven, eight, and NINE!

The last one was much more powerful than the others, so powerful it shook the destroyer hard enough to break crockery.

The captain of *Bainbridge* began to have an inkling of the true situation.

By six-thirty that evening, nearly all the ships of the convoy were safe in harbor. *Esso Augusta* was still outside, hurt, and waiting for the help that had been promised. A Coast Guard cutter circled her to protect her from the submarine that might still be menacing the approaches of the bay.

As the men of *Esso Augusta* waited, up came a tiny convoy from the south; trawler H.M.S. *Kingston Ceylonite* was bringing up a damaged freighter, S.S. *Delisle,* which was towed by the tug *Warbler.*

Suddenly, before the eyes of the men of the other ships,

Kingston Ceylonite blew up and sank. One moment she was there; the next the sea was covered with debris.

That sight shocked all those around.

The tug *Keshena* reached *Esso Augusta* just before nine o'clock that night, but it was a very long night for them all. They did not get the damaged tanker in to safety until the following morning.

By that time, the word was out that mines were in the channel. Fifth Naval District closed the port and ordered mine sweepers to sweep them away, and in the morning, the sweepers began to work in pairs.

The authorities divided the area into three segments, which they called A, B, and C.

The problem, the commander of the mine sweepers said, was the large area involved. He did not have enough mine sweepers to cover the whole in less than two or three days.

They could use the sweepers from the Navy Mine Warfare School that was nearby, said Fifth Naval District. That ought to help speed up the job.

All day long, in Area A, Fifth Naval District's sweepers worked, making 111 runs, each run of each vessel carefully plotted so that they would, together, cover every square foot of the sea in their area. Those sweepers picked up and exploded five magnetic mines, which had been laid to float at a depth of 50 feet. The mines were definitely identified as enemy.

At noon, the sweepers from the Navy Mine Warfare School appeared and were assigned to sweep Areas B and C.

They found no mines.

On June 17, the port was opened to shipping once more. The channel was safe, authorities said.

The south-bound convoy departed.

S.S. *Santore,* heading for Cristobal with 11,000 tons of coal, was in that convoy. The ships passed along the channel at 7:40 in the morning, near the buoy where *Esso Augusta* had been struck in Area B. Eight minutes later, *Santore* struck a mine and went down.

The mine sweepers of the Navy Mine Warfare School had misunderstood their instructions. They had swept only Area C.

In the investigation that followed, the officers involved

learned a great deal about mine sweeping and the protection of shipping. It was pointed out to them, in no uncertain language, that shipping had been disrupted at Hampton Roads for several days, that three ships had been sunk and four damaged, all because of bad sweeping, bad convoy practices, and bad port management. There should have been constant harbor patrols to discourage the mine-laying submarines in the first place. The supply of pilots should have been certain and prompt, as Admiral Andrews had ordered two weeks earlier, so that the convoy would not be milling around the entrance to the harbor, as had happened with convoy KN-109.

Admiral Andrews, Admiral King, and all the others on top of the heap had much to say, and almost the least of it was an injunction to the commander of the Fifth Naval District to overhaul his organization, which was tantamount to a reprimand.

But it was apparent there was a good deal more that needed overhauling than just Fifth Naval District.

U-BOATS OFFSHORE

THE NEVER-BEFORE-TOLD STORY OF HITLER'S STRIKE AGAINST AMERICA

Admiral Karl Doenitz might well have won the war for Germany had he been given all the U-boats he requested for operations off the American coast (above). Admiral Adolphus Andrews commanded the territorial waters off the U.S. Atlantic coast (right).

Kapitaenleutnant Hardegen's U-123 sank eight ships and damaged several others in January 1942.

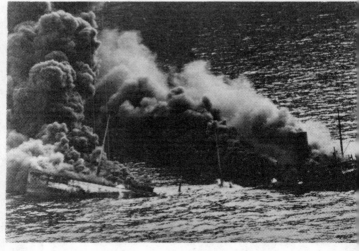

A freighter in distress (above). The tanker SS *Dixie Arrow* burning (left).

All submerged speeds 6-7 Kts

Type II (250 tons)

Speed on Surface 11 Kts
6 Torpedoes

North Sea Boats
50 built

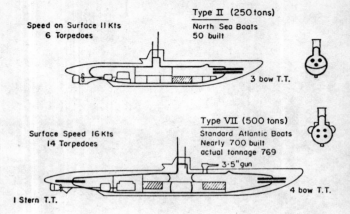

3 bow T.T.

Type VII (500 tons)

Surface Speed 16 Kts
14 Torpedoes

Standard Atlantic Boats
Nearly 700 built
actual tonnage 769

3·5" gun

1 Stern T.T.

4 bow T.T.

Type IX (750 tons)

Surface Speed 17 Kts
19 Torpedoes

Long Range Boats
Over 150 built
actual tonnage 1051

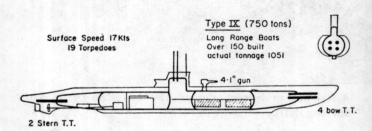

4·1" gun

2 Stern T.T.

4 bow T.T.

Type XIV (U-tanker)

No Torpedo Tubes
635 tons fuel to replenish
up to a dozen other
U-boats

Supply U-boats
10 built
1688 tons

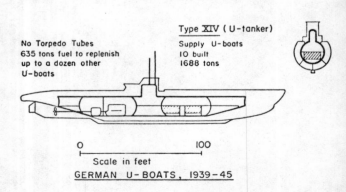

```
0                    100
```
Scale in feet

GERMAN U-BOATS, 1939-45

CONFIDENTIAL

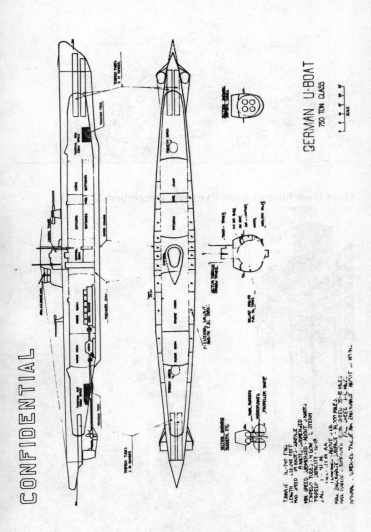

GERMAN U-BOAT
750 TON CLASS

SCALE

TONNAGE 7l-750 TONS
LENGTH 225-245 FEET
MAX SPEED 19 KNOTS-SURFACE
                14 KNOTS-SUBMERGED
MIN SPEED SUBMERGED 4 KNOTS
TORPEDO TUBES 4 BOW 2 STERN
TORPEDO CAPACITY their
GUNS 1-4.1 IN. AA

MAX RANGE ABOUT 8,000 MILES
MAX SURFACE ENDURANCE 75-85 DAYS
NORMAL SUBMERGED TIME AT MIN SPEED 4-10 HRS.

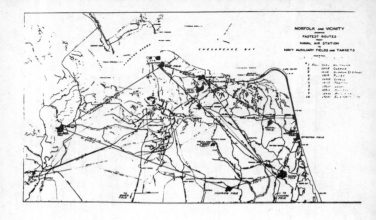

Dual launching of escort vessels, December 20, 1941.

A "Kingfisher" about to land at Norfolk (above). A Navy patrol airship (right). Blimps helped to shepherd convoys (below).

U.S.S. *Toucey,* DD 282 (above). One of the British trawlers
lent by Churchill when America's submarine defenses were
inadequate early in the war (below).

U.S.S. *Pope,* DE 134 (above). The nemesis of the wolfpack (below).

The innovative "hedgehog" threw depth charges *ahead* of the escort vessel. No longer did a ship have to pass directly over a submarine to make a kill (above). Rough positions of ship sinkings in the western North Atlantic from January 1942 to May 1943 (below).

PBY hauled up on ramp at Jacksonville (above). Low altitude PBY patrol bomber (below).

U-boat under attack.

Attack on German submarine U-134 (above). Survivors of a sunken German submarine (below).

Nazi U-boat survivor taken ashore (above). Nazi submarine officers in the custody of the Coast Guard (below).

24
THE AMAGANSETT INCIDENT

The events of the winter and early spring had convinced the whole Nazi military establishment that America's defenses were paltry. The Germans knew that the long coastline of the United States could not be easily defended. When Doenitz's reports of February indicated no defense at all, German intelligence came up with a plan to take advantage of the unprepared and apparently naive new enemy. They would send saboteurs to the United States in Doenitz's U-boats. The saboteurs would land, make their way to the big cities, and disappear into the "melting pot." Then they could begin a campaign of destruction of U.S. defense industry and transportation.

In May 1942, the plan was put in motion.

By the second week in June, the submarines assigned had crossed the Atlantic.

Just after midnight on the morning of June 13, S2c. John C. Cullen set out from the Coast Guard station at East Amagansett, Long Island, for his assigned patrol. It was his duty to walk east from the station along the beach for 3 miles and return. When his tour was finished, another sailor would take his place. They walked alone, these sentries, day and night, not only unaccompanied but unarmed. Yet they were the second line of defense of the U.S. coastline, behind the paltry handful of patrol craft. Small wonder the Germans were contemptuous of American defenses.

Five miles down the beach from the East Amagansett Coast Guard Station and just as lonely in the dunes stood the post of the 113th Mobile Infantry Unit of the Army Coastal Defense Command. The 113th, with 100 officers and men, was the strongest defense force in the area. Weakest was the naval radio station at Amagansett, a shore station whose duties were to maintain radio watch for ships at sea. This night the station was manned by one operator.

From the Coast Guard station, Cullen walked along the beach in pitch darkness. It was a moonless night, and the fog was drifting in to chill the sailor as he strode along the sand.

This beach was a deserted place, miles and miles of sand, broken by the silhouettes of a few cottages and shacks set back beyond the high-water mark, most of them dark, many of them unoccupied on a mid-June evening in wartime.

Seaman Cullen moved quietly. He had gone barely 300 yards along the familiar path before he nearly stumbled over three men laboring around a small boat at the water line. As he came up, Cullen saw that two of them were wearing bathing trunks, which seemed a little odd just after midnight. The third man was conventionally dressed in a civilian suit, which also seemed a little strange.

"What's the trouble?"

There was no answer. The man in civilian clothes stepped forward.

"Who are you? What are you doing out here?"

Still there was no answer. The man came closer.

Cullen kept his flashlight in his pocket. He reached for it. The man stopped.

"Wait a minute . . . are you Coast Guard?"

"Yes. Who are you?"

"A couple of fishermen from Southampton. Run aground."

It seemed almost logical.

"Come up to the station and wait for daylight."

The man looked at him hard. The fog rolled in wispily. It was dead quiet on the dark beach.

"Wait a minute. You don't know what's going on. How old are you? Have you got a father and mother? I wouldn't want to kill you . . ."

The torrent of questions was stopped by the arrival of a fourth man. He, too, was wearing bathing trunks, and he was dragging a bag behind him. He spoke to the other. The language was German, Cullen was sure.

Seaman Cullen looked at the bag. "What's in it?"

"Clams."

That's when Cullen knew they were lying. There were no clams for miles along that south-shore beach.

The man in civilian clothes joined in. "Yes, clams. That's right."

Cullen said nothing. He knew his danger.

The man in civilian clothes looked at him sharply. "Why don't you forget the whole thing?" He held out his hand. "Here's some money. A hundred dollars."

"I don't want it."

The man peeled off more bills. "Then take three hundred."

To refuse would be to raise suspicion. There were four of them. They had already talked of the possible need of killing him.

"O.K." He took the money.

The man in civilian clothes stepped close.

"Now look me in the eye. Would you recognize me again?"

"No."

The man seemed satisfied. Cullen turned and walked slowly away, not looking back until he was sure he was out of sight. Then he ran all the rest of the way to the Coast Guard station.

Inside, Boatswain's Mate 2c. Carl Ross Jenette looked up from the desk. Cullen told his story. Jenette picked up the telephone. Warrant Officer Oder, in charge of the station, was off duty that night. Jenette called him, anyhow. He also called Chief Boatswain's Mate Warren Barnes. That call was completed just 15 minutes after young Cullen had set out on what seemed to be a routine patrol.

Jenette rounded up the other men at the station, armed them all with .30 caliber rifles, and led them toward the beach.

To their relief, they found nothing. They returned to the station.

Shortly after, Chief Barnes arrived and took charge. He took the men back to the beach, and there he said he saw a long, dark object lying offshore. A submarine. Not knowing the strength of the enemy force, he dispersed his men behind the dunes. They waited. The beach was silent. The sea was empty. They returned to the Coast Guard station.

There Cullen insisted on giving Barnes the money the man had given him, and Barnes gave Cullen a receipt. The man had said the bribe was $300. He had shortchanged Cullen by $40.

Barnes put through a call to New York Coast Guard headquarters at 42nd and Broadway. He spoke to the duty officer, Lieutenant Ninshel, who warned Barnes to secrecy. Ninshel then called the district Naval Intelligence office. The assistant duty officer there, Ensign Fitzgerald, telephoned the assistant duty officer at the Eastern Sea Frontier. In the morning, Admiral Andrews was informed.

By that time, Andrews was told the Coast Guard had "a hundred men on the scene," which seemed adequate. Actually, eight nervous Coast Guardsmen had been joined by an army lieutenant and 20 men from the 113th up the beach.

But what had prompted them to show up if security was as tight as it was supposed to be?

Actually, the security existed only in New York City. For as Cullen was talking to the man on the beach, at the Amagansett Naval Radio Station, Chief Radioman McDonald heard diesel engines just off the beach. What else he heard, what he saw, what he guessed, were never fully disclosed, but he was so fearful that then and there he packed his family off to Amagansett village and called the Coast Guard station. He reported hearing a U-boat almost on the beach.

"I'm sorry. We can't discuss enemy activity," said the Coast Guardsmen who picked up the phone. He hung up.

Chief McDonald then called the 113th. He wanted help.

"I'm sorry," said the soldier who answered the phone. "I can't leave without the captain's permission."

He hung up the phone.

Chief McDonald stayed at the radio station and worried.

All night long, telephones buzzed. The assistant duty officer at the Eastern Sea Frontier telephoned the FBI office in Manhattan. The duty sergeant of the 113th telephoned the FBI, too. Agents were routed out of bed.

When the light of day came, the Coast Guardsmen took courage and began searching the beach where Cullen said he had met the strangers. They found a package of cigarettes half buried in the sand. The writing was in German.

They found a pair of wet bathing trunks a little farther down the beach. They found signs of dragging. Someone had pulled a heavy object along the soft sand and left a deep furrow.

They traced the furrow and dug where it disappeared. Soon they unearthed four wooden cases, two heavy and two light. The heavy cases were bound in marlin, with marlin handles. They opened one. Inside was another case of metal. They waited for higher authority to open that. Later, it was found to contain high explosives.

The searchers found another disturbed area in the sand. Digging again, they discovered dungarees, a reversible civilian coat, overshoes, and a gray overseas cap with a swastika.

By six o'clock, they were finished and waiting. Soon others began to arrive on the scene, for in spite of "secrecy," every command in the area knew about the landing.

At Riverhead, the command point of the naval zone of Third District, the officer in charge launched an investigation. Naval Air Intelligence launched an investigation. At Third District headquarters, Naval Intelligence dispatched three undercover agents to the area. They arrived at Easthampton at three o'clock that afternoon. One agent disappeared, and in his place appeared a young German-speaking civilian who sought a job as waiter at the restaurant owned by a German-American family that had long been under Naval Intelligence survey.

A second agent disappeared and was replaced by an unkempt young man in dirty clothes who found a job on a fish truck that served the whole eastern end of the island.

The third agent disappeared, and a new attendant was hired at the gas station at Montauk Point.

A week went by.

The District Naval Intelligence office had sent four other agents into the field. They were investigating, but they learned nothing except that the FBI was around in force, and the agent in charge announced that the FBI was taking over.

Naval Intelligence did not like that. The District Intelligence officer complained to Admiral Andrews. He called the FBI agent in charge. The agent complained that the navy people were getting in the way, and the Coast Guardsmen were actually withholding evidence.

That latter charge was true. Several of the Coast Guardsmen had decided to solve the mystery themselves when they were brushed aside. They found a vest that no one else noticed on the beach. They took it to New York and consulted the New York police about labels and laundry marks. These "private sleuths" then tracked down an innocent American and accused him of sabotage.

Meanwhile, all kinds of other disturbing facts came to light: A U-boat had sent out a transmission from a point not 30 miles from the Amagansett radio station at 8:53 on the night of the landing at Amagansett. The transmission had been noted and reported to Washington, where red tape delayed it for two and a half hours before it was forwarded back to the New York area for action.

And three days after the Amagansett landings, early on the morning of June 17, *U-584* landed four other saboteurs on the lonely beach south of Ponte Vedra, Florida, in an operation that was totally unobserved by any Americans.

The saboteurs were rowed ashore by one of the submarine crew in an inflatable rubber boat. Like the Amagansett Germans, the Florida saboteurs were in bathing suits, and they, too, carried four heavy wooden cases ashore. In them were clothing, forged identification cards, nearly $100,000 in U.S. currency, and enough explosives to last them an estimated two years while they blew up basic elements of American industry.

About 200 feet east of U.S. highway A1A, the Germans buried the boxes near an abandoned house. They walked down the beach toward Jacksonville Beach, then dashed into the surf as if they were young men on vacation.

No one noticed anything unusual about them.

At Jacksonville Beach, they put on clothing over their swim trunks and walked to the main highway to take a bus into Jacksonville. They aroused no suspicion with the bus driver or any of his passengers.

They split up in Jacksonville; two went to the Seminole Hotel and two to the Mayflower, two blocks away, on Bay and Julia streets.

They stayed one night and made one telephone call to

New York. But neither by action or accent did they arouse the slightest bit of suspicion.

Then two of them headed for New York and two for Chicago, according to the plan laid out back in Germany.

Even as they headed north and west, the forces were in motion that would bring them to arrest.

They were being betrayed by one of their own number.

Naval Intelligence, Army Intelligence, and the Federal Bureau of Investigation clashed over the investigation of the Amagansett saboteurs. Knowing nothing of the second group from Florida, their whole quarrel centered around Long Island and New York. But the investigation was getting nowhere. The Germans had simply disappeared as the Abwehr had ordered them to do.

They were in New York City. One of them, George Johann Dasch, was distinctly uneasy about the mission. Although he was a German national, born in the old country in 1903, he had been a resident of the United States for many years, until 1939, when he was caught in Germany by the war. Furthermore, he was married to an American citizen, and he had a strong affection for the United States.

All Dasch's doubts were increased by the narrow escape the Germans had when they had encountered Seaman Cullen on the beach. Dasch did not want to kill anybody. He wanted out of the whole mess. He decided to give himself up and turn state's evidence before something serious occurred. He would go to the FBI.

Dasch telephoned the FBI office in New York on Sunday evening. The person who answered the phone thought he was a crackpot and got rid of him.

Dasch really began worrying. How could he get anyone to take him seriously? He worried for three days. Then he decided he would go to the top, J. Edgar Hoover. He went to Washington on Thursday. He telephoned J. Edgar Hoover. But Hoover did not talk to crackpots. Dasch was turned aside.

Somehow, the German was able to convince someone at the FBI that he was worth talking to. And once he laid out the plan for them, even the FBI was convinced.

Up in New York, the FBI, the navy, and the army were all exchanging recriminations and getting nowhere in the investigation when suddenly the case was solved. By June

27, the last of the Germans was found and arrested, following the information given the authorities by agent Dasch. Eventually, they were all tried, found guilty of espionage, and sentenced to death. Dasch and Ernest Peter Burger, another who turned state's evidence when captured, were given prison terms. The others were all executed.

Sensational accounts of the adventure appeared in *Life* and other publications, indicating that the FBI had once again saved the nation. The public was a long time in finding out what had really happened, and they were never told of the delays, confusion, and interservice bickering that hampered the case from the beginning.

If agent Dasch had not gone to the authorities voluntarily, and if he had not been able to convince the FBI that he was not a crackpot, it would have been months, perhaps years, before the Germans would have been caught. The Abwehr plan was simple enough to have succeeded.

As it was, the failure of the Abwehr plan was brought about by the queasiness of one agent who respected America and a young recruit seaman who had the luck to encounter the agents on that deserted beach and the good sense not to alarm them into murdering him.

25

"GOD BLESS THE COMMONWEALTH OF MASSACHUSETTS . . ."

The quarreling, the errors, the duplications, and the misunderstandings that hampered American defenses were not confined to the military. They seemed to permeate the whole American effort along the shore.

For many months, the American Red Cross had been performing admirably in assistance to military authorities in the care and treatment of merchant seamen.

In April, when the survivors of the S.S. *City of New York* had been brought to Norfolk by the destroyer *Roper,* the Red Cross took over. Mrs. Desanka Noharovic and her new "lifeboat" baby were taken to St. Vincent's Hospital, along with other sick and injured. The Red Cross supplied clothing, transportation, razors, and toothbrushes. Dr. Albert Crosby, chairman of the Norfolk chapter, even appeared at the hotel to which some survivors were taken to treat them for minor ailments.

In Norfolk, the Red Cross arranged for a myriad of services; one man had his glasses repaired, and the gray ladies made appointments with the hotel beauty shop "to fix the women's hair." The ambulance corps and the nurse's aides pitched in with everything from books and candy to morale-raising alcohol rubs.

That Norfolk story represented a typical Red Cross performance; in these port cities, the organization had been at the work for two and a half years already, since the day that Hitler marched into Poland. They did the job without seeking attention or thanks.

The increasing tempo of the war along the American coast brought new pressures. In May, for example, the Key West

Red Cross cared for survivors from 14 different ships sunk by submarines in southern waters.

Somehow the Red Cross always seem able to cope. They cared for the badly burned men of the Mexican tanker *Faja de Ora*, whose 27 survivors landed at Key West. They helped the burned, half-drowned men of *Samuel Q. Brown*, and when one of the young boys died of his burns in the Marine Hospital, the Red Cross provided the $111 needed to send his body to Princeton for burial. They managed in shortages and the heavy outlay of money that had to be made at the expense of the volunteers until the Washington headquarters could get around to reimbursements.

They made friends almost immediately with Naval Intelligence, which found the Red Cross useful in a dozen ways.

But in the broadening of the war, soon the Red Cross was not alone among civilian assistance organizations. The Office of Civilian Defense came into being, and it spread its tentacles into the states. Its local organization in Massachusetts was the Massachusetts Committee on Public Safety (MCPS).

On Cape Cod, the new committee was industrious and very eager to participate in the war.

With the increase in sinkings in the spring of 1942, more survivors began to come ashore, and in spite of the new government policy of suppressing much of the news, the word got around by word of mouth.

In May, Aaron Davis, regional director of MCPS in Hyannis, fretted over the priority given the Red Cross when his organization was ready and willing to do everything needful for survivors of torpedoed ships.

Davis decided to do something about it. He paid a call on Lieutenant Ireland of the Coast Guard station at Provincetown. He complained that when survivors were brought in, the authorities always called the Red Cross. He wanted them to call the committee, too.

Lieutenant Ireland agreed that next time he would inform the committee as well as the Red Cross.

He was as good as his word. On Tuesday, June 16, survivors of the torpedoed transport S.S. *Cherokee* were being brought to shore by S.S. *Norlago* and *P. G. San Bernardino. Cherokee* had been hit 46 miles off Cape Cod light—the Germans were in that close—and she had gone down fast, taking nearly 200 men with her. The survivors might come to the Cape Cod Canal. They might come to Provincetown.

When the call came just after 6:30 in the morning, the war-wise Red Cross volunteers got ready to do the jobs they did best: provide canteen service, clothing, and transportation for the stricken men.

When the call came to John Rosenthal, Provincetown chairman of MCPS at 6:45, he swung into action. Lieutenant Ireland said he did not know the exact number of survivors. He also asked that the news be kept from the public in the national interest, and Rosenthal listened carefully. Then he got on the telephone.

He called his chief air raid warden and the deputy chief air raid warden, the chief of auxiliary police, the chairman of the First Aiders, the head of the medical department, and Drs. Cass, Hiebert, Perry, and Corea of Truro.

They all stood by for further orders.

He summoned the head of ambulances to the Report Center, and the head of ambulances and all the others telephoned the workers in their units to stand by.

At 7:30, Rosenthal had at his disposal seven ambulances with drivers, four first-aid workers with each ambulance, and Mrs. Comee and Mr. Law of the Red Cross. Rosenthal made sure all the equipment was parked behind the post office "so that the public would not know about the same."

Rosenthal then kept summoning workers. Mrs. Baumgardner, the head of the canteen, came to headquarters. She waited with the rest. Rosenthal had another call from Lieutenant Ireland. It was definitely Provincetown, not the Cape Cod Canal. The lieutenant still did not know how many survivors there would be.

Chairman Rosenthal dispatched his chief air raid warden to see Mr. Cashman, the manager of the Town House, a local hotel, and to take it over as a refuge for survivors. If Cashman did not want to cooperate, Chairman Rosenthal said, the chief warden was to tell him that Chairman Rosenthal would take it over, anyhow. The display of power was unnecessary. Manager Cashman said he would be glad to let them use his hotel.

Rosenthal then dispatched Mrs. Baumgardner and her 25 canteen workers to Town House along with Mr. Marshall, the chairman of food supplies. They took over the kitchen of the hotel and the dining room and "immediately started on food supplies." Graciously, they accepted the assistance of Mr. Law of the Red Cross. He delivered the food.

At eight o'clock, Deputy Chief Air Raid Warden Pigeon was placed in charge of the Report Center because Mr. Rosenthal had important things to do.

The rescue ship was coming in!

There was no danger in leaving his post. Pigeon was there in charge, and he had seven telephone operators standing by for orders, as well as two Boy Scout messengers.

Dr. Hiebert, who was also public health officer, went out in a Coast Guard boat to board the ship. Dr. Cass, who was chairman of the medical division, stood by to await Mr. Rosenthal's orders, which would be transmitted at the Report Center by Pigeon—Warden Pigeon.

Dr. Perry and Dr. Corea were sent to the Town House to stand by with five registered nurses and four first aiders.

Chairman Rosenthal took Chief Air Raid Warden Hallett to Lieutenant Ireland's office on the end of the town pier. The chairman used the telephone there to check in with the Report Center and the Town House. They were standing by.

The radio crackled. The survivors had been taken off the ship *Norlago* and were being brought into Provincetown. Immediately, Chairman Rosenthal was on the telephone. He ordered Dr. Cass and the ambulances to leave the Report Center and come to the town pier.

Dr. Cass and his ambulances arrived almost immediately, and Cass was dispatched to the *Norlago* by Coast Guard boat to help Dr. Hiebert.

From the Report Center, Deputy Chief Air Raid Warden Pigeon had been summoning the flock, and by nine o'clock the entire auxiliary police department of 50 officers was on duty. Main Street was roped off from the town pier to the Town House, all traffic was diverted, and when the first boatload of survivors arrived, they were rushed into the ambulances and hurried the little way to the Town House where Dr. Perry and Dr. Corea had now assembled 5 registered nurses, 4 first aiders, and 35 home nurses to help them.

By this time, Chairman Rosenthal had learned that there were 44 survivors, including two hospital cases.

"We served coffee," he said, "and the Red Cross had on hand a supply of dry clothing."

The doctors examined the survivors. Fourteen were suffering from shock or had suffered minor injuries. They were assigned to beds. They had the services of two doctors, 5 registered nurses, 4 first aiders, 35 home nurses, and now Chairman Rosenthal assigned 4 air raid wardens to serve as male orderlies. Never let it be said that Massachusetts did not know how to take care of its guests.

Since the Town House was the place of action, the seven public safety telephone operators were hurried there. They displaced the Town House operators, and Mr. Gott, the district manager of the New England Telephone Company, soon had the hotel switchboard hooked up so the seven public safety operators could control it.

Chairman Rosenthal put his people on watches: three hours on, three hours off until further notice.

At 11 o'clock the second boat-load of survivors arrived, and the people were hustled to the Town House.

It was midmorning, and Provincetown was wide awake. People were beginning to wonder what all the excitement was about. Chairman Rosenthal assigned a number of his auxiliary police to guard duty around the Town House. Only "authorized" persons were to be admitted, and the authorization would come from Chairman Rosenthal.

Other auxiliary policemen stood inside on guard to be sure the survivors did not give out any information to anybody—not even the public safety workers.

Just before noon, the last two survivors arrived. They were the hospital cases. The seven public safety operators had called the Truro ambulance, and Chairman Rosenthal dispatched it to the Boston Marine Hospital. He sent a first aider and an auxiliary policeman along with the driver and ambulance orderly to see that the injured survivors did not tell anybody anything. Chairman Rosenthal was as conscious of the need for security as anyone.

All this while the chairman had maintained his command post in the Coast Guard office at the end of the pier. From time to time, he and Chief Air Raid Warden Hallett made several trips back to the Town House to check on operations. They were going very well. They were going so well, in fact, that he could not use all the new first aiders and public safety workers who began to turn up to help.

The Red Cross had supplied magazines, playing cards, games, cigarettes, and candy, and "from then on first aiders, home nurses, and canteen workers that could be spared performed a marvelous job of helping to keep the morale of the survivors up, by playing cards, checkers, etc, with the men, taking their minds from their recent experiences," said Chairman Rosenthal's report.

In the early afternoon, three officers from Naval Intelligence arrived, along with an officer from Army Intelligence. Chairman Rosenthal assigned them a private office in the hotel. Lieutenant Ireland was also allowed to use it.

As evening approached, the Town House livened up. The canteen workers moved about dispensing orange juice, hot coffee, oranges, candy, and cigarettes; the 45 first aiders and 35 home nurses played cards and checkers and talked brightly to keep up morale. The 42 survivors were having a wonderful time.

Early in the evening, two army ambulances and an army truck appeared, and the officer in charge ordered out the soldiers in the group. It was hard for them to leave.

They all said what a fine rescue it had been, and the senior sergeant made a little speech. He said that although he had spent his lifetime in the army and had traveled all over the world, he had never received such hospitality as he had from the MCPS at the Town House in Provincetown. Everyone was sorry to see the soldiers go.

Mrs. Baumgardner, in charge of 27 canteen workers, had by this time been on the alert since seven o'clock in the morning. Chairman Rosenthal suggested that she go home.

Mrs. Baumgardner was obdurate. Go home? She knew where she was needed. She refused to be relieved, and so did her trusted workers. They would labor into the night for the rescued.

That evening, Red Cross Disaster Chairman Howard Hinckley came down from the Hyannis office of the Red Cross with three other Red Cross workers, bringing more clothing for the survivors. It was gratefully accepted. But what was happening at Provincetown was the MCPS show, not the Red Cross's. That was made very clear to Hinckley.

At eleven o'clock that night, Chairman Rosenthal was still going strong. A mine sweeper arrived at the pier, carrying the bodies of two soldiers it had picked up after the sinking of the *Cherokee*. Chairman Rosenthal accompanied army, navy, and Coast Guard officers to the pier and made arrangements for local undertakers to handle the bodies.

While they were on the pier came more disastrous news. A naval vessel was headed into port with 40 more bodies. Chairman Rosenthal got on the telephone. He called the mayor and made arrangements to use the town hall as a morgue. He called more undertakers, in Wellfleet and Orleans, and they hastened to the scene. The chairman assembled his air raid wardens and auxiliary police and ambulance drivers.

In half an hour, on the pier were ten ambulances and trucks, each with air raid wardens detailed as stretcher bearers. Chairman Rosenthal told them to stand by for further orders.

They stood by until midnight, then until one o'clock on Wednesday morning. At 1:30 came the word: The vessel would not come in because of fog. She would be dispatched to another port.

On Wednesday morning, Chairman Rosenthal had to call on the Red Cross once more, for he needed a special bus to pick up the merchant seamen and take them to the Boston Seaman's Institute. The Red Cross responded immediately. The bus arrived at ten o'clock with a state police escort.

As the survivors came out to get on the bus, most of the public safety workers came out to bid them farewell.

"Many of the survivors, with tears streaming down their cheeks, remarked that they hoped some day to get back here again to renew their acquaintances, and all expressed their heartfelt appreciation of the kind and friendly treatment they had received," the chairman's report said.

The bus doors closed, everyone waved, and the state police escort led the survivors away on the road to Boston.

At 2:30 that afternoon, the last bit of scrub-up was finished, and the Town House was returned to the management of Mr. Cashman. The hotel operators got their switchboard back. The 4 doctors, 5 registered nurses, 5 orderlies, 45 first aiders, 35 home nurses, 27 canteen workers, 7 telephone operators, 4 Boy Scout messengers,

4 ambulance drivers, 50 auxiliary police, 25 air raid wardens, and 20 members of the staff went home.

Chairman Rosenthal gave credit where credit was due. Mrs. Baumgardner, he was quick to point out, had not closed her eyes or rested from seven o'clock Tuesday morning until after 2:30 on Wednesday afternoon. Modestly, he said nothing about his own labors during the long vigil, and two days later, when he wrote his report, he was lavish with his praise of all concerned. Comdr. A. D. Turnbull, the first chairman, he said, deserved much of the credit for his thorough job of organizing.

It had been a major operation.

During the 32 hours after the MCPS pre-empted the Town House, the canteen workers served 500 meals, 1,000 cups of coffee, and 250 sandwiches, plus quantities of fruit juice, oranges, candy, and custard. Food had come into the kitchen from all over the community. The Red Cross had contributed heavily. So apparently had the Town House, for when the party was over, the total canteen bill submitted by Chairman Rosenthal was only $40.

Chairman Rosenthal was well pleased; Naval Intelligence, the captains of the two ships he had met, the Coast Guard, had all commended him for the fine job done by his workers.

He wrote out his report carefully, not forgetting to use both sides of each sheet. ("Paper must be conserved as a war necessity . . . please turn this sheet.") Then he sealed it up and sent it off to Aaron Davis, director of Region 7.

David read and admired what he read.

In a military manner, using the last unfinished sheet of Chairman Rosenthal's Report, he endorsed it and sent it on to Boston headquarters.

"I can add no word to this.

"God bless the Commonwealth of Massachusetts.

"It should be proud of its Committee on Public Safety."

The report was sent to J. W. Farley, executive director of the MCPS. On June 25, the report was given to the Boston newspapers, and it was printed verbatim by the Boston *Globe*.

The Red Cross was furious.

William H. G. Giblin, director of Disaster Relief Service for the North Atlantic Area reported to his Washington office that the Red Cross had, as usual, been on hand, ready to supply canteen service, clothing, shelter, and transportation.

The Red Cross people learned that Chairman Rosenthal and his workers had commandeered the Town House. They were shut out in the cold. They provided the canteen service and the clothing and all their usual supplies. The workers took them over. They provided the food. The workers took it, and everybody ate it.

What infuriated the Red Cross most was the report in the Boston newspapers.

"From reading the report the casual reader would fail to understand that most of the work was rendered by the Red Cross but would infer that the Red Cross only supplied certain supplementary service on a very small scale."

It was not just Giblin's pique working. The repercussions all through New England were serious: Many chapters began to question their viability. Was the Red Cross still the responsible agency for the care of survivors of the disasters of the sea?

The question could not be answered immediately by the authorities that counted, the naval commands. And the MCPS was riding high.

On Friday, July 3, at 8:30 in the evening, the Hyannis Red Cross office had a call from the Coast Guard to inform them that some time after ten o'clock 31 victims of a torpedoed ship would arrive at Woods Hole Navy Yard.

The request was routine: cots, blankets, and clothing. The Red Cross made routine of filling it as it had done so many times before.

Frank Holmes, the general field representative, set out for Woods Hole, and there met Howard Hinckley, the disaster chairman, and Milfred Lawrence, his assistant.

Hinckley and Lawrence were very angry. The MCPS was moving in on them again.

Hinckley said that he had a call from the Falmouth chairman of the MCPS, demanding the cots and blankets to be turned over to them because the committee did not have any.

And when the Red Cross men arrived at the scene, the safety committee chairman was there, with 150 workers, an ambulance corps, a canteen, taking over again.

Aaron Davis was in charge himself this time. He scurried about making arrangements. He arranged for ten MCPS workers and two Red Cross people, Hinckley and Lawrence. He had made no arrangements for Frank Holmes, and he told the field representative that he could not have a pass to the navy yard.

Holmes did not say a word. He turned on his heel and headed for Coast Guard headquarters. There he conferred with Lieutenant Whitmore, the commander of the unit. The lieutenant gave him a pass without hesitation, and Holmes went into the yard to confer with the naval authorities in charge of rescue and survivors.

They told him that the rescue ship had just radioed that it would not arrive until morning because of heavy weather.

So the Red Cross men left their telephone numbers and went home. Outside the base, Director Davis dismissed his workers, and they went home, too.

Holmes and Lawrence returned to the navy yard on Saturday morning. This time there were no MCPS workers in sight.

They waited.

At three o'clock in the afternoon, the word came. The ship would arrive in half an hour. When the survivors came in, the Red Cross was there, with clothing and underclothing, money, and comfort. Three of the men had escaped stark naked and needed everything supplied for them.

The ship's captain was among them, and he asked the Red Cross to supply transportation to New York, which was done. The Cape Cod Motor Corps was rallied and took the men to Providence in cars and station wagons, where they were put on the train to New York City, with tickets purchased by the Red Cross. The Red Cross gave the money to buy meals for the men on the train.

The Red Cross men went back to the Naval Intelligence office then, and there Lieutenant Good, the officer in charge, remarked on the disgusting display of Aaron Davis and his workers at Woods Hole and at Provincetown. In the future, he said, the local Navy Yard, at least, was going to call only the Red Cross.

In Hyannis, Aaron Davis fretted. He complained to higher authority in the MCPS in Boston.

In July, Joseph Loughlin of the U.S. Office of Civil Defense called a meeting in Boston to try to iron out all the difficulties. After the commotion in June, Loughlin felt it necessary to clear the air so the MCPS could take over its proper responsibilities for aid to victims of war disaster without Red Cross interference.

Loughlin invited representatives of the army, navy, and Coast Guard to a meeting. The list included 16 admirals, generals, captains, and colonels, a number of Civil Defense officials from Massachusetts and Washington, and one representative of the Red Cross, Charles Gates, director of the Massachusetts emergency field office.

When the room was quiet, Loughlin handed around a prepared memorandum that "proved" that the civil defense office was entitled to the responsibility and authority to handle all victims of the war offshore. Then his assistants began to improve on the case orally.

The head of the medical division of the MCPS pointed out how good the medical division was.

An official of the Social Security agency up from Washington explained how important Social Security was.

Other officials of the MCPS explained their operations and proved once again that theirs was the proper organization to handle these matters.

After about an hour, a Lieutenant Wilson of the Coast Guard leaned over to Gates.

"You're with the Red Cross?"

"Yes."

"What the hell is the idea of all this? Isn't the Red Cross doing its job?"

"Yes. But apparently some other people want the job."

The meeting lasted another hour. Loughlin had expected it all to be settled here, but the admirals, generals, captains, colonels, and Lieutenant Wilson were not convinced. Charles Gates suggested that the Red Cross was doing just fine.

The issue was not resolved; the meeting broke up in exhaustion. Finally, the quarrel had to be taken to Washington. Admiral Waesche of the Coast Guard, Admiral Land of the Maritime Commission, and DeWitt Smith, director of domestic operations for the Red Cross argued the case with Paul McNutt, federal security administrator, and with representatives of the Office of Civilian Defense. The navy and commission representatives told the civilians to leave the Red Cross alone.

And only then did the MCPS subside and let the Red Cross get back to its job.

26

"WHO'S IN CHARGE HERE, ANYHOW?"

From the beginning of the war, the army and the navy had quarreled over command responsibility for protection of the U.S. coast from enemy attack.

At first the quarrel was not meaningful because none of the services involved was well enough organized to undertake the task. Perhaps, for that reason of unpreparedness, the admirals and generals failed to rise above service pettiness.

The navy began the war with 170 vessels, equipped with sound gear, a sonar expert whose rank, Chief Radioman W. A. Braswell, indicated the value the admirals placed on sonar, and only a handful of sound operators. Nor, as noted, did they have any system worth writing about, so they did not. There were no antisubmarine-warfare manuals.

The submarine and surface sailors quarreled among themselves over the importance of the undersea weapon. The surface men won, as they had in the past.

Just as troubling was the clash between the army, represented by Gen. George C. Marshall, the navy, represented by Admiral King, and the new army air forces, represented by Gen. H. A. Arnold.

That quarrel had really begun with the invention of the airplane by the Wright brothers and had never been settled. In the 1920s, Col. William F. Mitchell epitomized the struggle in his claim that bombers could sink battleships. The navy denied the claim, the ebullient Billy Mitchell proved it, the navy called his proof a fluke, Mitchell was routed out of the service, and, on his death, the concept of air power was returned to its "proper place" far down on the scheme of strategy. Both sides overstated their

181

cases. The air-power advocates said navies were obsolete. Naturally, when the life of the navy was threatened, the admirals fought back with every weapon at their disposal.

And so, when World War II came to the American coast, neither sea power nor air power was available. The state of tension that existed between the navy and army air forces was such that there had been no consideration of mutual coastal defenses. That was the nub of the particular problem that faced America combating the submarines off the East Coast.

Neither the navy nor the air force's First Bomber Command was ready for the U-boats in December 1941. Those first army planes that supplemented Admiral Andrews' handful of ships carried demolition bombs that had little impact on a crash-diving submarine. Their crews were trained no better than the navy's for the task. But that was the technical side of it.

In mid-January, Rear Adm. John H. Towers, chief of the Navy Bureau of Aeronautics, asked General Arnold to allocate 200 B-24 bombers and 900 medium B-25s and B-26s for naval use when they were produced.

General Arnold was so irked by the request that he did not even reply to the letter.

In March, Admiral King took over the argument. He and General Arnold exchanged several letters on the subject of naval air power. The nub of the matter was that General Arnold insisted on the pre-eminence of the air forces in all shore-based air operations. In other words, the army air force wanted control of the air aspect of offshore defenses.

In result, it became clear to Admiral King that General Arnold would do nothing to help the navy with its antisubmarine warfare in the air unless the air force could have control. Admiral King then went to General Marshall, for under the existing military organization, the air forces were army forces, and Marshall was the senior officer.

By the time the discussion got so far, it was May, and the U-boat menace was so serious that Prime Minister Churchill was sending his many messages on U-boats to President Roosevelt.

Marshall answered that last King letter only after 16 days had gone by, and then his reply was merely an acknowledgment.

As July began, that is how the matter stood on a strategic command level. On the operational level, it was the same.

The burning question was: Who shall control antisubmarine warfare off the East Coast?

On March 26, when the sinkings were intolerable, Admiral Andrews had his way and gained control of all the planes of the air force that were available to fly antisubmarine search-and-destroy missions. Temporarily, the matter was resolved by discussion at the highest levels. The commanding general of the 1st Bomber Command agreed to serve as a task group commander in the naval scheme.

The system worked that spring but not very well. As noted, the lines of command were a hindrance rather than a help to the job at hand, which was to find and sink German submarines.

In July, the army became restive again. Lt. Gen. H. A. Drum complained to Admiral Andrews (with copies to his own higher authorities) about the duplications of effort in the navy air program. The sensible thing, said Drum, was for all navy and marine shore-based units to come under 1st Bomber Command.

Andrews wrote swiftly and coldly that he could not agree and sent his copies to Admiral King, who, of course, supported the admiral's view.

The quarrel continued.

Nor were the disagreements confined to interservice rivalries. The navy still had its own internal vested interests, and they did not respond readily to changes in operational needs.

The submarine tracking program was the outstanding example of the difficulty in the early summer of 1942.

The British had developed a highly efficient tracking program, which the Americans were just now becoming sophisticated enough to appreciate. The landing of the German saboteurs at Amagansett brought the matter to attention.

The submarine that had brought the Germans to the U.S. coast had made that radio transmission shortly after eight o'clock in the evening, just a few miles offshore.

If the radio-tracking system had been hooked into the coastal defense system, the submarine could have been hunted down and perhaps sunk before it left American waters, perhaps before the saboteurs were landed.

But it had not been. The note that a radio transmission had been heard and the position were bottled up in the system, and no patrol vessel was sent to the area that night, although one was available.

The shock of the actual landing of enemy personnel on American shores, however, brought Admiral Andrews' attention for the submarine tracking program.

Early in the spring, when the war offshore was going so badly, Andrews had begun bombarding Washington with demands about antisubmarine tracking. The principle was simple enough. Under the Doenitz system, U-boats rose to the surface as regularly as possible (every night if they could) and gave weather and patrol information to the U-boat command, which in turn transmitted convoy and shipping information and changes in orders. These transmissions could be located by triangulation when three or more radio stations got a "fix" on them. Thus, a system of high-powered receivers located around the shores of the Atlantic could keep track of Doenitz's U-boats as they headed for the Western Hemisphere, but only if the British and the Americans could work together.

The real problem in the spring of 1943 was not British versus Americans, but New York against Washington.

On March 6, Captain Kurtz, the chief of staff to Admiral Andrews had written to Capt. Frank T. Leighton, the submarine tracking officer for the navy high command in Washington. He was complaining about a dispatch relative to a U-boat, a dispatch that reached Washington late in the afternoon of March 5 and was sent out at 4:49. It did not get to the operations office of the Eastern Sea Frontier in New York until 9:30 on the morning of March 6. The reason: The dispatch had been sent by the British to Washington in their code and forwarded still in British code to New York for action. It took four hours for the cryptologists in New York to decipher the British code. If the whole had been sent up to New York in the U.S. naval code, it would have taken 20 minutes.

Leighton was a headquarters man and did not like to be questioned from the field. No, he said, the U.S. code would not be used. "It will not be done for reasons I do not feel free to discuss." Leighton did not say the reasons were too secret to discuss or too important to discuss. In service sign language, he was simply pulling the rank of the commander in chief's office on the Eastern Sea Frontier.

Admiral Andrews did not stop bombardment of Washington on the need for close coordination, efficiency, and speed in matters dealing with the U-boats offshore.

In May, when Comdr. George Dyer took over, the submarine-tracking organization in Washington began to show some improvement.

Still, the system was far from perfect. At a meeting on Governor's Island on May 6, the navy men discovered that as inexperienced as they were themselves, the army was in even worse shape. Fixes obtained by army stations and pilots might vary within 200 miles, where 25 miles was regarded as the useful outside margin for error.

In June, Admiral Andrews became more insistent with Washington about the need for the improvement of the radio network. The Amagansett incident played right into his hands. He got King's undivided attention, and the situation improved. In June, the work of the antisubmarine-tracking section of Andrews' command became so much more satisfactory that it was really useful in warning convoys and merchant vessels along the coast, and the assemblage of "killer groups" could go after the U-boat enemies before they settled in along the coast.

On July 22 came an incident that had to convince even Washington.

A U-boat was located by radio transmission at 1:17 P.M. at 39° N, 67°30′ W. At 7:45 on the morning of the twenty-third, Halifax reported a plane had sighted a U-boat on the surface at 41°03′ N, 66°58′ W. Almost certainly, it must be the same boat, heading for the American coast, moving southwest.

The tracking stations kept alert, and at the Eastern Sea Frontier Lieutenant Hess, the tracking officer, made his chart and showed the progress of the U-boat. At four o'clock on the morning of July 24, Lieutenant Hess estimated, the submarine would reach 40°05′ N, 70°00′ W.

At this point, she was close enough to call for action. Andrews ordered U.S.S. *Captor* to "rendezvous" with the submarine. Also, H.M.S. *Northern Chief* was summoned to the fray.

When all this was done, Andrews and his staff waited.

Just before midnight, the duty officer at Church Street had a message from the junior duty officer of the commander in chief, U.S. Navy Submarine Tracking Office, Washington.

Why had *Captor* been ordered out to the high seas?

The junior duty officer of the Eastern Sea Frontier Ships Plot section replied: "The estimate of the forecast position of the submarine was made by Lt. Hess."

The junior duty officer of the commander in chief's tracking section wanted to know what made them think up in New York that there was anything out there?

"A crystal ball, tea leaves, and an Ouija board," said the junior officer of the Eastern Sea Frontier Ship's Plot section.

No more was said that night. But as any student of the naval hierarchy knew, the junior officers of Ship's Plot and Lieutenant Hess had staked much on their estimates.

At 3:30 on the morning of July 24, U.S.S. *Captor* sent a message back to Andrews' office. A torpedo had just crossed her bow. She was at 40°22′ N, 69°00′ W.

Submarine Plot was in action in a moment. Patrol craft *SC 672* was ordered to the scene from Block Island. Army and navy planes began to fly as soon as dawn came.

They did not get the U-boat this time, but from Washington's submarine tracking section came a deep and significant silence.

27
A MATTER OF TRADITION

The U.S. coastal defenders gained confidence, but there was still a long way to go to catch up; after all, the Germans had three years more experience than the Americans at U-boat warfare.

But as the Americans learned, their efforts were more successful than they had been even though the day of rash claims was ending. On July 3, for example, when S.S. *Alexander MacComb* was torpedoed in a convoy, H.M.S. *Le Tigre* (one of those trawlers) went after the U-boat with the ferocity of her namesake. She approached at high speed to within 300 yards of the U-boat before it could dive and then dropped a full pattern of depth charges where *Le Tigre*'s captain thought she ought to be. The sea erupted in green water, oil, and even some debris. But the captain of *Le Tigre* did not claim a sinking. The report listed a U-boat as "probably damaged." That was British understatement. A few months earlier, when the destroyer *Ellis* and a number of planes had gone after a U-boat, they had claimed a sinking, but on this same day, when the U.S. destroyer *Lansdowne* encountered a U-boat off Cherry Point, and attacked, huge gouts of oil came up, and the contact stopped right there in 1,100 fathoms of water, the captain of *Lansdowne* claimed only a "possible." The claim was given credence that night by the tracking stations: One of Doenitz's regular callers from that area did not turn up on the radio. But *Lansdowne* still did not make any exorbitant claims. As the navy men learned, they became war wise; they substituted wisdom for blind enthusiasm.

On July 14, two Coast Guard planes flying at 2,300 feet spotted a U-boat a mile and a half away. They saw it crash dive as they came up, and with depth charges set at

187

50 feet, the first plane bombed. The submarine was lifted out of the water for a moment before it recovered and dived. The second plane attacked, and a quantity of oil came to the surface. A few weeks earlier, the pilots would have claimed a sinking. Now they claimed nothing, and the Eastern Sea Frontier, instead of congratulating them, pointed out that if the first plane's charges had been set at 25 feet, the PBY might have had a U-boat.

This new toughness extended to the convoy system, too. Andrews was trying to speed the learning process. In that regard, some old naval traditions were going to have to give way, such as blind respect for rank.

Convoy KS-520 was a nineteen-ship group heading south from Lynnhaven Roads. It was accompanied by two destroyers, two Coast Guard cutters, one corvette, and two patrol craft. On the morning of July 14, as the convoy headed out of Chesapeake Bay southward toward Cape Hatteras, two planes circled overhead, too. The protection was certainly adequate by the standards of that winter and spring.

On the afternoon of July 15, the convoy was off Ocracoke Inlet, 20 miles at sea. The Coast Guard cutter *Triton* had a contact on the starboard beam at four o'clock.

S.S. *Chilore,* one of the transports, was leading the Number 2 column and had gotten out 600 yards ahead of station. Suddenly, she was torpedoed twice.

The commodore of this convoy was a retired navy captain, regarded by his contemporaries and most of the officers of the escort service as the "best in the business." From the bridge of the transport *Mowinckle,* he saw the torpedoing of the *Chilore* and then was nearly knocked off his feet when a torpedo struck *Mowinckle* in the stern, blasted away her rudder, and destroyed the steering. A hole 20 feet square was smashed in the ship. One man was killed, and 20 were injured.

In the confusion of the dual attack, the other ships of the convoy scattered and fell out of line. *Bluefields,* which had so narrowly escaped in an earlier adventure, was the last ship in the sixth column. She was hit.

The U-boat was in the middle of the convoy. The two planes came in to bomb near the stern of *Mowinckle.* The destroyer *Ellis* dropped two patterns of depth charges. Up to the surface came the U-boat, just yards from the convoy flagship, but almost immediately she went down again, apparently blown to the surface but not out of control.

For 40 minutes, the ships of the convoy milled about while the escorts searched for the enemy. *Bluefields* sank.

At the end of that time, the commodore took stock. *Mowinckle* could not steer except with her engines. *Chilore* was badly hurt but still operable. Both ships needed to get into shoal anchorages as soon as possible.

At 5:00 P.M., the commodore asked the destroyer *McCormick* to send a doctor. The commodore then told the escort commander that he intended to leave the convoy and asked for an escort to protect the ships. The commander ordered the U.S.S. *Spry* to the job.

With the departure of the little group from the convoy, the convoy commodore ceased to have any authority. He had turned all that over to the vice commodore, who remained with KS-520.

But since the commodore was a highly experienced naval officer and convoy commander, he remained on the bridge of *Mowinckle* and was actually still in command of the subconvoy of three.

He directed the ships to take a course of 315 degrees. The problem was to get to shore quickly and with as little maneuvering as possible because *Mowinckle*'s steering by engine was so difficult a task.

The only trouble was that, that course would lead them directly into the Cape Hatteras minefield, which extended in an arc of 10 miles out to sea from Hatteras on the north to 2 miles out below Ocracoke Inlet on the south.

Near the south entrance was a swept channel, but the commodore did not know that.

On May 20, the shipping instructions called "Notice to Mariners No. 175" had mentioned the minefields off Hatteras. But the commodore was not a ship's captain in the sense of having his own command. He was supernumerary, installed for the safety of a convoy traveling to a particular place. He had access to the "Notices to Mariners" but no compelling reason to read them. He had not read No. 175 and knew nothing about the minefield.

The commander of *Spry* was an experienced and able regular naval officer. He knew of the minefields. All warships had overlays of the fields. But the commander of the *Spry* did not know his own position at the moment.

This was not surprising, for the convoy escorts spent their working hours roaming the edges of the convoy, boxing the compass several times a day. Where they were or where they were heading was of little import to them. They fixed on the convoy, and the convoy led them where it was going. So now, having spent an hour chasing about the sea looking for the submarine that had attacked the convoy, *Spry* had no idea of her position.

The commander of *Spry* could only figure his position by dead reckoning, and that is what he did. He estimated and came up with a position that was 60 miles south of his actual position. Given that reckoning, the commodore's course of 315 degrees was perfectly safe. It would take them in below the minefields.

And, of course, the commander of the escort believed the commodore knew about the minefields.

The commodore was, in truth, a little uneasy. He had just undergone a vicious submarine attack. Men were wounded, and one was dead.

He spoke to the master of the *Mowinckle*. In the back of his mind was a nagging doubt. Had he not heard of something about danger west of Hatteras?

The ship's captain replied. There had been something, he said, but it had been taken care of. No more danger existed there.

Reassured, the commodore kept on.

At 6:10, the commander of *Spry*, being a careful man, checked with the commodore.

What was their position?

The commodore did not hesitate. He gave them their position. But his mind was not on it. At the moment, he was radioing for a plane or a boat to be sent to Hatteras Inlet so that the wounded could be transferred immediately on their arrival and rushed to the hospital.

The commander of *Spry* got the message about position and saw that they were headed directly into the minefields.

He sent a hurried message to *Mowinckle*.

They should change course, he said. He suggested the proper course.

There was no answer.

In naval tradition, a subordinate had every right to question his superior officer—once. It was the custom for a superior to deny the questioner simply by failing to reply. It was much simpler that way than engaging in discussion, which might end in unpleasantness and even a reprimand for the junior officer.

This tradition was certainly in the mind of the commander of *Spry* at the moment. He had questioned his superior, a convoy commodore and a retired naval captain. There was no answer. He did not question again.

On the commodore's part, he was the victim of error by the radio operator of *Mowinckle,* who misread some figures in the message. The commodore and the captain of the merchant ship plotted the suggested course that they believed *Spry* had given them and found that it put them in to shore in an exposed area north of Hatteras.

Mowinckle asked *Spry* for a repeat on the message. It did not come.

Both ships sailed on.

The minefields off Hatteras were usually patrolled by three patrol craft. On this day, *PC-462, PC-463,* and *PC-480* were on duty. But *PC-463* had been detached to hunt a submarine that was reported not far away. *PC-462* had gone off to assist another patrol boat that had run out of gas.

So *PC-480* was the only patrol craft operating off the minefield to prevent the unwary from straying inside.

En route, the little convoy passed *PC-463,* 8 miles east of the minefields.

A blimp appeared overhead and dropped smoke bombs, apparently trying to warn the ships to change course. The commodore believed the smoke bombs were to warn them that there were submarines in the area, so he, in turn, ordered a sharper watch.

The convoy kept on, heading straight for the minefields.

PC-462 came back to the patrol area, having gassed up the stalled craft. Her captain now saw three ships heading directly into the minefield. He put on all possible speed; he tried to signal by blinker and by radio and to catch the attention of the men who were heading into death. No one saw him. He fired his guns. They were of such small caliber that no one paid them any heed.

Then, it was too late. The night air was rent by a series of explosions, and water leaped high against the sides of *Mowinckle* and *Chilore*.

The commodore sent the message: Abandon ship. The men of both vessels took to the boats and rowed to safety.

PC-462 caught *Spry* in the middle of the field and warned her of the danger. *Spry* turned obediently and followed *PC-462* out into the safe water outside. Then, with her two charges sinking, there was nothing more to be done here, so she headed off to rejoin KS-520.

Two tugs were sent out to the sinking ships in the hope that they might be salvaged. One, the *Keshena*, struck a mine coming into the deadly water and sank. The other two managed to handle both vessels and bring them to Orcacoke. They were patched up and sent south, but *Chilore* capsized on the way out of the inlet and sank. *Mowinckle* finally managed to make Hampton Roads and was put up for salvage.

On the day after this accident, Admiral Andrews rushed down by air to Fifth Naval District at Norfolk to discover what had gone wrong. Two responsible, cautious naval officers had apparently gone mad in midsea and had caused the destruction of three vessels and untold damage to the war effort.

They had endangered hundreds of lives. Whatever was wrong must be corrected, and immediately.

And it was then that Andrews learned how frail was his convoy system. The captain of *Mowinckle* knew nothing about the minefield because, although the ship was a Standard Oil tanker, she sailed under Panamanian registry (to avoid taxes and hiring rules) and thus did not receive the "Notices to Mariners." The commodore, not having a ship of his own, was not on the mailing list.

And the captain of *Spry,* being a "regular," did what regulars do in the face of superior rank.

The young escort captain came out of it probably worst of all. For he was reprimanded, which put a crimp in his hopes for promotion and a better command and made it almost certain that he would never receive his flag as admiral.

But as all (including Admiral Andrews) knew, it was the system that was at fault. It took time to build a workable convoy system. The Americans were learning that. One thing you had to do was strip away some of the hoar of tradition.

28
THE LIGHTS OF MIAMI

One could not really charge that Miami did not know there was a war on, although many a naval and merchant captain felt that way as they sailed by the lights of the city, beaming miles out to sea every night and knew that their vessels were silhouetted against this bright blaze for any U-boat to see.

Miami was close to the Caribbean and many a foreign shore. Among the people of so many varied nationalities as there were in the Antilles, the Germans could certainly count on some support, and Miami was aware of it.

One day, an American pilot, W. W. Wipprecht, flying his plane back from Nassau, swooped across a three-masted schooner about 35 miles east of Miami. The schooner was lazing along with sail only on the mainmast. The pilot looked down and saw the hatches, which were uncovered. They were filled with oil drums, almost as if the schooner was some sort of supply ship. He circled. The drums must be empty, he decided, because the schooner was riding high in the water.

On one leg of the fly-over, the pilot saw something else quite close by, a U-boat on the surface. He put two and two together, and when he got to Miami, the first stop he made was in a telephone booth to call Naval Intelligence and his friend W. D. Diamond, a civilian intelligence agent.

Two days later, two men were arrested when the schooner pulled into Miami, and they were charged with carrying supplies to U-boats operating in the Caribbean.

That story did not get much attention; it was kept secret by Naval Intelligence, but rumors got around Miami. And sometimes they were based on fact.

One day, for example, the navy blimp K-74 found a U-boat not far from Miami. The blimp crew decided to attack, but instead of diving and waiting for the depth charges, the U-boat surfaced, and the crew manned the deck guns. One shot struck the gas bag, and the blimp deflated and fell into the sea. The ten-man crew went into the water to struggle and wait for rescue. A destroyer came along and saved nine of them. One man was lost. The U-boat got away, and the story was all over Miami.

Miami had its civilian warriors, too. Very early in the war, Sixth Naval District (Charleston) organized its own antisabotage patrol. It consisted of a volunteer group of some 400 yachtsmen and fishermen. They sailed the inlets from Jacksonville to Wilmington, North Carolina, keeping an eye on the beaches from dusk till dawn. There were 350 boats, ranging from battered shrimpers to luxurious cruisers. They took the war seriously; the 75 most suitable craft were treated to a coat of battleship gray paint, and the letters CGA (Coast Guard Auxiliary) were painted on their sides. They were given the honor of patrol assignments along with the regulars, and Coast Guardsmen were assigned to the craft to work along with the civilian crews. Not to be outdone, Seventh Naval District organized 600 boats. Sixth District's fleet was divided into 13 flotillas, 4 of them at Jacksonville, and 3 at Savannah, with the rest scattered along the coast. Sixth District's civilians took the war more seriously.

Up in the Ocracoke area of North Carolina, the civilians had the memories of H.M.S. *Bedfordshire* to live with and much else. The auxiliary here worked as hard as anywhere, but so did the ordinary people, whose life was really the sea in war or peace. On July 17, four ships were torpedoed off the North Carolina coast in a few hours, and 104 men came ashore in lifeboats at the village of Ocracoke. The Red Cross supplies were totally inadequate to meet the needs, so people of the village organized and made a house-to-house canvass to find shirts, trousers, shoes, razors, and toothbrushes for the men.

The war was very definitely a part of life in Ocracoke.

"This submarine warfare is a ghastly business and the condition of these seamen when brought to shore is a sobering experience," said E. R. Mosher, one of the more educated residents of the village, in a letter to a friend. "I wish everyone in this country could know how close this war is to us."

His wife had been one of the organizers of the house-to-house canvass. Her war was reduced to absolute essentials. She had been reading the newspapers and learning, thus, about benefits in Miami and the continued comings and going of film stars and stage stars and radio stars, who paused here and there to give performances for the war effort.

"With all the horse play going on to impress people that we are at war," she wrote the Red Cross just after she had made a vain effort to find a supply of kerosene to get the oil off survivors of the *William Rockefeller,* "why isn't something being done where war is? Surely these seamen . . . should have recognition. I'm not asking for Hollywood stars to sing to them. What is needed are pants and shirts and a wash house equipped with soap that will cut this oil. . . ."

That, of course, was not Miami's war except for the likes of Mrs. Grady Stevens at the Good Samaritan Hospital in West Miami Beach. But not so very many around Miami saw that side of it. To most citizens, the war was what they read in the newspapers. To the hotel operators, the war was a mess of oil that washed up on their beaches and threatened the whole resort business.

For three months, ships had been burning and sinking so close to the city that many of the attacks were actually seen by bathers on the beaches. And still the lights burned brightly every single night, beacons from the beach-front hotels.

As the oil from the tankers stained Lummus Park Beach and blackened the groins of the marinas, some of the civilian warriors became as concerned as were the military authorities about Miami and the war.

But these Miami sailors were for the most part very much the amateurs. And their efforts were largely confined to patrolling the harbor, watching for U-boats that apparently might come up and try to shell the city.

One day, a submarine patrol boat off the shore of Miami Beach, about a mile and a quarter off 74th Street, suddenly veered off course. In the bow stood a sailor, pointing and shouting; the pointing could be seen from shore. Eyes followed the pointing, and on the patrol boat, they came to rest on an oil slick on the surface.

"Submarine," cried the lookout.

The captain headed for the slick, calling up the shore on his radio telephone to warn the naval air station. The crew readied the "ash cans" aft and dropped their charges as the boat passed over the spot.

Soon three Catalina flying boats converged on the area. They, too, spotted the slick and the patrol craft knifing the water about it. They came in to bomb, and the harbor erupted in geysers of sea water.

The slick grew heavier on the surface.

Suddenly, the captain of the patrol boat remembered he was in 40 feet of water. Shamefaced, he turned around and headed away as fast as he had come. The Catalinas dispersed.

The slick remained.

An hour later, Andrew Kelpsh, superintendent of the Miami Beach city sewer system was called to come down to 74th Street and see what was going wrong with the sewers. A terrible oil slick was staining the harbor.

Kelpsh hurried down, and a launch met him and took him out to the end of the 7,000-foot sewage-disposal line that carried the noxious wastes out safely past the bathing beaches so they would not pollute Miami Beach's waters.

Sure enough, there was the oil slick, dark and greasy.

Kelpsh went back to his offices and ordered divers sent to check the damage to the sewer line. The divers reported that the line itself was intact, although it had been strained at the seams apparently, and some damage had been incurred. But the sand had been excavated for 100 feet all around the sewer outlet.

That tale submerged in the archives of Miami Beach, not to surface for 20 years. Certainly, the captain of the patrol boat was not going to tell the story of his "submarine."

And Miami continued in her wicked ways. The businessmen would not turn off those lights at night.

To be sure, after strong representation from the military, they "darkened" the beaches, but people drove along the coast road flashing their lights, looking for submarines and excitement by night. The businessmen said they would turn out "some" of their lights, but the city still stood as a beacon against the land. It was a national disgrace, a regional disgrace, and little by little it began to become a local disgrace.

On July 12, Columnist Jack Kofoed of the Miami *Daily News* devoted his entire article to an angry attack on his townsmen.

"It seems that no small number of people in our town fail to comprehend that the war is at our doorsteps. There have been ships torpedoed within a few miles of the beach hotels. All of us have seen members of the crews in our streets. It has been pointed out that the lume [sic] for the city lights offers an excellent background for predatory submarines. Everyone knows that the ships silhouetted by that lume are vital to our national welfare. . . ."

And more because of this column than anything that had been said before, by General Drum, Admiral Andrews or any of the others, this attitude began to seep through into the consciousness of Miami. Finally, in midsummer 1942, even Miami gave up pursuit of the dollar to turn attention to the grim reality of the war. The lights went out for the first time since Pearl Harbor.

29
FORGING A WEAPON

In the near panic that seized the East Coast in the first weeks of war, the defenders had turned to any and every possible weapon to stave off the U-boats. Not the least of these efforts was the requisitioning of civilian craft. But it took time and yards of red tape, and so it was summer before the navy managed intelligent use of civilian sailors who were clamoring to help guard the shore of their homeland.

There were thousands of these civilians, yachtsmen, fishermen, and Sunday sailors. Admiral Andrews' staff had proposed a double-barreled system: Make a picket patrol of civilian sailors; make an observation patrol of fishermen to spot U-boats.

But spring had gone by, and so many other things came up to demand Andrews' attention that the planning stalled. The principal moving force was Commander Astor, the millionaire yachtsman, who was dealing with the Cruising Club of America, an organization of people with boats large enough to brave the open sea. What the club wanted—and Admiral Andrews approved—was the commissioning of 50 or 75 big boats that could go to sea, work with guns and depth charges, and in effect become parts of the real American defense force.

The members of the Cruising Club were volunteering. Astor reported that at least 50 vessels of size suitable for offshore work had been offered the navy. But as this plan was moving forward, another force was moving in a similar direction in Washington. The Coast Guard's organization reached its height in the Seventh Naval District, which claimed 500 boats with 600 volunteers to work them; people who could give 12 hours or more at a stretch for patrol work.

In the Fourth Naval District, they were actually using the volunteers by the third week of March. They patrolled as far as 5 miles out from Manosquan to Cape May.

When the reports of the Coast Guard about the appalling loss of life in sinkings came to Admiral King's desk, that program began to have more appeal than ever in Washington. Too many seamen were dying because after their vessels were torpedoed offshore, there was no way that help could be sent. In these desperate weeks, Admiral Andrews had no ships to spare for search and rescue. And so, while Andrews favored the picket-boat idea, he found that Washington much preferred the plan to use civilian craft for search-and-rescue work.

Andrews felt impelled to retract the encouragement he had been giving Astor, and Astor had to communicate the disappointing news to his friends.

But if Andrews was not to have his pickets, then he wanted control over the search-and-rescue program. He pointed this out in a letter to King, and the commander in chief agreed. The organization began to function, and congress helped by passing a bill authorizing the use of civilians for voluntary duty without pay. (Without such legislation, there was no way civilians could be given gasoline and supplies from naval stores.)

Still the competition between the navy and the Coast Guard for boats and captains continued, with the Coast Guard winning because it had the organization and less red tape than the navy.

In mid-June, Admiral King finally authorized the use of the "pickets" that Andrews had been trying for so long to get. King suggested that the boats ought to carry at least four 300-pound depth charges and a machine gun, preferably a .50 caliber.

The order came on the heels of another, authorizing the arming of the Coast Guard beach patrols and ordering that hereafter the patrolmen travel in pairs. It was not hard to see a correlation between both orders and the Amagansett incident.

So even the navy could be responsive if the challenge were great enough and obvious enough.

On the basis of this change, Navy Public Relations outdid itself in a story given *The New York Times* on June 26.

The armed forces (navy and Coast Guard) already had 1,200 small boats at sea, said the navy, covering the East Coast from one end to the other. The implications were that these craft were armed and ready to do battle with any submarine that came along. Soon, said the spokesman, another 1,000 boats would be put into service.

But the fact was that by mid-July there were only 49 such boats on patrol and another 23 in harbor, ready to do the kind of service the article described.

Nor would there ever be many more. For when the officers of Admiral Andrews' command set out to implement the new order, they discovered that no vessel under 50 feet could use depth charges. No vessel making less than 10 knots had any business having them aboard, either, for depth charges could blow the bottom out of a small boat. A boat dropped a charge and then had to move fast to escape the effect of the blast. Certainly, no small boat dare set off a charge that would explode closer than 50 feet under water.

By trial and error (to the destruction of several small craft), the naval officers of the Eastern Sea Frontier soon discovered that their plan left much to be desired.

Admiral King canceled his instructions about depth charges, and the craft were armed only with machine guns. That left them quite powerless to combat a U-boat; they were worse off than poor old *YP-389* had been, when deprived of her 3-inch gun.

A far more sensible and potentially effective weapon against the U-boats than the civilian "picket" craft was the fishing fleet.

Now the fishing fleet became a vital part of the American economy, a role it did not usually enjoy in peacetime. The breakdown of Britain's fishing industry on the other side of the Atlantic meant that tons of canned fish were shipped each month to England. This meant canned fish was an item in short supply in the stores, and fresh fish became an important part of the American diet because it was not rationed.

So important did the fishing industry become that in Washington, when in the first weeks of the war there was talk about mobilizing the fishing fleet to use as antisubmarine vessels, Secretary of Agriculture Claude Wickard objected. Let the fishermen alone.

The temptation was great to use anything at hand, but reason prevailed; the navy officials soon saw that if they did use the fishing fleet to fight the submarines, the moment the Germans discovered that the fishing boats were armed enemies, they would set out to destroy them. The repercussions could be severe.

But the fishing fleet could be useful in another way, as Admiral Andrews suggested. Let the boats be given radios and instructions and told to warn the authorities when they sighted a U-boat at sea.

As the need persisted, Admiral Andrews sent Commander Astor in U.S.S. *Vagrant* to various ports along the coast to survey the possibilities. Astor went first to Block Island. After a few days there, he reported back to his superior he had found 20 fishermen who were competent, eager, and had everything but radios. The plan would certainly work.

"The loyalty of the men is unquestionable, and I am inclined to think that they have a good fighting spirit too," he wrote. "Some of them come from families who have lived on the island for generations. One of the leading ones with whom I had a talk told me that he not only would report on an enemy submarine, but would trail it and chase it until he had been shot full of holes and sunk."

But, in New Bedford, Astor came across several cases of remarkable bureaucratic stupidity. The fishing boat *Ronald and Mary Jane* had made ready to go to sea for cod. The crew was aboard, the stores were loaded, including a supply of fresh meat, and the ice had been stowed to pack away the fish. The captain was waiting for the tide when the navy appeared and announced that as of that moment the ship was commandeered for naval service. The hull would be paid for, but the fishermen would lose the cost of their supplies.

At one boat yard, Astor saw a fine new fishing boat on the ways. She had been completed and was ready for outfitting when the owner was informed that she had been "processed," which meant the government would buy her, willy-nilly.

That word had been received two months before, but

since that time, the boat had sat in the ways. (Admiral Andrews must have winced at this reminder of his earliest program for the civilian craft.)

And just three weeks earlier, having done nothing about the new craft, the navy "processed" two more fishing boats in New Bedford. That meant two more crews on the beach, two more captains without employment.

"If you or I had our car taken from us and we then saw it sitting idle in a parking lot, we would probably not be very happy," Commander Astor wrote his admiral.

It disturbed Astor that the navy was not even intelligent about what it did. Astor encountered two captains who were security risks (one of them was on the Fourth Naval District blacklist as an Axis sympathizer), and neither of the captains had lost his boat. Instead, these two were allowed out whenever they wished to fish (and perchance to signal a submarine). All this while men of unquestionable loyalty were deprived of their boats and kept ashore.

Astor's vigorous protests produced some results. The disloyal fishermen were beached for the duration. Some of the wrongs done loyal men were righted, and fishermen gained new enthusiasm to go to sea with radios and help the navy.

That summer, one day, a fisherman called in to report that he had just sighted a U-boat on the surface off the Massachusetts coast, and he gave a position.

A new weapon had been forged.

30
THE THIRD U-BOAT . . .
AND FOURTH

It was a hot summer along the U.S. coast for the U-boats, much hotter than anyone had given them reason to expect. Back at Lorient and Le Havre, the crews of the earliest waves boasted of their exploits and denigrated the Americans. Thus, *U-701* set course for America with high expectations. Her commander, Kapitaenleutnant Horst Degen, was one of the new breed. He had been in the navy half his 29 years but only two years in U-boats. Still, he knew *U-701* from torpedo tube to propeller shaft; he had been assigned to her during construction and commissioned her and taken her on two previous patrols.

On the first patrol, *U-701* had been assigned to the northwestern approaches to England. She had sunk the *Baron Erskine,* a 3,000-ton freighter, but that was all, in five weeks at sea. The British antisubmarine-warfare units made the going hard.

On the second war patrol, in March 1942, *U-701* had hunted off Iceland. Degen claimed four sinkings, all armed trawlers, and British sources seemed to confirm at least three of these.

The third patrol had begun at the German U-boat base at Brest on May 26. A band had stood on the quay side and played as she pulled out, and two German patrol boats and two Messerschmitt fighters escorted her out to sea and stayed with her as she headed for Lorient to take on fuel. Two days later, she was at sea, fully fueled and carrying 14 torpedoes.

They crossed the Atlantic on the surface, but when they approached the American shore, Degen became more cautious. He took the boat down as they came into the Cape Hatteras area.

Degen's first attack had been made on June 16, when he sighted a south-bound freighter, a big one, about 8,000 tons. He fired two torpedoes, but both missed, and he had to dive because of approaching aircraft and lost the target.

On June 19, Degen's *U-701* was the submarine that sank *YP-389,* a victory so easy it embarrassed the Germans. But after *YP-389,* the U-boat had bad luck. One convoy came by, and then another. But Degen never seemed to be able to get into position to intercept, for the ships were protected by patrol craft and escorts, and they zigged and zagged on schedule and changed speed as ordered.

On June 27, Degen did encounter a southbound convoy and worked into position at periscope depth. He fired two torpedoes at a medium-sized freighter. The crew heard one explosion, but Degen could not see what had happened because the escorting destroyers turned on the submarine and began an attack. *U-701* dived and was depth charged so severely that the electric motors were knocked out, and gauges in the conning tower were smashed. The damage was repaired in short order, and the submarine got away, but Degen had gained considerable respect for the destroyers. The ship that *U-701* had attacked, *British Freedom,* managed to make Norfolk for repairs.

The next day, June 28, Degen trailed a big tanker. He was very careful and stayed below the surface. When he got into position, he fired one torpedo and then dived because the tanker had an air escort. The aircraft immediately came in to attack, but Degen managed to get away. That night *U-701* returned to the scene and saw the tanker there burning. (It was *William Rockefeller,* whose crew had been brought into Ocracoke.) Degen fired another torpedo into her and sank her. Afterward, on the surface, Degen radioed word of his sinking back to Admiral Doenitz in Germany. It was his last success.

In the days that followed, *U-701* was attacked so frequently by American planes that Degen kept the U-boat on the bottom during almost all of the daylight hours. But, occasionally, the air grew so foul that he had to bring the boat up. It was always dangerous, and several times they barely escaped destruction.

U-701 spent most of July 7 on the bottom, off Hatteras. By early afternoon, the air was foul and the men were breathing with difficulty. Just after three o'clock, Degen decided to chance it and came to the surface. The lookouts were posted on the bridge as the conning tower broke water, and the ship came up to an even keel. They poured out as the fresh air poured in, and the men took great gulps.

Then, out of nowhere came an American bomber. A lookout shouted the warning, and Degen pressed the alarm button. The klaxon sounded, men hurried back down the conning-tower hatch, and Degen blew the tanks and began to dive as the bomber roared in above them.

The bomber was piloted by 2nd Lt. Harry J. Kane of Squadron 59, who had lifted the Lockheed-Hudson off the runway at Cherry Point air station about an hour earlier. Kane had climbed to 1,500 feet and then begun the search pattern in a sky dotted with fleecy cumulus clouds.

Suddenly, he spotted something on the surface about 10 miles away and turned to investigate. As he came closer, he saw that it was a submarine, deck completely out of the water. He was lucky enough to have the sun behind him, and the submarine was slow in response as he began his attack.

When the bomber was 2 miles away, the submarine began its crash dive, but then the bomber was on it. The first depth charge fell 25 feet short, but the second and third were right on target, and they blew the pressure hull apart. Water began to pour into the aft compartments.

Captain Degen blew the tanks and ordered the men to abandon ship.

Then he fell and struck his head and blacked out.

The main lighting failed, but the emergency lights remained on in the forward and middle compartments. In a few moments, water was waist-deep throughout the boat, with the after compartments completely flooded. Two men escaped from those parts of the U-boat.

But from the midsection and the forward torpedo room, 15 men managed to get to the conning tower and open the hatch and scramble through. The captain was unconscious and was pulled up by his men.

Lieutenant Kane circled. He counted 15 heads and then another two a little farther off. He dropped four life rafts and a lifeboat and then went out to find other help for his enemies. He passed a Panamanian freighter, and the radioman on the bomber managed to make contact with the radio operator on the ship. He gave the position and asked the freighter to stop and pick up the survivors. He gave the position. The Panamanian acknowledged, but her captain was not about to stop in "submarine-infested waters," and the Panamanian freighter sailed straight on.

Lieutenant Kane finally located Coast Guard cutter *472* on the emergency frequency and gave the information. But the cutter's operator had the wrong coordinates, and the cutter did not find the German survivors.

Kane now went about his patrol and at the end of it landed at Cherry Point and reported the sinking of the U-boat.

The Germans struggled in the water. The life rafts and lifeboat were dropped too far away and drifted so that they were of no use. Some of the men had escape lungs. Some had life belts. Kapitan Degen had neither, and he would certainly have drowned had his men not taken turns to support his head and keep it out of the water.

At the end of the first day, the men began to slip away, exhausted. Oberleutnant Bahr, the engineering officer, went mad and screamed deliriously before he finally choked and sank.

They were in the Gulf Stream and drifting rapidly away from the point of sinking. Oberleutnant Junker said he could see the land, and he persuaded Leutnant Bazies and Unteroffizier Lange and one rating to swim for shore. They set out and were never seen again.

First Mate Gunter Kunert said they were crazy; the men had to stick together if they were to survive. He held the captain's head in his brawny arms, along with Machinist's Mate Ludwig Vaupel and Radioman Herbert Grotheer. Fireman Bruno Faust stuck with them.

A little way off were Fireman Schwendel and Fireman Seldte. They had escaped miraculously from the after torpedo room when the others believed every man had drowned. Each had a life preserver.

At the end of the second day, the survivors were down to these seven, and they had nearly given up hope. They had drifted more than 60 miles south of the point of sinking, carried by the current. Their rescue came about purely by chance when, on the morning of July 9, the airship *K-8* spotted the seven men in the water north of Wimble Shoals light buoy and lowered a raft, then blankets and first-aid gear. That afternoon, the men were picked up by a Coast Guard seaplane and flown to the naval air station at Norfolk.

The sinking of *U-701* came just at a time when Doenitz was being pressed by Hitler to divert U-boats to other areas. It was a decisive factor; Doenitz saw that the "happy time" on the American coast had ended. The introduction of the convoy system had made the American area far less attractive, and the pressing need just now was for operations against convoys in mid-Atlantic where the allies could not successfully manage air cover. Doenitz's emphasis now was on wolf-pack attacks on convoys, and the war moved, at least temporarily, away from the American coast.

The sinking of *U-701*, then, symbolized what had happened to American defenses in seven months. *U-85* had been sunk by a sheer lucky fluke. The chances of a patrol craft's coming upon a U-boat at sea were and remained infinitesimal, but *Roper* had done just that, and her captain had been lucky in every way. The usual performance of the period was more like that of *Hamilton* and *Triton*, which had spent a whole day and thousands of dollars worth of ammunition on a sunken wreck.

The sinking of *U-382* by *Icarus* had been another piece of luck, compounded by the carelessness of the German U-boat commander, who had been lulled into believing that because the U.S. defenses were so slight, there was no danger to his U-boat in shallow water.

But the sinking of *U-701* was accomplished by an aircraft pilot and bomber crew who knew precisely what they were doing and did it well. The depth of the charges was properly set at 25 feet, not 50. The approach was masterful and caught the U-boat by surprise, although the captain had been careful. Lieutenant Kane's performance was an indication of the speed with which the Americans were forging the weapons they needed to drive Doenitz away.

And when it became apparent that the pressure of the U-boats had lessened off the East coast at the end of summer, Admiral Andrews and his staff did not relax. Quite the reverse, they continued to develop their weapons and techniques preparing for the time when they were sure Doenitz would send his U-boat captains back for another try.

The most successful antisubmarine measures were being carried out then in the Caribbean by combined British-American hunter-killer teams. U-boat sinkings were still numerous in the area that summer, but so were the number of attacks on U-boats.

U-94 came to the Caribbean just then with an impressive record of sinkings on nine previous successful war patrols, including one off the U.S. coast in which she had sunk 40,000 tons of shipping.

On August 7, *U-94*'s captain, Kapitaenleutnant Otto Ites began tracking a convoy that was moving between Cuba's Guantanamo Bay, where the U.S. maintained a naval base, and the U.S. base at Key West.

All day long, *U-94* had dodged PBY flying boats with ridiculous ease. Ites could dive and be far out of range before the lumbering aircraft could get around to attack. It was the captain's first real encounter with PBYs, and he did not think much of them. Before this day was over, he announced his contempt: He told his executive officer that if he sighted any more of these aircraft, he would not bother to submerge until the very last minute.

That night, *U-94* surfaced. The moon was full and yellow, but Ites was contemptuous of his enemies in American waters. Although visibility was good, and the wind and sea were both light, Ites was maneuvering within the convoy screen, on the surface!

Then one of the lookouts sighted a plane.

"You are seeing ghosts," said the executive officer. "The Americans do not fly at night."

But the ghost was a U.S. Navy PBY and it came steadily along. Ites saw it, waited as promised, till the last moment, and then submerged.

The PBY dropped four depth charges and a flare. The first three charges shook the submarine as it went down to 60 feet. The fourth depth charge exploded below the U-boat and drove it back up to the surface.

What Captain Ites did not know was that this and other PBYs in the area were parts of hunter-killer teams of aircraft and surface vessels, trained to work closely together. This PBY was paired with the British corvette H.M.S. *Oakville*. Having attacked, the PBY signaled *Oakville*.

S was the letter flashed by the Aldis lamp. S meant submarine.

H.M.S. *Oakville* charged up toward the flare burning in the water and arrived just as *U-94* broke the surface. *Oakville* rammed the U-boat and then turned and began firing with her guns. A shell smashed into the conning tower. Another carried away the U-boat's deck gun. *Oakville* rammed the U-boat again, then dropped depth charges against the hull as she moved away, came back, and rammed a third time abaft the conning tower.

The U-boat was mortally wounded and filling with water. Men came pouring up into the conning tower and out the hatch, leaped off the sinking submarine, and began to swim. In a minute, *U-94* sank.

Oakville picked up five of the Germans and a third member of the hunter killer team; the U.S. destroyer *Lea* picked up 21 more. The rest died either from the attacks or by drowning, victims of captain Ites' arrogance and ignorance.

Those hunter-killer teams changed the whole war picture.

31
MYSTERIES OF THE SEA

The German presence continued all summer, only just enough to remind the Americans that the U-boats were still deadly if otherwise occupied at the moment. But instead of the horrors of U-boat warfare, the defenders now had the leisure to be preoccupied by mysteries of the sea.

On the evening of August 10, patrol vessels off St. John's River, near Jacksonville, heard gunfire and saw green flashes on the horizon. But when the boats went to investigate, they found nothing at all. Not a ship, not a submarine, not a trace of anyone at all.

In St. John's River, on the morning after the mysterious green flashes had appeared, the mine sweeper *AMG-67* was working in this area. It was part of her routine duty, now that the minefield laid by the U-boats had been found off Chesapeake Bay. She was near St. John's lightship, about a mile east, when, at 9:15, she struck a mine. Luckily, she was not seriously damaged. The Germans had sneaked in and laid mines. How many and where, no one knew. That was the problem. Those mines had to be swept out, and there were no other sweepers available. The navy had to order up one from Savannah and one from Charleston. They were two days in coming and then two more days in sweeping the area. Meanwhile, shipping at Jacksonville was at a standstill.

There were ten mines in the water, and when a mine disposal unit from Potomac River Naval Command came down to Jacksonville, the officers examined the fragments picked up in shrimpers' nets and found that they were German S-type mines, which had an 80-day clock in them. That meant they would self-destruct at the end of that period. It also indicated that Admiral Doenitz intended that his submarines would return to these waters and did not want his U-boats to run afoul of his own mines.

Since the sinking of *Bluefields* in that action that involved *Mowinckle* and the commodore, not a single ship had been sunk off the American shore by enemy U-boat action. A whole month had passed, and the U-boats had not made a kill.

On September 12, three mines were exploded by sweepers off Cape Henry. Norfolk port was closed down for two days. Where had they come from? Nobody knew.

On September 24, three more mines were exploded off Charleston. Again there was no damage, but where were these U-boats?

The naval planes, in vastly increased numbers, flew 8,000 hours with but a single sighting. The blimps flew 1,000 hours without any; the army reported one sighting in 3,750 flight hours, and surface vessels, which reported by far the most questionable contacts, said there were a dozen and they made five attacks. But the elusive U-boats laid their mines and escaped. Or were they U-boats at all or a surface ship? No one ever discovered.

September was a fearsome month in the U-boat war elsewhere. Eighty-five ships were sunk, from the Gulf of St. Lawrence to the Murmansk run.

But as for American waters, Lieutenant Hess, the tracking officer at Andrews' headquarters, said there was only one U-boat off Hatteras reporting convoys for a few days and one boat that hovered around south of Long Island for a week, then moved 100 miles off Nantucket, where is was "spooked" at night five times by Coast Guard Reserve picket boats and went on homeward without accomplishing a single sinking. It did not even seem to try, and so it was a mystery to Admiral Andrews and his men how St. John's River ever got mined.

An important factor in keeping the attacks on shipping to a minimum had been diversion of shipping to inland and coastal waters to safeguard the ships from any possibility of U-boat attack. An integral part of this system was the Cape Cod Canal, which cut 120 miles off the trip from the south to Boston. No more did ships have to skirt the dangerous waters of the Cape, made more than doubly dangerous now by the enemy U-boats. The canal served the double purpose of saving time and saving ships.

But the canal was narrow, only 480 feet wide, and its current changed with the tides and the winds. So it took a skilled pilot to manage this water, and even a skilled pilot was not always safe.

One summer night, the merchant ship *Stephen R. Jones* reached Cleveland Ledge Lighthouse at the entrance to the Cape Cod Canal, on the Buzzard's Bay side. The Wing's Neck light was against him, which meant traffic was coming from the other direction, so the master anchored in the east anchorage at Wing's Hook and waited. In the course of routine, a Coast Guard officer boarded the ship, examined the papers and checked the radio seal to be sure the ship had been observing radio silence.

The officer asked the captain if he wanted a pilot to take him through the canal. But the captain had made the trip six times since January 1942, by himself, and had navigated the canal 24 times altogether. He held a canal endorsement on his master's ticket, and he did not feel the need for a pilot. It would simply cost his owners a good bit of extra money.

At 1:30 on the morning of June 29, the captain had the green light, and half an hour later he had raised anchor and was clear. In 25 minutes, he entered Hog Island Channel at full speed. He reduced speed to 45 knots to go under the railroad bridge and moved cautiously toward Bourne Bridge. He cleared that bridge at 3:08 in the morning.

He was moving along when suddenly he was met by a change: A 2.5-knot current came from out of nowhere and sheered his bow in toward the bank to port. The captain ordered full speed, the helm hard a-starboard, and then full reverse. But it did no good. The ship was in the grip of the current, and it went aground on the bank. Immediately, water began to come in through the forward compartments.

The captain ordered the bow anchors dropped, and the ship came up and hung parallel to the shore about 110 feet out.

The captain went ashore and called his owners, the Mystic Steam Ship Company, and then came back aboard. Meanwhile, the Coast Guard tender *Kickapoo* and a tug of the Merritt Chapman and Scott Wrecking Company came up and tried to stop the swing of the ship, but they could not. Soon she was moved around so that her stern jutted out into the canal; the bow was aground, and it blocked all but 100 feet of the canal. Shipping had to be stopped. The convoys were stalled. Ships on both sides must either go around into the dangerous waters off the Cape or wait.

Meanwhile, when the ship began to go down to the bottom of the canal, the men jumped over the side and began to swim ashore.

One of the officials of the Mystic Steamship Company had come to the canal to see what was happening to their ship, and he had brought along his 15-year-old-daughter, who was dressed up for the occasion.

Several of the men began to founder in the water. Thereupon, the 15-year-old leaped in, saved them, and swam ashore, wet to the skin but otherwise all right. The men of the ship were so grateful they presented her then and there with the ship's mascot, a little cross-breed dog. He was aptly named: Shipwreck.

By nightfall, they had all gone, and all that was left of the ship was stuck there in the canal.

The company and the authorities were nearly a month getting her out and getting the canal cleared for ocean-going traffic. During that month, the convoys were routed around the cape into the deep water offshore, left to face the dangers of the U-boats.

At the court of inquiry, the captain was blamed for carelessness, although he had not been careless. (His owners, making their own inquiry, absolved him of all blame.)

All told, the affair was, in fact, another of those unfathomable mysteries of the sea: the emergence of that 2.5-knot current just at the wrong time in the wrong place for the ship involved.

Another mystery was the radio hoax of November 25, 1942. Late that afternoon, the Coast Guard base at Greenport, Long Island, picked up an S O S from a vessel that identified herself as the British freighter *Southampton* and reported her position as 76 degrees west, 41 degrees north.

Soon the radio traffic increased in tempo: The ship reported in again, and then on came the British steamer S. S. *St. George,* also reporting that she was torpedoed.

Then came a message, apparently from a U-boat to a ship: "You escaped us this time. Next time we will sink you," it said. "Heil Hitler." What ship? Where was the U-boat?

Twenty minutes later, Coast Guard cutter *609* intercepted another message.

"We were torpedoed and shelled four hours ago. Send an escort to conduct us to New York. S. S. *Southampton*." And it gave coordinates.

But there was no *Southampton* out there, nor any *St. George*. Planes from Floyd Bennet Field flew to check the coordinates and found nothing. There once had been an S. S. *Southampton,* but she had been torpedoed and sunk earlier in the year. There was no ship afloat that bore that name.

And when the Coast Guard got down to some fine-tuned checking, by the best estimates, they found those distress broadcasts were coming from inland Connecticut. But from what station? It was never found.

These were some of the mysteries of the war that were never solved.

32
CONVOYS

That summer, the Americans improved their convoy practices and protection so that they were almost as efficient as their British cousins.

The navy men knew what they were doing, and they did it well. Many a ship was saved by the exercise of group effort and plain common sense, and not all the danger of the sea these days was posed by U-boats. There were many other perils.

The military transport *Wakefield* was traveling in convoy from Glasgow to New York on September 3 with three other big troop transports. They had delivered human cargo to England and were coming back for another load. *Wakefield* was carrying 1,505 passengers and crew, including the survivors of the S. S. *Almeria Lykes,* sunk at sea, who were coming back to the United States for another ship.

The convoy was guarded by the battleship *Arkansas,* the cruiser *Brooklyn,* and eight destroyers.

The day was clear, the passage had been uneventful so far, and no submarines were reported. It seemed almost like a peacetime crossing. But at 6:32 that evening, fire was discovered in a compartment on B deck of this converted luxury liner. (She had been the S. S. *Manhattan* before the war.) Two civilian passengers found a blaze and tried to fight it with hand extinguishers. When they saw that they were not controlling the fire, they pulled the alarm.

On the bridge, Capt. Harold G. Bradbury ordered distress flags raised and the whistle blown to indicate *Wakefield*'s situation to the convoy. Seven hoses were hauled out to play on the fire. But the oiled wood paneling caught, and so did the linoleum in the ship's public rooms, and the blaze sent out an oily black smoke that made it hard to get near the fires even with gas masks. The fires began to spread, and 10 minutes later, flames were reported on A deck and C deck.

The ship's engines were stopped, and she was brought into the breeze to stop the draft. The rest of the convoy decided to move on, leaving *Brooklyn* and three destroyers to help the stricken ship. *Brooklyn* moved aft and began to take off passengers.

Captain Bradbury turned to fight the fire, although the flames rose as high as the stacks. The destroyers came in close, and *Mayo* took off 22 men and officers caught amidships by the flames. Those forward were rescued by *Madison.*

At 8:33, Captain Bradbury was taken off, too, along with Lt. Comdr. Roy L. Haney, his executive officer. But they stood by on the *Madison*, waiting for a chance to reboard their ship and save it.

Soon *Brooklyn* had 1,174 passengers aboard, and the passenger ship was deserted. It had been a successful rescue. All were saved. The most serious casualty was a sailor aboard *Mayo* who broke his arm.

The *Wakefield* burned for four days, and the other vessels stood by waiting while they sent back to the United States for tugs and salvage ships. Finally, four tugs took her into Halifax, where she was beached in McNab's cove, still burning. It was noon on September 12 before the fires were all out.

Then *Wakefield* was floated and taken to Boston for the job of rebuilding.

The convoys continued up and down the coast as well as across the Atlantic, and they were real convoys, adequately protected. There was always human drama in a convoy; there always were tales to tell of ships that fell out of line or had to be left behind or of near collisions or of mishaps that occurred to men.

One September, a convoy was heading from New York to Guantanamo Bay, and among her escorts was the destroyer U.S.S. *Broome.* That day, a distress call came from the S. S. *Genevieve Lykes,* one of the ships in the convoy, and *Broome* responded. A medical officer was wanted.

Lt. Harold W. Fleischer was the medical officer of the *Broome,* and he was quickly transferred to the merchant ship. There he found Steward John Lance in considerable pain. Lance was suffering from appendicitis; on examination, Fleischer ascertained that the appendix had burst about 12 hours earlier.

The situation was serious. Unless something was done, Steward Lance would soon be dead. But the merchant ship was no place for an operation. The medical officer decided it would have to be done aboard the *Broome.*

They took the patient back to the destroyer. Usually, in such situations, the ship would be stopped, but not this time. *Broome* was in submarine territory, and she had an obligation to continue her patrol and protection. So she moved at 25–30 knots, and the doctor would have to work out his procedures accordingly.

Lieutenant Fleischer took his patient into the ward room and strapped him to the table. Only one other man aboard, a chief pharmacist's mate, knew anything about surgery. Several of the others would have to learn in short order.

So men were enlisted for the operation: The engineering officer became chief anesthetist, and Fleischer's nurses were a chief commissary steward, a ship fitter, and a mess attendant. The sterilizer for the instruments was the big copper kettle from the galley.

In the heat of the badly ventilated destroyer ward room, Lieutenant Fleischer and his assistants worked. He made the incisions and removed the ruptured appendix. Peritonitis had already set in, he observed gloomily, as he sewed the patient up.

"Operation successful. The patient will die" was the prognosis, unless heroic measures could be taken.

Steward Lance was 36 years old and had been in good health. Now he was dehydrated and suffering from massive infection. He must have immediate aid in the form of glucose to restore the body liquids and sulfanilimide, the most effective treatment then known against infection. The captain of *Broome* broke radio silence and told Norfolk navy base what was needed. Eight hours later, a PBM (medium-sized flying boat) bomber circled the convoy and came in. *Broome* sent out a launch, and the PBM dropped a parachute that landed nearly on target; all the supplies were in the package, and not a bottle broke on impact.

Lieutenant Fleischer and his "nurses" worked on Lance for hours. They tended his glucose drip. They made sure he had the sulfanilimide. Still he seemed to be sinking. Preparations were made for a burial at sea; a piece of canvas was brought out and the sewing begun.

Then, as hope seemed lost, Lance began to rally. But the glucose was nearly gone. So another call was sent to Norfolk, and another mercy mission was flown by a PBY. Steward Lance survived the convoy and was delivered alive to Guantanamo naval hospital.

Then, on the way back, with a rough storm kicking up off Hatteras, the S. S. *R. H. Colley* signaled the destroyer that she had a sick man aboard. Lieutenant Fleischer got on the voice radio. It was a case of appendicitis again.

This time, the storm was raging so fiercely that no man could be transferred, even by breeches buoy. So, for 24 hours, Fleischer radioed treatment instructions, and the men of the merchant ship gave the sick man the treatment. The next day, he could be moved, and he was taken over to *Broome*.

The seaman had been packed in ice, and Fleischer believed that this treatment had been successful. But, in a few hours the man began to show signs of extreme distress, and Fleischer knew another operation was in order.

The whole procedure was repeated: strapping the patient down on the ward-room table, the scrubbing and instructions to his voluntary staff. The "nurses" were full of themselves this time and bragged to one another about their "technique."

When Fleischer made his cut, he saw with satisfaction that the appendix had not ruptured, although it was very near to that point. Carefully, he extracted it, powdered the cavity with sulfa, and sewed up the incision. The man was on his feet before the convoy reached New York.

33

THE GREAT NANTUCKET
U-BOAT HUNT

In October 1942, the American coast was free of submarines except for a handful of U-boats that crept along the coast like ghosts, checking the convoys, reporting to Doenitz on the weather, and stealing away into the night.

The change in U-boat tactics cost the Americans their British trawlers. On October 17, the 18 trawlers were ordered to Africa. Traveling at 12 knots, they turned toward Trinidad, where they would fuel and then move on to Freetown.

As seemed bound to happen in the momentum generated in the spring and summer, the defense commands began to expand. First Bomber Command was christened Army Air Forces Anti-Submarine Command and given a new status under Brig. Gen. W. T. Larson. The Eastern Sea Frontier moved into bigger offices to house the scores of new officers assigned.

Nantucket was regarded as a key watch point for U-boat activity from the beginning of the war. "Madaket Millie," a doughty Nantucketer, braved the winter winds for which the island was famous, the rain and the sleet and the pounding surf, and she gave the Coast Guard reports on anything that moved within her purview.

But actually very little did move. One day, an English cargo ship was torpedoed not far from the island, and two bedraggled boatloads of Chinese sailors and British officers made their way to Nantucket. They were towed into the harbor by a Coast Guard cutter and taken to the Congregational church gymnasium to be bedded down. Nantucketers scurried around to find mattresses, blankets, and old clothes for them. The 43 survivors stayed two days, then left by ferry for Woods Hole.

The same submarine then sank the American freighter *Plow City* with three torpedoes.

Radioman A. R. Daniel Delaine kept working his key as the other 29 survivors left the ship. One man, Second Mate Fred Martin, was killed in the explosion of the second torpedo. All others escaped, and Delaine jumped from the sinking hull as she went down.

The ship's three boats maneuvered to pick up all the men. The captain was setting a course for Long Island when the submarine surfaced in the midst of the little flotilla, capsizing one boat.

The Germans rescued the men from the water, hauled them on to the deck of the submarine, and gave them each a tot of rum.

The U-boat commander then apologized for sinking *Plow City*. "But this is war," he said tersely. Then he ordered the Americans put over into the other two boats and let them move away.

Then came the story of J. P. Mulligan and Carl Hoffman, two merchant seamen whose ship was torpedoed off Nantucket. Only one boat was preserved, and the survivors crammed into it until its gunwales were nearly slopping water.

Mulligan, the ship's bosun, looked over the side into the threatening sea and announced that it looked cold. It was cold. Nantucket water is always cold in the springtime and hardly even warm in summer.

"Unless a couple of us get out of this boat," said the bosun, "we'll all be drowned." He pointed to the ship. "There's some rafts back there. I'm going back and get one."

Then Carl Hoffman, a wiper in the engine room, stood up. He said he would go along, for it was obvious that Mulligan needed another hand if he was to get the life rafts off the hulk of their ship.

The pair kicked off their shoes, dived over the side of the lifeboat, and swam to the ship. The men in the boat could see the life rafts; they had broken loose at the ends and were hanging down the sides of the hull, banging. All it would take was the effort to climb up, slash away the ropes, and they would float.

Mulligan and Hoffman swam on and reached the side

of the ship. The men could see them there, against the hull. But only for a moment, for just then the ship gave a convulsive shudder, cold water struck her red-hot boilers, they blew up, and she broke in two. Both halves of the ship fell away and sank in whirlpools of water and flotsam. Mulligan and Hoffman were right there, at the side, and they were dragged down. The men watched, but no heads came up.

But all this activity was no more than preparation for an event that came to be known in naval parlance as "the great Nantucket submarine hunt of November 1942."

By November, the antisubmarine-warfare men of the Eastern Sea Frontier had begun to learn how to do their job efficiently, and they were eager for action.

There was little action because Hitler had ordered Admiral Doenitz to divert his submarines again, this time to the Murmansk run.

Yet as Lieutenant Hess and his submarine-tracking people knew, the logical route for the deployment of U-boats almost always passed by Nantucket. Off Nantucket, the U-boats split off and made their way into the grid areas that their admiral had assigned them as hunting grounds. Off Nantucket, too, the U-boats clustered and sent their weather data to the German submarine command.

The great submarine hunt began on the morning of November 5. An army B-25 medium bomber from Westover Field was on routine patrol about 15 miles southeast of Nantucket Shoals Light when the pilot spotted an oil slick.

"Submarine," he said.

He reported it to his base and circled while he waited for instructions.

At 11:30, navy OS2U planes from Quonset Naval Air Station arrived on the scene and confirmed the finding. Quonset reported that it was sending along an unarmed PBY with a new experimental echo-ranging device aboard. The B-25 continued to circle. The OS2Us circled.

The B-25 eventually grew low on fuel, and so the pilot headed back to his base, leaving the navy in charge of the submarine.

For by now all concerned were certain they had a damaged submarine under observation.

At 3:10, there seemed no doubt. The PBY made a contact with the echo-ranging gear: The submarine was moving east at 2 knots at a depth of 100 feet. The position was 40°30′ N, 69°27′ W.

"Send attack group immediately," radioed the PBY.

Quonset swung into action. By radio, the air station was in touch with Newport Naval Base, which got a surface fleet ready to move. At the Eastern Sea Frontier, the operations and tracking office studied the charts and disposition of ships. The Destroyer *Champlin* was en route from Boston to New York. Admiral Andrews' men were in touch with Washington: *Champlin* was assigned to Atlantic Fleet, but could they not have her for 24 hours to destroy this submarine?

Washington said yes.

Andrews ordered *Champlin* to the scene.

Meanwhile, the PBY, with sound equipment, was shadowing the submarine. At four o'clock in the afternoon, the PBY reported the submarine changed course to 105 degrees. Another PBY came up, this one armed, and dropped smoke bombs and two depth charges on the U-boat. More oil came up.

At 5:10, another plane arrived and dropped more depth charges. More oil appeared.

Quonset dispatched a PBY5a and four OS2Us, and they soon arrived to mill about in the air.

Newport dispatched the U.S. Coast Guard cutter *General Greene* and the patrol boat *SC-672* and PT boats 63 and 64.

At 9:34 that night, Andrews told U.S.S. *Captor* to join. She had been patrolling in the general area.

The radio-equipped fishing vessel *Indicator # 107* reported at about this time that she had sighted a U-boat 20 miles southeast of this position. The word was relayed to *Champlin* and *Captor*.

At 1:38, on the morning of November 6, *SC-672* arrived in pitch blackness off the light.

At 2:00 A.M., *General Greene* arrived.

At 7:52, *Captor* arrived and reported to headquarters immediately on the oil slick.

Then up came *Champlin*, the biggest of the bulldogs, and her captain, being senior officer present, took charge.

Champlin made a series of attacks. In fact, she made 14

attacks and dropped 66 depth charges in the next few hours.

SC-672 made a number of attacks as ordered by *Champlin* and dropped 15 depth charges.

Captor made five attacks.

General Greene made two attacks.

SC-704 and *705* came up from New York, and *SC-761* came from New London, and they joined in the attacks.

In all, the surface vessels dropped 133 depth charges on the location of the submarine, with its attendant oil slick up above.

At noon, on November 7, *Champlin* reported back to Admiral Andrews' office.

"No movement. . . . I am convinced that the submarine is definitely sunk. . . ." The captain reported he had put the *General Greene* to work taking oil samples, which could then be analyzed to show that the oil was of the type carried by German submarines.

Nine hours later, the captain was still as confident.

He had the U-boat trapped on the bottom, he said, but he did not believe he had yet given the German ship its death blow. He would continue.

General Greene, by this time, was running short of fuel and had to head back to base. *Captor* and *SC-762* were out of depth charges. *SC-761* attacked the submarine just then and reported that it was moving very slowly.

That night, up came the S.S. *Anton Dohrn,* the scientific vessel of the Woods Hole Oceanographic Institute with a patrol boat for an escort. At eleven the next morning, the men of *Anton Dohrn* made contact with the sunken U-boat by fathometer. *Anton Dohrn* was carrying underwater photographic equipment. With this, they could get a good picture for Admiral Andrews to see how a U-boat looked on the bottom, where it belonged.

That evening, from New London came the supply tender *Sardony,* carrying more depth charges, with *YP-440, YP-449,* and *PT 95* and *PT 141,* all to help out with the task.

At 6:11, on the evening of November 9, *Anton Dohrn* was finished with the photography and headed back toward Woods Hole, escorted by *General Greene,* which had returned to the scene. Just before she left, for good measure,

General Greene dropped two more depth charges on the now-still form below.

One by one, the ships dispersed, *Champlin* heading back to claim a submarine sunk.

When the underwater photos were developed on November 14, they showed a seamed, welded hull. That was quite in order; it was the way the U-boats were constructed.

But this seamed, welded hull was covered with debris and marine growth that took months to accumulate, and it was upside down, and it did not seem to be a whole ship.

That was the word from Woods Hole.

From Washington came words for *Champlin* to preen by, high praise:

"It appears probable that USS *Champlin* and later on her assisting craft accounted for death of an enemy submarine by applying persistent dogging tactics as often recommended . . . submarine . . . sunk. . . ."

Admiral Andrews got the photos and the statements from fleet. His officers checked the charts and wrecks and the history of the area.

Somebody remembered that one day in 1937 the Nantucket lightship had been anchored at about 40°30′ N and 69° 27′ W, when, in a dense fog, up had come the steamer *Olympia* and rammed her amidships, cut the lightship right in two, and both parts had sunk to the bottom of the Atlantic.

Welded hull . . . covered with marine growth of the sort that takes four or five years to accumulate . . . there it all was. A dozen ships and planes, enough depth charges to sink a fleet of submarines, and they had spent three days playing with an old wreck.

That was the Great Submarine Hunt of November 1942.

34

MYSTERIOUS MINES—
AND SABOTAGE

Miami was blacked out. The other cities along the East Coast were dark. Still the newspapers suppressed weather reports so as not to give aid and comfort to the enemy. And if he had moved away from the American shore, that did not mean his presence was no longer felt. If the defenders ever tended to become negligent, then some incident would suddenly explode to shake them from lethargy.

Everyone said the Germans had gone, and then, on the night of November 13, *YMS 20*, a mine sweeper operating off Ambrose light, exploded a magnetic mine while making a dull routine sweep just 4 miles from the lightship. For weeks, the sweeper had worked the area, and nothing had happened. But this day, there came a tremendous roar, and a column of water shot 200 feet in the air.

That brought the rest of the mine sweepers out to cover the entire port-entry area, and they worked all night. The port of New York was closed down until the task was finished, which meant no ships sailed or were allowed to enter for 18 hours. They stacked up outside the light, and warships had to be brought in to patrol against submarines. Sailings were delayed and convoy schedules wrecked. That single mine was a cheap investment for the Germans.

The German minelayers had been canny enough to reap the maximum harvest from minimum effort. Another mine was detonated in the area on November 15 and still another on November 16. Then a fourth mine blew up under a sweep on November 20 and a fifth on November 21. They kept the whole command off balance even though no ships were sunk.

Where did the mines come from? That was the question. There did not seem to be any submarine activity offshore.

But that week, the steamer *Pan Crescent* reported two mysterious wakes she had passed close by, 190 miles southwest of Nantucket light.

Between November 13 and 20, the sweepers exploded more mines in Ambrose Channel near New York. It was almost reminiscent of the days when Hardegen's *U-123* was lurking in the area: German submariners swore they saw pictures taken in those early months through the periscope of Hardegen's submarine that showed the Statue of Liberty! But if the submarines came in close, they were careful not to mount attacks, just now, against the gathering defenses.

The Coast Guard cutter *Tallapoosa* made a contact on November 18, and so did *Y-605,* an auxiliary sailing picket of Commander Astor's force.

The defenders were on the attack, there was no doubt about it, and their enthusiasm was boundless. On November 23, 19 miles off Charleston light, four patrol craft and a PBY attacked a contact and brought up quantities of oil. But that was all.

The defenders were also becoming far more discerning in their knowledge of the habits of the enemy. On November 25, the Civil Air Patrol, out off the St. Johns River of Florida, reported seeing a submarine dive 15 miles off Atlantic beach. At the Eastern Sea Frontier, Lieutenant Hess, who had been following that submarine on its odyssey down the coast, estimated it was time for the U-boat to go home for supplies. And he said she would take the great circle course if he knew what she was up to. On December 3, the lieutenant estimated, the submarine would be about 100 miles south of Sable Island.

That day, the S.S. *Empire Dabcheck* was torpedoed and sunk just there.

On December 11, the ships of a slow convoy, which would be named UGS-3, assembled in New York Harbor in fog and rain. The weather was so sloppy that although the commodore of the convoy was anxious and eager to be gone, the pilot of the flagship refused to move through the Narrows, and so the convoy had to be delayed a full day in hopes that the fog would lift.

Lift it did, and on the dawning of the twelfth day of December, the ships slipped through the Narrows, down the swept channel to the lower bay, and began to form up in columns.

The ships moved about, apparently aimlessly, until they found their places, hustled and scolded by the escorts that would take them out into the Atlantic until they met the sea contingent of protectors coming from the other side.

The sky grew dark, and night fell as they were ready to move. At five o'clock that evening the convoy began moving at 9 knots.

Not particularly noticeable in the pack was the 7,000-ton tanker *C. J. Barkdull,* owned by the Standard Oil Company but operating under the Panamanian flag. She was a latecomer, substituted for another ship that had been detained at the last moment. She made her way into the line and began to move along with the others.

At two o'clock on the morning of December 13, the convoy found itself 100 miles southeast of New York, in a sea that was growing increasingly rough and unpleasant.

That augured more attention from the officers on their bridges, sleepless nights, and constant worry. But not just yet, perhaps. They were still close inshore, out of the danger zone that winter, and so many a captain left his bridge for what might be his last good sleep for nights on end.

One such was the captain of *Anthony Wayne,* the lead ship in the sixth column. The watch changed at two, and the captain, who had been on the bridge, yawned and went below to his stateroom for some sleep. The second officer had the watch.

Ten minutes went by, and then the "second" saw that his helmsman was getting off course. He shouted a corrective order, the helmsman spun the wheel, and nothing happened. The ship was suddenly heading hard to starboard, which would put her in danger of collision with the lead ship in the seventh column.

The second mate grabbed the wheel himself and tried to spin it. It would not move. It was jammed tight.

Frantically, the mate rushed into the chart room, grabbed up the sledgehammer that was standing there against the bulkhead, and did what his captain had ordered in case of emergency: He smashed the sledge down on the steel deck directly above the captain's bunk, once, twice, and a third time.

The captain was up in a moment, slipped into his shoes, and ran up to the bridge as fast as he could pelt. As he came up, *Anthony Wayne* was just describing the last arc of a complete circle. With her helm jammed over, she had come clean around and was now heading back into the column, but in such a manner as to threaten the second ship in line, the *Mt. Evans*.

On the bridge of the *Mt. Evans*, the captain saw this black shape looming out of the night and heading straight for him at a 30-degree angle off his starboard bow. He sounded the general alarm and yelled to the helmsman to put the wheel hard a-port.

Inexorably, however, the *Anthony Wayne* came down on them. The captain of *Mt. Evans* had guessed correctly, and the blow that struck was glancing and did virtually no damage to either vessel. They sheered away from one another, and *Anthony Wayne* managed to avoid the other ships in the columns and fell out of line.

But in moving to escape *Anthony Wayne*, *Mt. Evans* put herself directly in the path of the *C. J. Barkdull*. They collided with such severity that *Mt. Evans'* stem and bow were stove in, and her captain stopped engines and let her go dead in the water. He was uncertain for a moment whether to abandon ship or not. But inspection proved she was seaworthy if not now a candidate for a transatlantic voyage, and she collected an escort and limped back toward New York Harbor for repairs.

Before she left the convoy, the captain was in contact with *C. J. Barkdull,* and the *Barkdull's* bridge reported that the ship was in satisfactory condition and could go on.

But she slipped out of line, began to straggle, and soon was lost in the darkness.

Anthony Wayne corrected her steering and made her way back into position and moved with the convoy toward Gibraltar. As daylight came on the thirteenth, the commodore of the convoy was informed that *Barkdull* was missing. To him, she was just another straggler left behind to brave the U-boats in mid-Atlantic as best she could. There was nothing to be done.

C. J. Barkdull was never seen again, nor were any survivors from her crew picked up. The only clue to her fate came in a broadcast by DNB, the German radio, announcing the sinking of a lone 7,000-ton tanker near Gibraltar toward the end of the month.

When the convoy reached its destination, the captain of *Anthony Wayne* was called before a board of inquiry to account for the strange behavior of his vessel in those first hours of the voyage. He had investigated, and he knew the answer:

When he had checked the rudder, and the wheel connections, he discovered the telemotor cotter pin had been taken out of its socket and the rudder jammed over hard right. The pin was lying on the deck intact. There was no way it could have fallen out or that the rudder could have jammed by accident. Someone aboard *Anthony Wayne* had committed a deliberate act of sabotage aimed at destroying the vessel and others in the convoy.

The men of *Anthony Wayne* had that pleasant thought to live with on the long voyage home.

35

THE TALE OF THE
WANDERING YAWL

In the winter of 1942–43, Admiral Andrews was singing his old tune: "Give me ships, ships, ships." But Admiral King did just the opposite. He took away Andrews' last destroyers, leaving the American shore defended by no vessel larger than a converted yacht. Andrews would have to depend on some 300 army and navy planes and the various small craft that had been assembled during the year.

Many of them were former pleasure boats, ill fitted for the heavy weather off North America in the winter months, and so there was many a hair-raising tale of adventure on the high seas. One of them made headlines all across America.

Coast Guard picket boat *CGR-3070* was the vessel involved; her tale was as hoary with rime as that of any vessel in the fleet.

The adventure began for her and her captain, Chief Boatswain's Mate Curtis Arnall, on November 27. Arnall and his little crew of seamen were to set out that evening at 5:30 on a routine patrol of a grid area not far from Greenport, L.I., their Coast Guard base. The schedule called for the craft, a 58-foot yawl, to remain out on patrol until December 3. Then she was to return to base.

All went well enough until the weather began to kick up; and soon a nor'easter was blowing. On December 2, the storm drove the yawl off her station, and before long, the mainsail had split and blown away, and she was traveling under bare poles.

On December 3, at ten in the morning, Chief Arnall radioed for assistance. The little yawl was not built for this kind of weather, not to brave the north Atlantic at her most wicked. Madaket station on Nantucket had the message and sent out a lifeboat. Another put out from Cuttyhunk. But they did not locate the yawl, although Arnall had indicated the vessel as close off Nantucket.

A bit concerned, the Eastern Sea Frontier dispatched a larger Coast Guard vessel from Newport to give assistance.

An hour and a half later, another distress call was picked up by the Madaket station. This time, it came from some point between Nantucket Shoals and Martha's Vineyard.

Then there was silence.

The silence came because Arnall's yawl had capsized. She was overtaken by a giant wave and knocked right over. The mizzen mast was broken off short; the radio was soaked and became useless. The engines died, and water got into the fuel. She came back up, good vessel that she was, and she began to run before the wind on the bare poles.

At 2:45 that afternoon, a B-25 bomber located the yawl and circled. By Aldis lamp, the plane was in touch with the vessel, and the captain gave a hint of the story. He had a man injured and two more in need of medical attention, he said.

Twenty minutes later, the Coast Guard cutter *General Greene* was heading out from Newport to try to help.

That afternoon, a PBY found the yawl, too. For more than three hours, the patrol bomber circled the area. The pilot could not see any sign of life, nor, when the darkness came, any lights aboard the craft. He sent up a parachute flare and tried to communicate. But he had little success.

That night, three Coast Guard vessels searched the area for the yawl, two out of Nantucket and one from Martha's Vineyard. They did not see her in the storm.

On December 4, the Coast Guard shore stations picked up another distress call from the yawl. The men had gotten her auxiliary transmitter working. But though she reported she was 30 miles off Nantucket, and vessels set out to the area, she was not found. Midmorning came and passed, and a PBY was sent out. The yawl reported she was drifting east at about 3 knots.

But the pilot did not find her that morning. He searched until dusk and still did not find her.

No one knew it, but at that moment, the rescue was complicated by the fact that two sailing vessels of the picket fleet were in distress.

The second was *CGR-3027*, a 60-foot gaff-rigged schooner, which was on patrol in the same general area in which *CGR-3070* was located.

CGR-3027, under Chief Boatswain's Mate Eugene Tompane, had sailed out late on the afternoon of November 28. The next day, when the weather roughed up, she was hove to under a trysail and double reefed fore staysail. But the weather cleared, and in midmorning, she was investigating smoke on the water 2.5 miles off Montauk Point.

The rest of the day was routine, with the schooner in constant radio touch with shore stations. There was little excitement, just the routine of patrol.

The weather was changeable, but they could tell that a storm was blowing. On December 2, they ran through heavy wind, lightning, and rain until dawn, and then around nine o'clock in the morning the wind rose to a gale.

They rode it out until just after one o'clock on the afternoon of December 3 (the day that *CGR-3070* fell into trouble), and then the high seas began sweeping over the deck. A wave carried away the ventilator and hatch cover. The vessel began taking water below, and soon the radio was drenched. The men were soaked; there was not a dry inch aboard the schooner. The pumps could not handle the load, and the water began gaining on them.

Fifteen minutes later, they sent a distress call in the clear English and warned that it might be their last, for the radio was fading fast.

Luckily, the men had been issued good foul-weather gear and were wearing it. So they survived, although some were very seasick, and all were cold and miserable.

On December 4, the Coast Guard cutter *General Greene*, which had been sent out to search for the yawl, found the schooner and stood by her. It was too rough that afternoon to rig a tow, but by blinker and radio, the captain of the cutter informed the schooner that he would tow her the next day.

The night passed. Tompane and his men had plenty of food, at least: crackers, prunes and raisins, and even apples and oranges. They also had fruit juices, so they suffered neither from hunger nor thirst as they waited out the night.

At daylight, the weather seemed to have abated a little, so *General Greene* put a line aboard the schooner and took her in tow. The tow was a great strain; it damaged the schooner more than the storm had done earlier, but in 40 hours, they were safe in Newport Harbor, and after a night in the hospital, the men of the crew were fit for duty once more. Meanwhile, the yawl was still out there, in distress.

One problem, which did not come to light until later, was that several aircraft that had reported sighting the yawl had actually seen the schooner, so the positions reported did not jibe.

On December 4, at one o'clock in the afternoon, the British warship H.M.S. *Caldwell* came across the yawl in a driving snowstorm and stood by while the captain of the escort vessel decided what he might do to help.

At four o'clock in the afternoon, he considered trying to take the crew off the yawl but had to give up the attempts as too risky in the high seas. He did manage to get a line over and took her in tow. He was heading for Halifax, and he radioed the shore stations that he had the yawl and that she had lost her sail and was leaking. Her engine was out of order, and she had "one injured rating aboard."

In spite of the heavy seas, for five hours the tow succeeded; then in one wrench, the hawser parted, and the yawl was adrift once more in the storm.

Two hours later, *Caldwell* had lost her in the darkness and the wind and the rain. Headquarters at Halifax wanted *Caldwell* to resume her journey. There were more important matters at stake than the little patrol craft.

Early on December 5, U.S.S. *Captor* joined the search party, and no fewer than 11 planes were out looking for the yawl.

Caldwell continued to search, and so did *Captor*.

For a time, the tense little group in Operations at Church Street believed all was well; the juxtaposition of messages indicated that *Caldwell* had the crew of the yawl safely aboard.

But when queried, the British ship reported that they had no one aboard. And, they said, the end of the tow-rope hawser appeared to have been cut loose.

All day long, they searched without finding the little cork that bobbed in the threatening gray seas of the northeast storm. That night, *Caldwell* was summoned officially back to Halifax for other duties; there was no more time to be lost from convoy work for a sea rescue of a handful of men.

On December 6, in response to calls from *Captor,* planes from Halifax and planes from Massachusetts and Long Island bases searched the seas off Nantucket, trying to find the stricken yawl.

Every hour or two, *Captor* gave her position to guide the searchers. The yawl was called up time and again. There was no answer.

Admiral Andrews now told Admiral King of the plight of the yawl and asked that all shipping be notified. It was a desperate measure, and no one had much hope that it would produce any results.

As *Caldwell* moved away toward Halifax, other ships were called by Admiral Andrews to come and help. *PC-556* was assigned, and Andrews asked for detachment of *PC-553* from a convoy to help out.

Her last estimated position was 41°20′ N and 63°40′ W, and she was believed to be drifting eastward at three miles an hour.

Somewhere out there were a petty officer and eight men, three of them reportedly injured, and if humanly possible, Admiral Andrews wanted them back from the sea.

Just after midnight, on December 7, the captain of *Captor* sent a discouraging message to Church Street. He had searched the area where she ought to be and had found nothing. But drift had changed to southeastward in the storm, and she might have gone elsewhere. What he was concerned about was her ability to live in this weather.

"Some doubts felt as to her ability to live through the rough seas and heavy squall in the last two days, especially if weakened while in tow."

Thus, another day passed, with *Captor* leading the search, calling on planes and patrol craft, and directing them to search areas and then to rendezvous with her later in the day.

But December 7, the anniversary of the beginning of the war, passed without positive result. The wind continued to howl across the sea, and the dire fears of the captain of *Captor* seemed to communicate themselves to the other searchers. The yawl was such a little vessel. How could she survive so long in such weather? Chief Tompane, safe ashore in Newport, found it hard to believe that his own craft had survived even two days of such buffeting, and she was a foot longer and considerably roomier than the yawl.

At noon, on December 8, it seemed a lost cause. That night, *Captor* and *PC-553* would have to head back for New York for fuel and supplies.

At 3:30 that afternoon, *Captor* told Admiral Andrews it was probably a lost cause: "Considering all factors it is our opinion chances yawl afloat remote."

But Admiral Andrews would not give up.

On December 9, Madaket station had a garbled message signed *WC-145*, the yawl's call sign. Block Island intercepted the same message and got it whole.

"Conditions favorable. Three men injured."

That was all. Efforts to get her position, to raise her again, were unsuccessful.

But the yawl was still out there; she was afloat, and men were living aboard her. That was enough. The search would continue.

The coastal picket *CGR-72*, on patrol out of Block Island, was ordered to try to make contact. Two shore stations were told to send out trucks to take bearings on the radio broadcasts. Twenty minutes later, another broadcast came in from the yawl almost insouciant in tone: "Satisfactory condition. Three men injured. That is all."

The optimism in the message veiled an important truth: Just then, *CGR-3070* lost the use of her radio. It was the last message she would send.

But that message aroused the shore defenders to new efforts. Lakehurst Naval Air Station was alerted to stand by with first-aid kits and food and water packets. Halifax and Newport were told that the yawl was still out there, that she might be in their seas.

No one really knew.

At 10:45 that morning, Lieutenant (jg.) Watson of *VP-31* at Quonset saw a black yawl under power and several men on deck. They waved. They did not seem to be lost or concerned, but he reported the vessel, anyhow. It was not *CGR-3070*.

The searchers began to lose hope again. The validity of that message of the morning was questioned. Her base had given her up as lost on December 3; how could she have possibly survived this storm was the question many were asking.

The Coast Guard said she was gone. Presumed lost were the sad words. But the radio shore stations were instructed to listen that evening, listen as carefully as they had ever listened.

All radio units were to remain silent at eight o'clock that night, and that meant New Moriches and Shinnecock, Shark River, and Fire Island, Fisher's Island, Greenport, Montauk, Rockaway, and New London.

They would listen.

Meanwhile, the war went on. Admiral Andrews ordered *Captor* to search until dark, then to return to Boston. *PC-553* would go back to New York.

At eight o'clock, radio interference made it impossible to hear if the yawl was sending. The listening was extended until nine o'clock.

There was no call that night.

On the morning of December 10 *PC-553* was continuing to search. That day, the call was sent out again, almost pleadingly: "*CGR-3070*: All stations East Coast will keep silent and listen for you to make a report at 2200-2215 tonight. . . ."

And the search continued all day long.

PC-553 announced that late in the afternoon she would head home, but U.S.S. *Sagamore* was called in to help from New London.

All day long, navy planes searched, when they could see through the clouds, scouring the area (they believed) around Nantucket and eastward.

They found nothing again that day.

On December 11, *Sagamore* came up, new to the search, new with hope. She searched from Nantucket Buoy to the north and then around the area. "Assume radio on *WC-145* out of commission since she is unheard."

There, that was not giving up. It was is if the search were beginning all over again.

For six hours, the navy planes were out, half a dozen of them under Lieutenant West, of VS3D-1 at Quonset, flying formation, 5 miles apart in a scouting line, at 1,000 feet of altitude. They spotted two two-masted vessels, but they identified themselves: the *Crawly* and the *Princess Alexandria Marie*.

On December 12, the search continued. *PC-553* had to leave for port, but *Sagamore* stayed on. The army bombers flew search missions, and so did the navy.

They found nothing.

On December 13, other matters began to interfere. The U.S.S. *General George Goethals,* disabled, was left behind by convoy UGF-3, and an escort had to be sent to her assistance.

But from this Admiral Andrews had a gleam of information: Convoy UGF-3 had passed the yawl on its way out, and a destroyer escort had communicated with her by blinker.

"Do you want to be taken aboard?" the destroyer asked.

"Yes," said the yawl.

But it was impossible. Thirty-foot waves made it so.

The yawl said she needed food and water. The destroyer dropped over two sealed drums, containing both, and then went on her way. The war called. She could not stop.

Chief Arnall could see the drums bobbing in the heavy sea, so near, so far, so impossible to pick up. They tried, but they could not beat into the wind to get windward of them, and then darkness set in. The drums were lost forever.

That information was delayed in reaching Admiral Andrews; the destroyer involved did not break radio silence for several hours.

The lagging search was immediately revived.

That night, as the S.S. *Irish Elm* passed what she thought was a derelict two-masted schooner at 37°27′ N, 64°14′ W. The message went to the Federal Communications Commission shore station and was transmitted to Admiral Andrews at Church Street.

This meant the yawl had now drifted to a point 568 miles from Cape Henry, 307 miles north of Bermuda.

What did she look like? Admiral Andrews asked *Irish Elm*.

She had a high mainmast, a small mizzen, she was gray, and she had a deckhouse aft.

That description matched the yawl.

Shortly before noon that day, Admiral Andrews asked the naval operating base at Bermuda to make an air search in the area designated by *Irish Elm*. The ship could do nothing to help further than she had; the weather was too stormy to board the "derelict."

But other naval authority intercepted the messages. Boston suggested that the derelict might be indeed just that, the *CGR-2522*, a sailing vessel that ran aground at Truro, Massachusetts, on December 2. The crew was taken off, whereupon the boat worked herself loose and "took off." She had not been seen since.

And sure enough, when the weather cleared enough for a fly-over, Bermuda was satisfied that the derelict was indeed *CGR-2522*.

So the mystery of the whereabouts of *CGR-3070* continued and grew more upsetting hour by hour. It was also expensive, this search, in terms of vessels and aircraft used and man hours spent. Had this incident occurred at the height of the offshore submarine menace, it is doubtful if nine men on a little yawl would have had so much attention.

On December 15, the search was renewed with all the vigor the command possessed. For the long-delayed message from the escorts accompanying UGF-3 came in when the destroyer *Parker*, sent back from UGF-3 to assist the limping *Goethals*, came to Ambrose light and risked breaking radio silence.

At five o'clock on the morning of December 15, Admiral Andrews had the forces in motion.

Six PBY patrol bombers and three B-17s were assigned to search in a pattern that should take them across the area where the yawl had last been seen two days before, and in a circle to account for drift and currents.

Atlantic Fleet entered the picture, telling the captain of *Parker* to assist in the rescue if it were possible to do so. That was a remarkable gesture by the usually stiff-necked fleet.

The U.S.S. *Overton* was dispatched at noon to find that position reported by the convoy and circle it in the hope of discovering the yawl.

By late afternoon, it seemed that the rescuers might have a break. The planes were out, in a scouting line, heading out from Nantucket, sweeping around, and then toward Montauk. The visibility was 6–12 miles, with scattered clouds at 2,000 feet. The sea had quieted, so that they referred to it as "moderate."

The problem had been complicated, however, for if the yawl was where she was supposed to be, she was in danger of collision with ships plying the shipping lanes. That evening, as darkness settled down over the chill waters of the North Atlantic, Andrews' operations office warned the *Esso Gettysburg* in that vicinity, that the yawl might drift into her track and threaten a collision.

By the morning of the sixteenth, even Admiral Andrews and his staff were beginning to lose heart. The yawl had been missing for 13 days, and by rights she should not have had aboard enough food for more than a week. She was, after all, near the end of her patrol when she fell afoul of the storm. If the vessel were still afloat, the men might have perished from exposure or weakness.

The search continued on the morning of the sixteenth, but the whole command was now skeptical. The night of December 13–14 had been one of the hardest of the winter, with even big liners and cargo ships straggling in the heavy seas. How could the little yawl have survived was again the question asked.

Andrews and the staff did not believe she had.

The messages continued to go out; the destroyer *Dickerson,* in the south, was told to look for her, and planes were sent from as far away as Elizabeth City to search the offshore waters, but the cause looked more doubtful every hour.

On the morning of December 17, the planes were searching once more. Conditions were very rough; a flight of three B-17s was supposed to begin the search at eight in the morning, but only two of them got off, and not until 10:15 because of serious icing on the wings.

Cherry Point reported that one PBT had to return to base because of wind, squalls, and fog. A little later, one of the B-17s that did get off the ground had to return, reporting the fog too dense to find anything at all on the water.

But that second B-17, heading toward 36° N, 69° W, found the weather a little better. The pilot, Lieutenant Lecompe, searched for four hours. At 2:55 that afternoon, coming out of the clouds, he looked down, and there below was the yawl, gray, her mizzen gone, flying a jib only. Three men were on deck, and they waved frantically to the circling B-17.

Lieutenant Lecompte continued to circle and dropped an emergency kit. He dropped supplies by parachute 150 feet ahead of the yawl. Then he saw the yawl raise her mainsail, reverse course for five minutes, and lower the mainsail and resume the course. He decided that the men had found and picked up the supplies.

He came in low and saw that the Stars and Stripes was flying on the gaff, upside down. Small wonder!

He tried to make radio contact. His radio operator had no luck at all.

He radioed base, but that message was never received. He stayed with the yawl for four hours, waiting for assistance and support that never came. Then he headed back for Langley, arriving hours late, as the field was alerted that he might be lost at sea. Only then did the word get out that he had seen the yawl.

As for the men of the sailing craft, their luck had not been as good as Lecompte believed. They had picked up the canvas bag with the supplies in it, only to discover the bag had broken on impact with the sea, and all the contents had been lost.

As the plane was circling, the men of the crew blinked

their Aldis lamp and tried to signal their plight, but the B-17 never replied. It just kept circling until darkness began to set in, and then the bomber flew away.

That night, Andrews sent messages to Cherry Point, Langley Field, and Elizabeth City, asking them to get planes up in the morning to search the area described by Lecompte. At last, they seemed to be getting somewhere.

The planes took off the next morning. Three B-17s from Langley searched for five hours, in rough air and rain and haze, with wind at 30 knots, and found nothing.

One PBY from Elizabeth City had a report almost the twin of Langley's. Another from Cherry Point also found nothing, although it remained out until dark.

Failure once more.

Andrews and his staff plotted the sightings of the yawl and came to the conclusion that she was offshore, trying to beat her way against unfavorable winds to the coast, with a damaged engine and quite probably damaged sails on her one sound mast.

The planes were out again on December 19, in cloudy and stormy weather. They found nothing.

The story on the twentieth was the same.

And the twenty-first.

On the evening of the twenty-second, Coast Guard cutter 462, on routine patrol, spotted the yawl just before dark. She told her to heave to for the night because she was nearing a minefield. Then a squall arose; the cutter lost the sailing ship in the rain and wind and did not see her again. She seemed as elusive as any ghost that ever sailed the waters off Patagonia, in the heyday of the dreaded Horn.

But at midnight, miraculously, the yawl appeared out of the murk, and the cutter was alongside her. They were near Buoy 6, off Ocracoke Inlet, North Carolina. The yawl, in 20 days, had sailed and drifted that far south of Nantucket.

All was well. She seemed in good enough condition, but the men were gesturing for supplies. Ocracoke base dispatched a motor lifeboat with a doctor and supplies aboard. The base also sent CGC-470 to help the other cutter, to take the yawl in tow and bring her in.

As the night wore on, the weather roughed up once

again, the seas began to run heavy, and the yawl tossed like a cork. One moment, she was alongside the cutter, the next she was gone, and when daylight dawned, she had quite disappeared.

She had been blown many more miles to the south.

At dawn, the planes were out once more, three navy planes and two blimps. They searched all morning long without result. But then, at 2:38 that afternoon, one of the blimps located *CGR-3070*, now 23 miles from Cape Hatteras.

Soon a plane from Cherry Point joined the blimp. The yawl was found again. This time, there was one difference with the "discoveries" of the past. The shore bases were in communication with the blimp and the A-29 plane that circled it. It was daylight. Visibility was good.

The plane dropped an emergency kit and saw it picked up. The pilot watched the half-dozen men on deck all gesturing wildly for food and drink.

In half an hour, five more planes arrived on the scene, one of them a navy plane with pontoons that would let it sit down on the water.

But by this time, two Coast Guard patrol boats were on their way to the scene and not far off.

The danger was not yet over. One plane noted that the yawl was moving dangerously close to the mine fields that had claimed *Mowinckle* and *Chilore* not so long before. The pilot wig-wagged and finally managed to get the yawl to change course and jibe about as the other plane led the two surface vessels to the scene.

Shortly after four o'clock in the afternoon, the cutters arrived, and the men of the yawl were taken off the sailing vessel, aboard *CGC-470*, and rushed to Ocracoke, where they arrived at eleven o'clock that night.

From Ocracoke, air transport was arranged to Elizabeth City, after they had been looked over by a doctor and pronounced fit for travel. A few hours rest, some hot food, and they were flown to New York, arriving at Admiral Andrews' headquarters on Church Street at 4:30 in the afternoon.

Then the press was called in, and the story was told of the remarkable odyssey of the yawl and the brave men who sailed her, sought her, and found her on the bosom of the cruel winter sea. And then, as darkness fell, the men were whisked away once again, this time sent to their homes for Christmas. It was a story to gladden the heart of a nation on a wartime Christmas Eve.

36

THE DAY THEY CLOSED
THE PORT OF NEW YORK

The months slipped by.

In January, the East Coast was plagued by storms but not by U-boats. The ardent searchers declared they had sighted 16 enemy submarines and had made 30 sound contacts with U-boats and 20 attacks, but the wise heads back on Church Street knew all this was myth. The tracking stations and other intelligence indicated that Admiral Doenitz's U-boats were all occupied elsewhere.

Church Street had other worries. One of them was the growing danger that merchant ships and warships ran in the crowded confines of New York Harbor. The port facilities were strained almost beyond belief. The proof of it was the number of collisions: 123 between September 1, 1942, and February 1, 1943. That was nearly a collision a day. Most of them were minor, hardly worth reporting, some of the captains said, but that they continued to happen was a constant worry to Admiral Andrews. By February, it became a matter of such import that it drew the attention of no fewer than five naval commands, including that of the commander in chief, Admiral King.

No one seemed able to agree on a sure-fire method of controlling ship movements so as to eliminate collisions.

The problem was one of plentitude: too many ships moving in these waters at the same time, coming and loading the wherewithal of war, which would defeat Hitler and send his U-boats to the bottom of the sea forever.

So while there were no submarines to menace navigators in these months of respite, there was danger a-plenty, and the worst danger of all was brought home to Admiral Andrews and his staff one night in March.

245

On the morning of March 26, the converted yacht that was *CG-5006* broke down in New York Harbor.

When Chief Boatswain's Mate Beal, her captain, began to investigate, he discovered that the 85-foot yacht had a clogged fuel line. It was as simple as that, and shortly after noon, the difficulty was corrected, and *CG-5006* was under way again, on patrol.

At four o'clock on the morning of March 27, Beal and four men of the crew were in the wheel house, and six others were below asleep in their bunks. A flash split the air, the yacht blew completely apart, and the five found themselves struggling in the water. There was no sign at all of their vessel or of their comrades. Only bits of flotsam floated about them.

The five managed to clutch on to one fair-sized piece of wood that came up from what was left of the yacht. But it was a cold night, they were suffering from shock and soon enough from exposure, and holding on was difficult.

One by one, the men began to slip off, to sleep, to lose their grips on the piece of wood, and to quietly disappear. By dawn, three were gone; only Chief Beal and one other man were alive.

As the day brightened, the other man lost his strength, and Beal watched him as he weakened. Then, one moment he was there, and the next he was dead.

Just before 10:30, Chief Beal was rescued; the freighter *Charles B. Aycock* came by, saw a man in the water clinging to a piece of wreckage, and stopped to pick him up. The sailors also picked up one body, but that was all.

The master of *Charles B. Aycock* reported the disaster to Staten Island shore station, and within an hour, the Coast Guard cutter *Kimball,* the patrol craft *SC-683,* and the Blimp *K-3* had hurried to the scene of the disaster to help with rescue. There was no one to rescue. They did recover three bodies the next day.

At Church Street, Admiral Andrews and his staff wondered. What could have caused the destruction of the converted yacht so totally?

The answer, of course, was a mine.

If there were mines in the channel and in New York Harbor, the potential for destruction was frightening. Suppose a munitions ship hit one; the triggering of explosions could conceivably destroy the entire port and set the war effort back months, if not years.

The admiral, the port director, the commander of the naval district, were all worried. Should they close the port of New York to traffic while they investigated? That decision could be taken only most reluctantly because to close New York even for 24 hours was to endanger the flow of material and men to Europe.

They decided to wait.

While they waited, the ships continued to move in and out of the Narrows, some coming to be loaded, some leaving in convoy or in lonely watchfulness, to travel to their secret destinations.

On the morning of March 29, the 10,000-ton *Esso Manhattan* sailed through the Narrows, heading out alone for Curacao. She moved southward and eastward, steadily at 14 knots. Then, at 12:05, the men aboard her felt a shudder, and she broke clean in half, as though a cleaver had sliced through her. There was no sound, no explosion. It was eerie, but she was cut in half, and the halves were pulling away from each other.

Then the steam pipes burst, and the ship was shrouded in steam, then in smoke, as fire broke out.

The captain gave the order to abandon ship, and the men took to the boats and the water.

Luckily for them all, the Coast Guard cutter *Kimball* was in the area, for this disaster occurred not 6 miles from the spot where the converted yacht had exploded two days before. *Kimball* had just been released by Eastern Defense Command from her search-and-rescue efforts in behalf of the missing men. She came up in a hurry and picked up the 25 men of the gun crew and the 48 crewmen of the tanker. Not a life was lost. In fact, the ship was not even lost, for the two halves were rescued by tugs, towed to New Jersey yards, and the process of rebuilding was begun.

But what had happened?

This second disaster in three days made it imperative that the port be closed. And so New York Harbor was shut down; no ships went in, no ships went out, while the mine sweepers tested the channel and the water about the channel, and the investigators came out to investigate.

New York's war stood still then for more than 24 hours.

It was far worse a jam-up than had been occasioned by the mine exploded off Ambrose light. The authorities were seriously worried that they had been attacked by some fiendish weapon devised by the Germans.

The cost of the closing of New York to the war effort was so immense that no one ever tried to ascertain it.

37

THE SECOND COMING OF
ADMIRAL DOENITZ

Admiral Andrews and his staff sensed that they were in for a new round of trouble. Doenitz was coming back to the American coast.

The German admiral had persuaded Hitler to let him make another attempt to stop Britain's supply by attacking at the source. On April 23, a U-boat torpedoed a ship 540 miles east of Jacksonville. That was a long way offshore, still out in the middle of the Atlantic, but it was clear that the sea war had changed. It triggered a reaction at 90 Church Street. Doenitz was up to something.

Three days after that sinking, the tracking section reported a submarine in the Caribbean, apparently moving toward the windward passage. That would bear watching. Was it the same U-boat?

No. Wait a minute. A navy blimp that day sighted a submarine on the surface, 120 miles out at sea, northeast of Jacksonville. The blimp attacked with three depth charges but could not even claim to have damaged the U-boat.

In the earlier days, Admiral Andrews and his staff might have questioned the report. Was it really a U-boat? But with the development of the antisubmarine-warfare sections, they had gained confidence in the reporting of the scouting forces and felt that in six months vast improvement had been made.

The first blimp's report was given substance next day when a second blimp saw a submarine in that same general area and attacked with eight depth charges. Once again, the blimp made the most modest of claims. And that day a plane from the base at Argentia in Newfoundland reported sighting a U-boat 180 miles east of Cape Sable Island. The plane attacked, the U-boat went down, and the pilot claimed the sinking of one submarine.

Perhaps.

What was important, more important than a claim of that nature, was the knowledge that so much activity must reveal purpose: Doenitz was bringing the war back to the American shore.

April 29 dawned with the really bad news: An American patrol plane flying out of Bermuda sighted ten submarines, and one much larger one that Andrews and his staff knew must be a "Milch cow." They were lying on the surface, like a school of killer whales, not more than 400 miles east of Bermuda.

There lay trouble for certain!

As the month opened, then, Admiral Andrews and the whole corps of defenders of the shore were greeted by what his report would call "rude shock." They had been planning, with Admiral King, a reduction and consolidation of the Eastern Sea Frontier. It had been nine months since a ship had been sunk close offshore, and the number of trained air and sea crews capable of antisubmarine warfare could very well be used in the mid-Atlantic and on the coast of Africa, where submarine activity was intense.

The Americans were improving antisubmarine warfare in every way. For example, in February, convoy ON-16 had been attacked by wolf packs between February 21 and 25 and had lost 16 ships. But three months later, when ONS-5 was attacked on May 4 and 5, the story differed. To be sure, 12 ships were lost, but the escorts and planes accounted for the sinking of 4 U-boats without question, and the serious damaging or sinking of 9 or 10 others. The defenders were learning their job.

They were needed out there in the mid-Atlantic, and the plan had been made to send them. But on May 1, the Germans were back again offshore.

A U-boat was located somewhere between Savannah and Cape Hatteras, the tracking office said. And so planes were out immediately to search.

On May 3, a storm stopped air operations. It did not prevent NK-538, a convoy of 11 merchant ships and 4 escorts, from moving along the 100-fathom curve near

Hatteras. Nor did it prevent NG-359 from moving the other direction a few miles away.

Late on the afternoon of May 3, the army transport *Oneida* was finding the going very difficult with NG-359 because of the storm.

She was about 80 miles off Norfolk when the situation grew really serious just before midnight. She was leaking badly, and the stern was settling a little. Shortly after midnight, the captain radioed that he was dropping out of the convoy altogether and planning to try to make the beach before his ship sank under him.

The shaft alley was flooded, and the engine room was flooding fast.

They kept going, heading toward shore, until 2:30 on the morning of May 4, when the captain decided they would not make it after all and ordered his men to abandon ship.

As they left the ship, he heard two thuds, and men on the seaward side saw a light 10 feet above the water not far away. Members of the ship's gun crew said they also heard gunfire, but there was so much confusion in the abandonment of the sinking vessel that no one paid any attention. The ship was going to go down, anyhow.

Fifteen minutes later, with all men off and safe but one, the ship sank. She may have been the first victim of the Germans off the American shore in 1943. No one would ever really know (unless scuba divers of a future generation investigate), for the *Oneida* sank as her captain knew she would and went down in deep water.

In the other convoy, NK-538, the 7,000-ton tanker *Panama* was having her troubles, too. She had been bedeviled by engine trouble all during the trip. Now she was heading down from Norfolk to Louisiana. She could not keep up, and she was soon left behind by the convoy.

At eight o'clock on the morning of May 4, an army bomber B-25 flew over and circled her. The pilot saw a wake streaking toward the ship's side, but he was too far away to do anything about it except watch.

The seven lookouts aboard the tanker saw nothing. The first they knew of any danger was when a torpedo struck with a smashing blow in the port side, drove into the engine room, blew up, wrecked the whole engine room, killing two men, and knocking out the whole ship's radio system.

The gun crew manned the guns, but there was nothing at which they could shoot. They scanned the horizon. They saw no traces of a submarine. The U-boat captains used different techniques those days, in the presence of that constant overflight of bombers and patrol planes. The submarine was staying down below and coming up only occasionally for a quick periscope look.

Ten minutes went by. The ship was rocked by another torpedo, this one striking amidships.

The captain ordered the men off, and they went. Some leaped from the decks. Most managed to remain and get out the three lifeboats; then they picked up their impetuous companions. All were soon in the boats, pulling away from the sinking wreck.

Another sinking. More death offshore. It was reminiscent of the year before when Doenitz's captains had come to the "happy hunting grounds," and the American defenses had been totally unable to stop them.

But 1943 was a different year, as the commander of the U-boat soon discovered. The B-25 radioed the report of the sinking and almost immediately was joined by two navy OS2Us and one patrol boat, *SC 664*.

When the report reached Admiral Andrews' office, he ordered out a killer group. Two 83-foot Coast Guard cutters with depth charges set out from Morehead City. They were joined by two patrol boats, and overhead, two B-25s, 10 OS2Us, and two blimps coming from Elizabeth City.

They searched, they attacked, but they did not claim to have sunk the submarine.

At Church Street, the submarine trackers announced that it was probable the U-boat would now go to the bottom and lie doggo for at least 48 hours, given so much activity in the hunt for her.

Apparently, that is what happened. For it was not until the morning of May 6, just after dawn, that a PBM, flying out of Norfolk, saw a periscope in that area, 65 miles east of Cape Lookout.

A swarm of aircraft, 31 planes in all, was dispatched along with a blimp and a destroyer and two patrol boats. Just before five o'clock in the evening, part of this contingent surprised a U-boat, obviously the same one, just 30 miles north of its morning position. Two of the planes attacked, with a ferocity and accuracy that the Germans had certainly not experienced the year before. The depth charges were put in the right places and with the right settings, and when the attacks were over, bubbles, oil, and debris indicated that the submarine had been damaged. The defenders never claimed any more than that.

On May 8, a B-18 from Langley Field had a contact and stayed with the submarine for two hours but did not manage to sink it. On May 13, there was another.

The patrol craft and other vessels were getting new weapons at this time for use against submarines, including the antisubmarine projector, which fired Mark 20 projectiles and was more commonly known as the "hedgehog."

Patrol boat *PC-552* was on escort duty on the fifteenth of May when she picked up a contact at eleven o'clock at night. She made a run and fired eight Mark 20 projectiles, one of them set to explode at 240 feet. The submarine had dived deep, which she could afford to do because she had 1,600 fathoms of water under her keel.

And apparently that deep-set charge was effective, for seven minutes after it went off, there came another explosion deep under water, so heavy that it knocked out the engine-room lights aboard the *PC-552* and was heard by other escorts 7 miles away.

This one went down as a "probable" in the navy book.

The U-boats were back, no doubt about it. But they were not happy with what they found this time.

On May 19, the Canadian barkentine *Angeles* was sunk by gunfire; it must have been a registration of the U-boat commander's frustration at finding other ships so well protected that he would waste time and effort on a sailing ship.

For this year, whenever a submarine seemed to raise its periscope, there were a flock of planes or a handful of escorts waiting right there.

On May 22, an army plane out of Newfoundland attacked a submarine on the surface and sank it. Almost immediately, the destroyer HMSC *St. Laurent* was on hand to pick up survivors.

On May 28, another submarine was spotted by a B-24 from Langley, on the surface at 9:25. It attacked, and another B-24 attacked, and they made the water spout oil for 30 minutes. However, old hands knew now that the Germans had ways of releasing oil under water to fool the escorts and search planes. So no one made any rash claims.

The end of the month came, and the plotting office of Admiral Andrews' command estimated that there was a submarine off Georgia, one off Hatteras, and one on the convoy lane off Cape May. But every one was having a hard time of it. That was the big difference that had taken place offshore in just a single year.

38
THE MIRACLES OF THE SEA

Some stories of the war at sea verged on the miraculous.

The Steamer *Moldanger* went to sea that summer and disappeared. She had been traveling alone, unwisely, and had been torpedoed 360 miles off Norfolk. The chances of survival for her crew were not very good: Nobody knew she was gone; the winds and currents in that area did not make it easy to make the North American continent. And yet, ten days after the sinking, HMS *Buctouche,* traveling across an unlikely bit of water to join an escort force, ran across a lifeboat and rescued 15 men. They reported six other men afloat in a dory and nine more on two rafts.

Admiral Andrews put out the word to every vessel the whole length of the American continent, and the search began.

Eighteen days after the sinking, an army bomber sighted the dory and its six survivors 100 miles east of Atlantic City. A blimp was soon on the scene, and two patrol craft came to pick up the nearly dead men.

But there was not word of the fate of the others until August 14, 47 days after the sinking, when the steamer *Washington Express,* again by chance, sighted two rafts and saved the nine men aboard them.

Thus, quite by accident, those men who had survived the torpedoing and the initial disaster of the sinking were preserved from the sea.

One of the problems in the early days was the lack of facilities, ships, and personnel to do the job that had to be done to assure any system that could help men thrown into the sea with so little to sustain them. In those days, Comdr. E. J. Moran was the "rescue officer," but the term referred to the ancient past of the navy. Rescue, in this sense, meant he was in charge of the rescue tugs, whose prewar duty had been to succor ships gone aground or in trouble at sea due to engine failure or other more or less natural causes.

Rescue in the war meant something entirely different.

It was late in April 1942 before Admiral Andrews was able to spare a young Lt. (jg.) A. E. Wolf and make him responsible for recording all sinkings and then the correlations of those records with rafts and boats reported by the searching planes and ships.

Thus, the command's performance and knowledge of men lost at sea offshore began to improve, slowly but steadily. It still left much to be desired, as the case of S.S. *Maiden Creek* in January 1943 had shown. (After *Maiden Creek* went down, the first lifeboat, carrying 31 survivors, was picked up in three days. But the second boat, carrying 23 survivors, was not found and drifted in the winter storm. Two more days went by, and when it was found, capsized and waterlogged, a single body was lashed inside.)

Timing, then, was everything in the saving of lives of the men cast adrift offshore. And by the spring of 1943, everyone concerned with defense knew it and was responsive to it. They had a little more time now, more attention to give to saving lives that once would have been forfeited to the sea.

And yet, even as the war offshore turned about, and the beseiged became as much hunters as hunted, there was still the cold, cruel sea to face.

Late in April, the *Rebecca R. Douglas,* a sailing ship owned by the Douglas Navigation Company of New York, headed out to sea. Perhaps she ought not to have gone at all. She was 50 years old, her timbers were ancient, and her whole 175 feet creaked and moaned as she was towed by tugs out to Nantucket lightship, where Captain Walter Wrightson ordered the crew to cast off her lines. She headed south for Brazil.

But within a matter of hours, a brisk wind and heavy sea had taken their toll. She began to take water up forward, and then the leakage spread beyond the ability of the pumps to handle it.

A plane came over, but the captain still had hopes that she would somehow seal her own leaks; sailing ships had done it before.

It was not to be. On the twenty-eighth, she was taking water so steadily that the captain gave orders to abandon ship. The first mate and two others climbed down into the dory, and the master and three others got into the 22-foot steel lifeboat. They cast off and tied the craft together. It was about eight o'clock at night.

During the night, the *Rebecca R. Douglas* sank, and next morning, when a B-25 medium bomber from Fort Dix passed over, the pilot was puzzled by the debris in the water. But he saw no boats, no men. That night, another B-25 flew by and sighted a red flare but nothing else.

The presence of these indications led the rescue officer of the Eastern Sea Frontier to presume that there was some reason for them. No one knew the whereabouts of every ship that passed by the North American shore. For example, a Canadian vessel, traveling alone, would have no particular reason to make her presence known to Americans.

And so it would not be surprising if what the B-25s had seen was the result of a sinking. That meant there might be men out there in the water somewhere.

On April 30, the word was out to the patrol craft to keep a sharp eye, and at 8:55 that morning, one B-25 spotted what its pilot called a "life raft." (Actually, it was the two boats lashed together.)

Then the hunt was on:

From Wildwood, New Jersey, Admiral Andrews dispatched the U.S.S. *Alabaster,* a yacht, and the *SC-715.* The destroyer *Greer* was called to help, and the S.S. *Mounta Aetna,* a freighter in the area, was pressed into service. So was the tug *Rescue* of New York. Their movement was watched by planes overhead.

But even as the vessels hurried toward the coordinates given by the sighting bomber in its report, the sea began to change. The wind struck up, and the waves grew high, and the two boats were broken apart when the lashing ripped asunder. They drifted then, swiftly, but were caught in different swirls and eddies until they were out of sight of one another.

The vessels searched, covered the area, once and twice, and broadened their circle. But they found nothing.

On May 2, when the weather cleared, the planes were out again, and the ships, and a blimp came along. The blimp had the luck and sighted the dory with two men in it. In a matter of hours, the men in the dory were rescued, two only, because the mate had become ill on the second night, began mumbling unintelligibly, and had simply slipped over the side into the water and was gone.

As for Captain Wrightson and the other three, they were traced, too, as well as men could be traced in the sea.

The skipper, said the rescued men from the dory, had announced, as they broke loose from one another, that he was going to raise sail in the lifeboat and head for shore. So the search took that pattern, and it was not long before a plane sighted an overturned steel lifeboat. It was the boat, said the rescued men. Unmistakeable.

And so Captain Walter Wrightson was found at last, lashed to the tiller, but he was long dead. Even the resources of an eager and alert group of defenders of the shore could not save a man from his fate, and Captain Wrightson had sealed his own when he took the battered old sailing ship out to sea.

39

THE TENTH FLEET

For many months Admiral Andrews and his staff had tried to secure establishment of a single command over all anti-submarine warfare. They wanted the command for themselves, of course.

Captain Thomas R. Kurtz, chief of staff of the Eastern Sea Frontier, suggested it to Washington. Admiral King said no. Yet, from one of King's subordinates, Kurtz had a glimmer of hope: When King felt the Atlantic was under control, he would be receptive to the idea.

In the spring of 1943, King decided the time had come. There was only one problem: King put himself in command.

Tenth Fleet was created to extend the war at sea beyond the dreams of Andrews and the nightmares of Doenitz. It would employ ships, aircraft, and even aircraft carriers. The blank spot in the mid-Atlantic, where patrol bombers came to the end of their range from either side, was to be eliminated by auxiliary carriers. The convoys would have "eyes" all the way.

The tentative experiments with hunter-killer groups off the coast had proved successful. Pilots were learning to drop depth charges properly. Surface vessels had improved their procedures for attack. There was some difficulty because army planes and navy ships were not under a single command, and this is what King proposed to rectify in his sweeping change.

One of the most important developments that must be produced and used in strength was the new method of delivering depth charges. The British had invented the "hedgehog," a device that enabled them to throw depth charges ahead of an escort vessel. In the first years of war, one grave disadvantage had always been the need for a destroyer or patrol craft to pass over the spot where the submarine was diving in order to release the depth charges for Y guns or rails. But with the hedgehog, the ship could attack a U-boat even as it dived with 30-pound charges of high explosive, enough to blow a hole in the side of the hull with a direct hit.

The Americans developed their own weapon, Anti-Submarine Projectile Mark 20, christened "the mousetrap." A destroyer or corvette, so equipped, could project eight of the 32-pound missiles 300 yards in front of the ship. Obviously, this was a far more effective way to hunt down U-boats than the old method, which took anywhere from one to two minutes after locating the enemy to make the attack.

The patrol craft SC-716 was equipped with the new experimental weapon in the spring of 1943. She came to Norfolk on April 1 and was given 16 mousetrap projectiles. They were installed by an experienced gunner's mate in the crew, but he was soon transferred out and not replaced.

The care of the mousetrap missiles, then, was given to Gunner's Mate 3c. Williamson, an intelligent but inexperienced man in the field.

His major problem was to take apart the warheads after each cruise and clean them so they would not foul.

The mousetrap was so new and experimental a weapon that tools had not yet caught up with it. It should have been handled with a special "spanner" wrench; instead, all Williamson had to work with was an ordinary Stillson wrench, and that is what he used to adjust his charges.

On the morning of May 17, when the SC-716 had just returned from patrol, the commanding officer told Williamson to overhaul his mousetrap charges that day.

Williamson secured the assistance of Seaman 2c. Miller, a shipmate who was a gunner's mate striker, or apprentice.

They took eight of the projectiles off the ship on to the pier to which they were tied and began to work with them. Williamson had cleaned up three by noon, and was beginning to work on the fourth.

Suddenly, a tremendous explosion shocked the whole port, the 2 men working on the mousetraps were literally blown to pieces as the missiles exploded, 4 other men of the ship were killed, and 10 were wounded. *SC-716* was seriously damaged.

If such incidents showed the difficulties of building a defense against the enemy offshore, the battle was beginning to turn toward the allies. The Germans made a major onslaught on convoy ONS 5, and although they sank a dozen merchant ships from the convoy, 4 U-boats were definitely sunk, 4 were probably sunk, and 9 or 10 were damaged. The score was becoming more even.

The men who took the convoys offshore were becoming expert at their job. On June 2, the escort *PC-565* was assigned to the port side of a New York-Guantanamo convoy. She was patrolling her sector at 12 knots as the convoy reached a point 120 miles southeast of Cape May, at noon.

Suddenly, she had a contact at 1,600 yards. In seconds, the crew was at general quarters, making ready to attack. The captain knew precisely what was happening; a U-boat beneath the surface, probably at periscope depth, was moving across the path of the convoy, so he could have a choice of targets.

Setting the depth charges for 100 feet, four minutes after the first sounding, the escort attacked with a five-charge pattern. She ran two minutes, 1,000 yards from the point of attack, and turned right just as the submarine came up next to her.

There was something wrong with the U-boat, the men of the patrol craft could tell that much. Her conning tower came out of water but not to the deck level, and then she began to sink just as the captain of *PC-565* gave the order to ram.

The men of the patrol boat tried to open fire, but Number 2 gun was shrouded in the smoke of the ship's rapid turning, and Number 1 gun misfired. The starboard 20 mm. opened up and made a number of hits on the conning tower.

The submarine began to submerge. The *PC* changed course and fired another depth charge 100 yards ahead of the U-boat. The submarine disappeared.

The contact lost, the captain stopped his engines, so his sound man might listen. He heard it, off the bow, 300 yards away. Then there was an explosion, and debris came to the surface in a cloud of oil. They moved forward into the oil slick and saw something white like a fish's belly. A man scooped it up and the pharmacist's mate identified it: It was part of a human chest and stomach. Soon, from way in the deep (they were in 1,500 fathoms of water) came a dull explosion, and then a large bubble came to the surface.

In the slick, they picked up one man swimming. He was Kapitaenleutnant Klaus Bergsten, the commanding officer of *U-525*, which had just been sent to the bottom. The first spread of charges had done the job. The captain had tried to bring the U-boat to the surface, but it had faltered and began to break up. He was the only man to make it out the hatch.

U-525 had been on station for just about a week. She had not sunk a single ship and had been destroyed by a lowly patrol boat. Her story was a microcosmic indication of what was happening in the sea war.

Yet death still waited out there offshore. The odds were changing; the defenders had the advantages, but the war had not changed so much as all that.

On June 9, a week after the sinking of *U-525*, the Eastern Sea Frontier counted three U-boats at its front door.

In the months since the U-boat war had slowed, many ship captains refused to wait for convoys and insisted on sailing along. One of these was Capt. Peder A. Johnson of *Esso Gettysburg*. The tanker sailed from Port Arthur, Texas, for Philadelphia, laden with fuel oil. Johnson felt relatively safe: The navy had supplied him with a big deck gun and an armed guard under Ens. John S. Arnold, II, of Tallahassee.

But on June 9, Captain Pederson was uneasy. All day, he had the feeling they were being shadowed by a U-boat. Shore stations obligingly sent out air patrols, and they flew around the ship and combed the area. They found nothing.

But at two o'clock that afternoon, two torpedoes slammed into the side of the tanker, and she burst into flames. The string of fire shot high above the deck and spilled over on to the surface until *Esso Gettysburg* was floating in a sea of flame.

Ensign Arnold came running out of the amidships deckhouse burned so badly that skin was hanging down from his chin and along his arms, literally dripping. Blood was pouring down his chest.

He headed forward and managed to load and fire a shell in the direction from which the torpedoes had come. It was an act of defiance, little more, for the submarine did not appear.

He had no time to fire more.

The second mate ran to the forecastle head and tried to get Number 2 lifeboat loose. He saw one life raft burning and could not free the boat.

Five minutes after the torpedoes hit the ship was an inferno, and then she capsized.

The men who survived the flames leaped off and swam through fire to the other side, to what safety they could find. Of the 48 officers and men of the ship and the 27 men of the armed guard, only two dozen or so were still alive. Out of the fire came a boat drifting toward them as they struggled in the water, but it was so hot from the flames that they had to splash water in it before they could enter, and then they had to cast over the side the roasted corpse of one of their comrades.

Eighteen of them survived, including Ensign Arnold, and he got into the boat.

Then began another ordeal, the terrible test of exposure and hanging on in the face of thirst and pain and the sense of loss and loneliness of shipwreck.

They were lucky. The next day, a B-25, escorting the U.S.S. *George Washington,* spotted the boat in the water and flashed a message to the ship. She changed course and picked up the survivors.

For three more days, the defenders strained their resources searching for "other survivors." Then a plane sighted a lifeboat, three charred life rafts, and a great slick of oil, drifting along with the Gulf Stream.

That was all.

40

"A WHOLE NEW BALLGAME"

The British had some success with antitorpedo nets, which they streamed along the sides of their ships, fore to aft. The problem was in turning; the nets sometimes fouled the propellers.

By the spring of 1943, the Americans had developed a sort of mine for which they had particularly high hopes. Two dozen Liberty ships were equipped with them, including the *William H. Webb,* which sailed east in a convoy on June 13. She was deliberately assigned one of the most dangerous convoy positions, as tail ship in the outside starboard column, and her captain was instructed that he was to act in a fashion that would convince any prowling submarines that *William H. Webb* was a straggler.

The night was dark and rainy; even so, halfway through the evening, the vessel to port of *William H. Webb* began blowing her whistle to sound the Morse S. S S S S S, she went, letting the convoy know that she had sighted a submarine.

The escorts came charging up, but they found nothing, and the convoy settled down to silence.

Just before two o'clock in the morning, there came a tremendous explosion 200 feet off to port of the *William H. Webb,* and a water spout followed. The ship lurched, and the blast so shook her that she lost several bearings and strained her shaft. She turned back then and headed for New York, where the captain reported to the shore authorities that the experimental mine had destroyed the torpedo intended for her.

No one believed the story. German Naval Intelligence did not even bother to check it out. The war was going too badly by that time. It was only much much later, when the victory had been won, that the record kept by the captain of

U-190 mentioned the strange tale, how he had fired a torpedo at a merchant ship in convoy just off the American shore, and the ship had somehow exploded the torpedo in midsea and gone blithely on, apparently unhurt.

That was June 1943.

The war offshore had changed completely.

In the Atlantic, it was a "whole new ballgame." The battle odds had switched. Only 22 Allied ships were sunk in the month of August. Meanwhile, three U-boat "milk cows" were sunk in the Bay of Biscay.

Three submarines might not seem a decisive number, but the sinking of those particular U-boats was the direct cause of crippling the German undersea effort against the West that month. Several U-boats hurriedly left the middle Atlantic and headed home when the German radio carried the word to them that they could not expect to be resupplied at sea.

On August 1, a B-17 Flying Fortress, operating out of Mitchel Field, Long Island, spotted a blip on the radar 120 miles off Montauk Point just before nine o'clock at night. It circled the area but made no further contact, although the pilot was sure they were on the track of a submarine.

Next evening, a PBM flying boat came upon a long wake, about 200 miles to the south of the spot where the B-17 had made contact. It moved in and was greeted by tracer bullets from a deck gun. The submarine submerged, and the PBM circled the area. The action took place about 30 miles from a Gibraltar-Norfolk convoy, but the convoy was unmolested, probably because of the swift action of the flying boat.

On August 3, another PBM spotted what the Eastern Sea Frontier Tracking Section was sure was the same U-boat, but once again, the submarine dived and got away.

On August 5, the submarine was tracking a convoy bound from New York to Key West, about 90 miles west of Elizabeth City. The convoy was escorted by several surface vessels and had an almost constant air screen of bombers.

The escorts included the U.S. Coast Guard cutters *Pandora* and *Calypso*, the newly built British tug *HMFT-22*, which was on its way to delivery in the south, and U.S.S.

Plymouth, which was W. K. Vanderbilt's old yacht *Alva* (the one with the sliding bar and bed). She was now serving under Lt. Ormsby M. Mitchel, Jr., a New York bond salesman who had enlisted in the navy and made his way upward swiftly for a reserve officer. Two months earlier, Mitchel had joined *Plymouth* as executive officer, having spent a few weeks at antisubmarine-warfare school. Now he was captain, an indication of the speed and success with which the regular navy was training citizen sailors to take their place in the war effort.

As if in contrast to the young bond salesman, with his first command, also with the convoy in escort was the Hon. Sir H. Meade-Featherstonehaugh, an admiral of His Majesty's Royal Navy, retired before the war but now doing his bit for king and country by bringing the new tug down from New York to the West Indies to join the British forces there.

Plymouth was on the starboard bow of the convoy, patrolling with her sound gear, when the sonar man made a contact. It was 3:35 in the afternoon.

Hardly, however, had Captain Mitchel been called and reached the bridge when a torpedo slammed into the side of Willy Vanderbilt's pride and joy and blew her half apart. One of the fuel tanks spewed forth its oil and caught fire, and the ship was quickly aflame forward.

Almost immediately, she began going down by the head.

Lieutenant Mitchel stayed on his bridge as long as he could. Then he had to jump down to the well deck, for the ladders to the bridge were all blown away by the explosion. Only then did his men discover that he had been badly hurt; the force of the explosion had thrown him against the bulkhead, and he had dislocated his knee.

Even so, Mitchel insisted on staying aboard, hustling his men off into the water, with life preservers on, and making sure the process of the abandonment of his command was carried out in a seamanlike manner.

Old *Alva* had heroes aboard that day. Ens. R. Keltch was in the engine room when the torpedo hit. He hurried his men out and helped them go. He stayed behind, trying to find others, and he never came out of the engine room. Soundman McGinty heard men shouting from the blazing armory and went back to help them. He never emerged.

Three seamen, whom no one could identify, gave up their life jackets and went back to the stowage compartment for others. When they got inside, the compartment flamed up; they were trapped and died there.

All this while, Lieutenant Mitchel was urging his men off the ship, half fainting with the pain of his leg. But he never gave up, and actually went down with the ship, but the life preserver he was wearing brought him bobbing back up to the surface, and he was saved.

The rescue was accomplished by the other escorts. The PBM circled overhead, the *Calypso* and the British tug steamed carefully and slowly into the water, picking up men among the debris of the converted yacht.

Calypso, as senior vessel, undertook the basic responsibility, and when her captain saw the British tug hauling down on him, he turned and shouted across the water with every bit of his lieutenant's authority:

"Get that goddam tub out of here."

And Admiral the Honorable Sir H. Meade-Featherstonehaugh turned to him with angelic placidity.

"Aye, aye, sir," said the admiral to the lieutenant.

But, in fact, he did not desert the area or the men struggling in the water but moved out of the way of the choleric skipper of the cutter and continued his rescue work. A few moments later, those in the water later swore, the admiral was out in a small boat himself, at the oars, saving the lives of men struggling in the oil and debris of what had been their ship.

It was a sore loss that day. Four officers and 87 men were lost in the sinking of *Plymouth*, although 8 officers and 84 men survived. A good many of them had a quiet, retiring man with a hyphenated name and a career long behind him to thank for their lives that day.

The submarine that had been the cause of it all continued to roam but began edging her way east, preparatory of going home. The targets in the waters off the American shore were nothing like they had been, and the dangers were intense. For her troubles, she had only a converted yacht to claim in the nightly broadcasts to Doenitz.

As the submarine headed east, 11 planes and a blimp were sent by Admiral Andrews' staff to find and destroy her.

One of these planes, a patrol bomber, was flown by Lt. (jg.) F. C. Cross. His copilot was Lt. (jg.) J. Taylward, Jr. The plane also carried a radio operator, machinist's mate, and ordnance man.

Early on the morning of August 7, the plane picked up a radar blip far out to sea and then sighted, 1.5 miles away, a submarine on the surface. Pilot Cross attacked.

The submarine was a big one of the most modern class, and she had three separate gun installations on deck. All of them were manned, and all were firing.

Machine-gun fire caught the starboard engine of the bomber as she came in and knocked it out. The same burst also wounded Cross and his copilot. They dropped their depth bombs, anyhow, and shook up the submarine harshly, but then they had to look to survival. The starboard propeller would not feather and was dragging them down. Twenty miles from the submarine, they landed in the sea, and although it was a gentle landing, soon the plane was sinking.

Apparently, the machinist's mate and ordnance man had tried to parachute out, but if so, their chutes did not open because the plane was too close to the sea.

The radioman made one last broadcast to fix their position and then escaped out the hatch with the two officers.

They floated for a while, and then Lieutenant Cross slipped from his life jacket and went under and did not come up again. The other two were there, surrounded by the green dye that they had used to mark their position when a PBM from Elizabeth City found and rescued them.

By this time, the submarine had a name at the Eastern Sea Frontier headquarters. On the big plot board, she was shown there offshore and marked Red A. The hunt was on.

The bombers went out, searched, found nothing, and searched some more.

At 11:53 on the night of August 7, one bomber, out of Floyd Bennet Field, reported to base that he was in the area where the Cross plane had gone down and searching. The plane was never heard from again. The next day, Admiral Andrews speculated that it, too, had run afoul of the sharpshooting gunners of the U-boat and had been destroyed so quickly that it could not even get a message away.

An hour later, the U-boat was spotted again by a plane from Quonset. The submarine fired a few rounds and then dived. The Quonset plane lost it in the dark.

The plane found it again, came in, attacked with four depth charges, and forced the submarine to the top of the water. This time, the crew could see smoke coming from the conning tower.

Another plane, a PBM from Elizabeth City, came up to bomb, and the submarine crew manned all three of its guns and began firing. The plane's depth-firing mechanism misfired on two runs, and finally the pilot dropped his bombs, all eight of them, manually, as the submarine dived. Once again, the explosion damaged the U-boat, lifted it out of the water, and forced it to remain on the surface. For a half an hour, plane and U-boat fought, without visible effect. The submarine got under way then, but she was out of trim, down by the stern, and moved slowly off on the surface.

But a half an hour more, and she managed to submerge, heading east once more.

That night, the tracking office was busy, and the next day called up a Gibraltar-New York convoy for help in running down the submarine. The U-boat, the trackers suggested, was heading for the convoy, anyhow.

That night, a PBM made contact with the U-boat, found her dead in the water, and tried to lead the destroyer *Laub* to the place. But the scheme had misfired: Another PBM came along, though it had spotted a U-boat on the water, and fired flares.

The flares turned night into day and illuminated the destroyer thoroughly for the glad eyes of the U-boat commander. He went down and stayed down. The destroyer escort *Lawrence* had a contact a few hours later and dropped a whole set of hedgehog charges, but the submarine got away and headed across the broad Atlantic.

The hunt for that enemy had failed, but in his own way, so had the enemy failed, for although he came across to the waters off the American shore, he never was able to make contact with what he sought, the ships that were carrying the materials of war that would turn the tide in Europe.

The Americans by this time were confident enough that they could even laugh at themselves a little.

On August 27, at Pier 9 on Staten Island's naval installation at Tompkinsville, a seaman was showing a group of student officers from Fort Schuyler around the big patrol boat U.S.S. *Pheasant*. He was particularly glowing in his description of the mousetrap that had recently been installed to fire depth charges forward, and he emphasized their effectiveness.

"To fire them," he said in closing, "all you do is press the button like this."

And he did.

Up into the air went the 16 antisubmarine missiles, carrying enough high explosives to blow a light cruiser out of the water, and down they came onto the roofs of the buildings alongside the pier, and through some of them.

Luckily, the explosive mechanisms were on safe, and so the missiles did not blow up. And the command was relaxed enough so that even the admiral could laugh about it.

And why not?

In September 1943, not a single ship was lost on the Eastern Sea Frontier, and for the first two weeks of the month, not even one in the whole wide Atlantic.

The weight of Allied skill and American industrial power had changed the balance.

Death had been driven from the American shore.

AUTHOR'S NOTE

The research for this book began in Washington at the Naval Historical Center's Operational Archives Branch. Dr. Dean Allard and his staff provided me with all the information available on the conduct of the war against the U-boats off the U.S. coast in the winter, spring, and fall of 1942, and again in 1943. Dr. Allard's people did everything from supplying me with microfilm of all the war diaries available to action reports, survivors' stories, and individual first names.

Also in Washington, I worked at the National Archives, and the headquarters of the American Red Cross, where the librarians were most cooperative. At the Department of Transportation, U.S. Coast Guard officials were as helpful as they could be, the problem being that during the war the Coast Guard was taken under U.S. Naval administration.

From Washington I went to Hyde Park, N.Y., to do research in the Franklin D. Roosevelt library there, and received every assistance from the archivists. Then the going became more difficult; the materials sparse and scattered.

Captain Earl Schwass of the U.S. Naval War College was most cordial. Dorothy T. King of the East Hampton, N.Y., Free Library, sent me materials and references. Mrs. Justine Postal of the West Palm Beach Public Library gave me an anecdote and many references to material in the library. I began a tour of East Coast cities and found that nearly all records pertaining to the events of World War II had long since either been destroyed or sent into the files of historical societies and libraries. Edith McCauley of the Portland (Maine) Public Library steered me to materials. I also consulted libraries in Portsmouth, N.H.; Gloucester,

Maine; Boston; Newport, R.I.; Charleston, S.C.; Jacksonville, Fla.; Savannah, Ga.; Daytona Beach, West Palm Beach, Fort Lauderdale, and Miami, where Sam J. Boldrick of the Florida Collection and others spent much time with me and my researchers. Key West's Monroe County Public Library was useful.

G. Christopher in the manuscript department of the Pennsylvania Historical Society gave me some information and I am also indebted to the following, for finding sources, and contributing tales or parts of tales and bits of the picture of the U.S. in this period:

M. H. Carpenter, Maritime Institute of Technology, Linthicum Heights, Maryland; Michael J. Eula of the U.S. Coast Guard; John G. Bunker of the Seafarers International Union, Brooklyn, N.Y.; C. H. Harris, Jacksonville, Fla.; John L. Lochhead, Librarian, the Mariners Museum, Newport News, Va.; Richard C. Kugler, Director, Old Dartmouth Society Historical Whaling Museum, New Bedford, Mass.; Everett S. Allen, New Bedford *Standard Times;* Samuel Thompson, National Maritime Union of America; J. L. Webb, U.S. Coast Guard; Gayle P. Peters, archivist, Federal Archives and Record Center, East Point, Ga.; George F. Johnson, U.S. Coast Guard; William R. Emerson, Director, Franklin D. Roosevelt Library, Hyde Park, N.Y.; Clifford S. Morgan, United States Lines; Anna M. Leotta, The Sailor's Snug Harbor, Staten Island, N.Y.; Bonnie Golightly, Joseph Conrad Library, of the Seamen's Church Institute of New York; Elizabeth Roland, of Gloucester Mass.; librarians at the Nantucket Atheneum; Palmer Hoyt, Denver.

Anyone who writes about the war at sea off the American coast has a special debt of gratitude to the naval historians of Eastern Sea Frontier, whose monthly summaries of activity are masterpieces of description. Professor Elting Morison of Massachusetts Institute of Technology was then a young reserve officer, one of whose tasks was to write the war diary. It recreates the atmosphere of the Church Street headquarters better than any official naval study I have ever seen does of any part of the war. It was so readable, and so coherent, in fact, that Admiral Andrews was chided by other commands for allowing his war diarist to dwell on detail, when all higher authority seemed to want was statistics. Without the Morison reports it would be impossible to give much of the detail that occurs in this book. The most important debt of all, to Olga G. Hoyt, my wife, researcher, and typist, can never be paid. I am also grateful to Diana P. Hoyt for research assistance.

CHAPTER NOTES

Chapter 1   Sea War

The accounts of the sinking of the *Athenia* and other liners during the first weeks of war are from the files of *The New York Times* for the period, as are the tales of what happened in New York, and at the Presidential press conferences. I was unable to track down the source of the Boston story of the intrepid U-boat captain, but I heard it so many times, that it has at least the validity of folklore. No navy records nor any others I could find would substantiate the tale but it was, I am satisfied, a true indication of the U-boat mystique that had arisen. The story of the Red Cross girls' crossing of the Atlantic and the tragedies that befell them are from the files of the American Red Cross, in the Washington D.C., library.

Chapter 2   Uneasy Peace

The story of Norfolk's entry into war is largely from the files of the Norfolk *Virginian-Pilot* for the period. The tales of Norfolk in 1940 and 1941 are from the newspaper files. The Kennedy-Roosevelt exchange is from the Presidential files in the Franklin D. Roosevelt Library at Hyde Park, N.Y. It is interesting to note that in William Stevenson's Book, *A Man Called Intrepid*, Kennedy was painted as defeatist and ignoble, a picture that does not come through in the Roosevelt papers. But, of course, Stevenson's biography of Sir William Stephenson, British wartime intelligence chief, would be likely to give a different view.

The references to the Neutrality Patrol and Admiral Stark's actions are to be found in FDR's papers, as well. The analysis of the German side of the war comes from Admiral Karl Doenitz's biography and Samuel Eliot Morison's history of U.S. Naval Operations in World War II, vol. 1. The story of the *Niblack*'s encounter is from the Navy Operational Archives. The tale of the *Texas*' near-incident is from Naval archives and Doenitz. The story of the *Greer* is from her action reports, as are those of the *Truxton, Kearny,* and *Reuben James.*

Chapter 3 War!

The story of the events in North Carolina, Norfolk, and Atlantic City is from newspapers in the files of the libraries in these places. The story of events in Times Square is from *The New York Times.* German activity is detailed in the Doenitz autobiography. The material about Admiral Andrews' defense command is from the war diaries of the Eastern Sea Frontier and from Morison. The Red Cross material comes from the Red Cross library in Washington. The statistics and accounts of sinkings are from the Eastern Sea Frontier War Diaries.

Chapter 4 The Drums Beat

Plan Z and the German progression is from Doenitz and from naval files in the historical division. The story of the *Allan Jackson* is from a report in the Mariner's Museum and from an article in ESSO's own history of the tanker fleet. The story of *Venore* is from the War Diary of Eastern Sea Frontier.

Chapter 5 Onslaught

The portion of this chapter that deals with the Churchill-Roosevelt correspondence comes from the files in the FDR library at Hyde Park. The arguments about anti U-boat warfare among members of the Presidential staff are indicated in papers and reports to the President, and memos from him to others. The notes about public reaction come from the various newspapers of the time. Secretary Knox's optimistic communiques were printed in the press. The story of *Indian Arrow* is from the war diary of Eastern Sea Frontier. The running battle between military men is hardly discussed in histories of the war. Morison makes some reference to it. The newspapers of the time and military reports of this period do not. Later the military would grow exasperated. But the civilian attitude was not openly admitted until after the war, when newspapers began telling tales of the "blackout." Atlantic City and Miami were particularly callous about their lights.

Chapter 6 When Defense Was No Defense

Admiral Andrews' views were made known in correspondence and the Eastern Sea Frontier War Diary. The story of the trawlers comes from ESF Diary.

The story of the disappearing destroyers comes from Eastern Sea Frontier files. Coast Guard Admiral Waesche's protests are recorded in naval files and in histories of the Coast Guard. The story of *Alva*, William K. Vanderbilt's yacht, is from ESF War Diary. The tragedy of Civil Air Patrol No. 8 is told in newspaper clippings in the files of the Charleston public library.

Chapter 7 The Admirals Take Stock

The Hardegen story is from the Doenitz book. The comparison of the damage done by five U-boats in a few weeks is from Morison's history of U.S. Naval operations. The worries of Prime Minister Churchill are detailed in his own history of the Second World War and in the correspondence with FDR in the FDR library. The mutiny of the merchant ships is from the New York newspapers. The complaints of the merchant seamen come from materials supplied by the NMU and from reports in the Red Cross Library in Washington. The movements of American forces by Admiral King are from Morison, and the ESF War Diary. Admiral Andrews' proposals about defense come from his correspondence with Admiral King and the War Diary. The anecdote of the condemnation of the Norfolk Country Club is from the Norfolk *Virginian-Pilot* files in the Norfolk public library.

Chapter 8 Oil on the Beaches

The Germans' pleasant surprise at the easy pickings off the American coast is reflected in all German submariners' accounts and in Doenitz. The tale of *U-504* is from ESF

War Diary, and the name of the submarine comes from extrapolation of German reports by the Office of Naval Intelligence. The Jupiter Inlet story is from *Graveyard of the Atlantic* and from clippings in the Miami public library.

The story of *Triton*'s exhaustive submarine hunt is from her action report of Feb. 28, 1942, and that of *Hamilton*.

Chapter 9 The Fate of *Jacob Jones*

The situation report in February is from the ESF War Diary, and the story of the sinking of the *Jacob Jones* is told in some detail in the War Diary monthly summary for February. Some details were supplied by Dr. Dean Allard of the Navy's Operational Archives section, from reports of the period.

Chapter 10 The Winds of March

Lt. Gen. Drum's order that lights be turned out is described in various histories of army and navy operations. ESF War Diary refers to it. The activities of the U-boats are from Doenitz ESF War Diary, and Morison. The story of S.S. *Barbara* is from the War Diary of Caribbean Sea Frontier. The Churchill-Roosevelt exchange is from the FDR papers. The newspaper headlines about sinkings come from the Atlantic City, Norfolk, and New York newspapers, of March 1942. Admiral Andrews' attempts to find search and patrol craft are detailed in ESF War Diary, as is the story of the early convoys. Admiral King's petulance is recorded in the FDR papers.

Chapter 11 "Shut off That Goddam Light . . ."

The story of S.S. *Liberator* is from survivors' reports and the ESF War Diary. *Dickerson*'s misadventure is recorded in her Action Report for March 18, 1942. Dr. Dean Allard supplied the name of the captain. The *Raritan* story is from the ESF War Diary.

So is the story of *Malchage*. The story of Carl Hermann Schroetter is from the newspaper accounts of the day and from clippings in the files of the Miami Public Library. The notes about German espionage, much more scanty than I would have liked, come from ESF Diary and the Operational Archives. Thirty-five years after the fact, the Office of Naval Intelligence still does not respond to queries on such subjects.

Chapter 12 "The Answer is NO."

The British concern over American laxity in reporting ship losses is apparent in the Churchill-Roosevelt exchanges. The story of the five tankers is from the ESSO Fleet at War and the ESF War Diary, from the Action Report of *Agassiz*, and *McKean*. The story of the Inshore Patrol is from ESF War Diary. Admiral King's answer is in ESF files.

Chapter 13 The Q-Ship Caper

The Q-ship story is sketchily told in ESF War Diary. Other information was provided by Dr. Dean Allard from Navy Operational Archives, including a memo to the Secretary of Navy from Admiral F. J. Horne on the loss of *Atik*.

Chapter 14 Fumbling

The newspaper accounts are from *The New York Times*. The account of vessel adventures is from ESF War Diary. The story of H.M.S. *Bedfordshire* is from the booklet *In Some Foreign Field,* which is a study of the ship's life in American waters, and from the diary of Eastern Sea Frontier.

Chapter 15 "No More Tankers Will Sail . . ."

The stories of the tankers are told in the ESSO book, and in various reports in the files of Operational Archives. The Mariners' Museum has an extensive file of such materials. The story of *Mackerel* is from her action report and ESF War Diary. The tale of *Victoria* is from *The New York Times* and ESF War Diary.

Chapter 16 The First U-Boat

The story of *U-85* comes from the files of ONI, which made a series of Postmortem Studies of Enemy Submarines sunk in U.S. waters, and from *Roper*'s action report.

Chapter 17   The End of H.M.S. *Bedfordshire*

The sinking figures are from Doenitz, as are the recorded movements of U-boats. The story of *U-558* is from *In Some Foreign Fields* as is the story of destruction of H.M.S. *Bedfordshire*.

Chapter 18   How Not to Fight a U-Boat

The tales of the Miami area are from the files of the Miami Public Library's material on World War II. The story of KS-500 is from ESF War Diary. The movements within Eastern Sea Frontier are from ESF reports. The establishment of the Anti-Submarine Warfare section is from ESF and other naval reports. *Broome*'s adventure is told in her action report of May 2, 1942.

Chapter 19   The Second U-Boat

The story of *U-352* is from the ONI postmortem series on enemy submarines, and the action report of *Icarus* for May 9, 1942. The communications snarlup was investigated by Eastern Sea Frontier and described as a "horrible example" in the war diary that month. The wasteful attempts to salvage *U-352* are described in various reports.

Chapter 20   The Juggling Act

The material for the early part of this chapter is from ESF War Diary, and from the action reports of USS *Ellis*.

Chapter 21   A Matter of Information

The progress of the convoy systems from ESF War Diary and press reports of Secretary Knox's conferences. The story of *F. W. Abrams* in the Hatteras minefield is from Eastern Sea Frontier reports.

Chapter 22   The Misadventure of *YP-389*

The failure of the Halifax convoy is from Eastern Sea Frontier reports and the war diary. The story of *YP-389* is the result of an investigation into the loss of that vessel, as detailed by ESF.

Chapter 23   This Harbor Is Mined!

The indications of German mine activity are from ESF War Diary, as is the story of Convoy KN-109.

Chapter 24   The Amagansett Incident

The story of the coming of the Nazi saboteurs to the U.S. coast has been told several times in *Fire on the Beaches* and *They Came to Kill,* and in newspaper and magazine accounts. The story of the inner workings of the naval and military and civilian commands comes from Eastern Sea Frontier's War Diary, and other files in the Navy Operational Archives department.

Chapter 25   "God Bless the Commonwealth of Massachusetts . . ."

The farce played by the Massachusetts Committee on Public Safety on Cape Cod is thoroughly detailed in reports in the library of the American Red Cross in Washington.

Chapter 26   "Who's in Charge Here, Anyhow . . . ?"

The Army-Navy quarrel over air power is so well-known as hardly to need documentation. Much of what appears here is from my *How They Won the War in the Pacific,* and from ESF war diary. The quarrel between Navy headquarters and Washington over submarine tracking is part of the ESF records.

Chapter 27   A Matter of Tradition

The story of the mixup between the commodore commander and the naval escort is told in ESF War Diary as a horrible example of relying on wormy tradition, and from *Spry*'s action reports.

Chapter 28   The Lights of Miami

The story of the pilot who saw the treacherous schooner is from W. D. Diamond's *Memoirs of Ships and Men.* The tales of Ocracoke are from clippings and articles in the collection of the Jacksonville Public Library. The story of the bombing of the sewer line is from the Miami *Herald,* in a story written long after the war. The clippings are in the Miami Public Library.

Chapter 29   Forging a Weapon

The story of the picket boats and Commander Astor's adventures among the fishermen is from Eastern Sea Frontier files.

Chapter 30   The Third U-Boat . . . and Fourth

The stories of *U-701* and *U-94* are from the ONI postmortem reports, and ESF War Diary, and *Oakville*'s story is from *Lea*'s action report.

Chapter 31   Mysteries of the Sea

The tales of mysterious explosions and mines are from clippings, and ESF War Diary, and from various naval reports. The story of the *Stephen R. Jones* is from ESF War Diary.

Chapter 32   Convoys

The story of *Wakefield* is from the naval operational archives. The tales of *Broome*'s medical team come from her action reports.

Chapter 33   The Great Nantucket U-Boat Hunt

The story of *Plow City* is from the SIU files. The Great Nantucket U-Boat Hunt was detailed in ESF's War Diary.

Chapter 34   Mysterious Mines—and Sabotage

The mystery of the mines was outlined in ESF War Diary. The tale of *Anthony Wayne* and sabotage is told in that same source.

Chapter 35   The Tale of the Wandering Yawl

The source here is the report of *CGR-3070* and ESF War Diary.

Chapter 36   The Day They Closed the Port of New York

Eastern Sea Frontier papers are the source of the story of the converted yacht that blew up in New York harbor.

Chapter 37   The Second Coming of Admiral Doenitz

The story of convoy NG 359 is from ESF's files. The other material is from the war diary.

Chapter 38   The Miracles of the Sea

The stories of rescues are from newspaper clippings and the files of *The New York Times,* and ESF War Diary.

Chapter 39   The Tenth Fleet

The story of The Tenth Fleet is told in great detail in Ladislas Farago's book of the same title. The story of the Mousetrap missiles is from ESF War Diary, as is that of *Esso Gettysburg* and Ensign Arnold.

Chapter 40   "A Whole New Ballgame"

The story of *William H. Webb* is from the navy operational archives. The death of the Vanderbilt yacht is told by ESF's War Diary, as is the tale of the unfortunate U-boat hunters from the air.

BIBLIOGRAPHY

The Battle of the Atlantic, Official Account of the Fight Against U-Boats. London: His Majesty's stationery Office, 1946.

Bloomfield, Howard V. L. *The Compact History of the United States Coast Guard.* New York: Hawthorn Books, 1966.

Bunker, John (ed.) *The SIU At War. True Experiences in the War at Sea of Members of the Seafarers International Union.* Seafarers International Union of North America, August, 1944.

Busch, Harald. *U-Boats At War.* New York: Ballantine, 1955.

Carr, Roland T. *To Sea in Haste.* Washington: Acropolis Books, 1975.

Dash, George J. *Eight Spies Against America.* New York: Robert M. McBride Co., 1959.

Diamond, Walker D. *Memoirs of Ships and Men.* New York: Vantage Press, 1964.

DuBois, Bessie Wilson. *Shipwrecks in the Vicinity of Jupiter Inlet.* Privately printed, 1975.

Frank, Wolfgang. *The Sea Wolves.* New York: Rinehart, 1955.

Halstead, Ivor. *Heroes of the Atlantic.* New York: E. P. Dutton & Co., 1942.

Hanna, Alfred J. and Abbey, Kathryn. *Florida's Golden Sands.* New York: Bobbs-Merrill Co., 1950.

History of Marine Corps Operations of World War II. Central Pacific Drive, Vol. III, 1966.

Hynd, Alan. *Passport to Treason,* New York: Robert McBride & Co., 1943.

Karig, Walter. *Battle Report,* Vol IV, "End of an Empire."

Langer, William L. and Gleason, S. Everett. *The Challenge to Isolation, 1937–40*. New York: Harper, 1956.

Lonsdale, Adrian L., and Kaplan, H. R. *A Guide to Sunken* Publications, 1964.
Ships in American Waters. Arlington, Va.: Compass

McIntyre, Donald. *The Battle of the Atlantic*. New York: Macmillan, 1961.

McCoy, Samuel Duff. *Nor Death Dismay*. New York: privately printed. American Export Lines, 1948.

Morison, Samuel Eliot. *History of the United States Naval Operations in World War II*. Vol 1. "The Battle of the Atlantic," Vol. X, "The Atlantic Battle Won," Boston: Little, Brown & Company, 1947, 1956.

Naisawald Van Loan. *In Some Foreign Field*. Winston-Salem, N.C.: John F. Blair, 1972.

The North Carolina Shipbuilding Co., *Five Years of North Carolina Shipbuilding*. Wilmington, N.C., 1946.

Rachlis, Eugene. *They Came to Kill*. New York: Random House, 1961.

Reisenberg, Jr., Felix. *Sea War*. New York: Rinehart & Co., 1956.

Standard Oil Co. of New Jersey. *Ships of the Esso Fleet in World War II*. 1946.

Taylor, Theodore. *Fire on the Beaches*. New York: W. W. Norton, 1958.

Tebeau, Charlton W. and Carson, Ruby Leach. *Florida from Indian Trail to Space Age*. Vol. II. Delray Beach, Fla: Southern Publishing Co., 1965.

Waters, John M. *Bloody Winter*. Princeton, N.J.: D. Van Nostrand Co., 1967.

Wheeler, W. R. (ed.) *The Road to Victory: A History of Hampton Roads Port of Embarcation in World War II*.

Wighton, Charles and Peis, Gunter. *Hitler's Spies and Saboteurs*. New York: Henry Holt & Co., 1958.

Willoughby, Malcolm F. *The U.S. Coast Guard in World War II*. Annapolis: United States Naval Institute, 1957.

Periodicals and Newspapers:

Oliver, Lt. Commander Edward F. "Overdue—Presumed Lost." *U.S. Naval Institute Proceedings*, March 1971.

Prior, Leon O. "German Espionage in Florida During World War II." *Florida Historical Quarterly,* April 1961.

———. "Nazi Invasion of Florida." *Florida Historical Quarterly,* October 1970.

———. "The Seven-Day Invasion of Florida." *Tropic* magazine, Miami, 1968.

Swanberg, W. A. "The Spies Who Came in From the Seas." *American Heritage,* April 1970.

Woolie, Martha and Martin, Pete. "Camp Boardwalk." *Saturday Evening Post,* February 27, 1943.

Wylie, Philip and Schwab, Laurence. "The Battle of Florida." *Saturday Evening Post,* March 11, 1944.

"The Eight Nazi Saboteurs Should Be Put to Death," *Life* July 13, 1942.

"Navy Tardy in Driving Off U-boats." *U.S. Naval Institute Proceedings,* August 1947.

Atlantic City *Press*

Atlantic City *Press-Union*

Charleston *Evening Post*

Charleston *News and Courier*

East Hampton (N.Y.) *Star*

Elizabeth City (N.J.) *Daily Advance*

Jacksonville (Fla.) *The Florida Times-Union*

Key West *Citizen*

Miami *Daily News*

Miami *Herald*

Miami Beach *Sun*

Newsday

The New York Times

New York *World Telegram*

Norfolk *Virginian-Pilot*

Palm Beach *Post Times*

Portland (Maine) *Sunday Telegram*

Southampton (N.Y.) *Press*

Suffolk (N.Y.) *Sun*

Tampa *Tribune*

Wilmington *Morning Star Daily*

Wilmington *Sunday Star News*

WAR BOOKS FROM PLAYBOY PAPERBACKS

_____ 21158	THE BATTLE FOR MOSCOW Col. Albert Seaton	$2.75
_____ 16629	THE BATTLE OF LEYTE GULF Edwin P. Hoyt	$2.50
_____ 16634	BLOODY AACHEN Charles Whiting	$2.25
_____ 16879	BLOODY BUNA Lida Mayo	$2.50
_____ 21103	CORREGIDOR James H. Belote & William M. Belote	$2.95
_____ 16609	THE DEVIL'S VIRTUOSOS David Downing	$2.25
_____ 16597	DUNKIRK Robert Jackson	$2.25
_____ 21197	HITLER'S WEREWOLVES Charles Whiting	$2.95
_____ 16716	POINT OF NO RETURN Wilbur H. Morrison	$2.50
_____ 21089	THE SECRET OF STALINGRAD Walter Kerr	$2.50
_____ 16655	U-BOATS OFFSHORE Edwin P. Hoyt	$2.25
_____ 21122	WAKE ISLAND Duane Schultz	$2.50

582-11

 PLAYBOY PAPERBACKS
Book Mailing Service
P.O. Box 690 Rockville Centre, New York 11571

NAME_____

ADDRESS_____

CITY_____STATE_____ZIP_____.

Please enclose 50¢ for postage and handling if one book is ordered;
25¢ for each additional book. $1.50 maximum postage and handling
charge. No cash, CODs or stamps. Send check or money order.

Total amount enclosed: $_____